FLORIDA TEST PREP
Math Skills Workbook
B.E.S.T. Mathematics
Grade 3

ISBN 9798482742167

Acknowledgements

Thank you to the following sources for providing graphs, charts, diagrams, and illustrations.

Evil Math Wizard
www.teacherspayteachers.com/Store/Evil-Math-Wizard

Innovative Teaching Ideas
www.teacherspayteachers.com/Store/Innovative-Teaching-Ideas

Hidesy's Clipart
www.teacherspayteachers.com/Store/Hidesys-Clipart

Rachelle McCracken
https://www.teacherspayteachers.com/Store/Rachelle-Mccracken

Teacher Trap
www.teacherspayteachers.com/Store/Teacher-Trap

Teaches Third in Georgia
www.teacherspayteachers.com/Store/Teachesthirdingeorgia

CONTENTS

INTRODUCTION
For Parents, Teachers, and Tutors

Introducing the B.E.S.T. Standards for Mathematics

In 2020, the state of Florida introduced the B.E.S.T. standards. The standards describe the skills and knowledge that students are expected to have and replace the previous MAFS standards. The new standards will begin to be introduced in 2020-2021 and will be fully introduced by 2022-2023. The state tests will assess these new standards beginning with the 2022-2023 school year.

About the B.E.S.T. Standards for Mathematics

The B.E.S.T. Standards are divided into six strands. These are listed below.

- Number Sense and Operations
- Fractions
- Algebraic Reasoning
- Measurement
- Geometric Reasoning
- Data Analysis and Probability

Within each strand, there are standards describing an overall skill and then benchmarks within that standard describing specific skills.

Complete Skill Coverage

This book covers all the standards one by one. Each section is focused on one standard and covers all the benchmarks within that standard. The standard and the benchmarks covered are listed at the start of each section. In each section, there are five complete question sets covering that standard. This provides complete and focused coverage of the new B.E.S.T. standards.

Developing Math Skills and Preparing for the State Tests

The organization of this book into focused question sets allows students to focus on specific skills as they are introduced and learned. The question sets can be used to practice skills, reinforce learning, determine and show understanding, or prepare for assessments and state tests. The five sets for each topic can be used to show progress and promote improvement.

From the 2022-2023 school year, the state tests will assess the B.E.S.T. Standards for Mathematics. The state tests will include a range of question types including multiple-choice, multi-select, equation response, written response, and graphic response questions that use online features. This book provides practice with all these types of questions and will prepare students for the state tests.

Number Sense and Operations

Place Value

B.E.S.T. Standards

MA.3.NSO.1 Understand the place value of four-digit numbers.

MA.3.NSO.1.1
Read and write numbers from 0 to 10,000 using standard form, expanded form and word form.

MA.3.NSO.1.2
Compose and decompose four-digit numbers in multiple ways using thousands, hundreds, tens and ones. Demonstrate each composition or decomposition using objects, drawings and expressions or equations.

MA.3.NSO.1.3
Plot, order and compare whole numbers up to 10,000.

MA.3.NSO.1.4
Round whole numbers from 0 to 1,000 to the nearest 10 or 100.

Place Value – Practice Set 1

1 Which number is the same as 25 tens?

Ⓐ 205

Ⓑ 250

Ⓒ 2,050

Ⓓ 2,500

2 Georgia lives in a small town with a population of two thousand five hundred and seven. What is this number in standard form? Write your answer on the line below.

Answer ________________

3 Which number is represented by the model below?

Ⓐ 24

Ⓑ 204

Ⓒ 240

Ⓓ 244

4 Complete the missing numbers to show 3,085 in expanded form.

________________ + ________________ + ________________

5 Randall plots a number represented by X on the number line below.

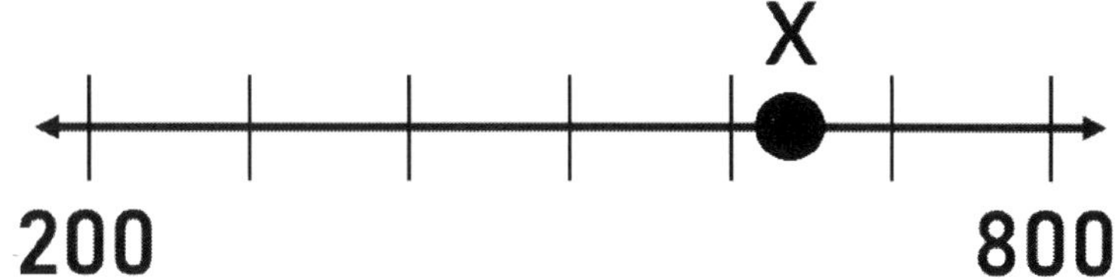

Which of these numbers could Randall have plotted?

Ⓐ 244

Ⓑ 521

Ⓒ 635

Ⓓ 782

6 What is the number 627 rounded to the nearest hundred? Write your answer on the line below.

Answer ____________

7 Which two numbers are the same as 7,600? Select the **two** correct answers.

- ☐ 76 tens
- ☐ 76 hundreds
- ☐ 760 hundreds
- ☐ 7 thousands + 6 tens
- ☐ 7 thousands + 600 tens
- ☐ 7 thousands + 6 hundreds

8 Write the symbol < or > in each box to make each statement true.

1,855 ☐ 2,855

2,906 ☐ 6,906

7,115 ☐ 7,105

9 Plot the number 35 on the number line below.

10 The table below shows the elevation of the four highest points in Florida. Complete the table by adding the elevations rounded to the nearest ten.

Point	Elevation (feet)	Elevation to the Nearest Ten (feet)
Britton Hill	345	
Oak Hill	331	
High Hill	323	
Falling Waters Hill	318	

Place Value – Practice Set 2

1 Which expression shows 50,208 written in expanded form?

Ⓐ 5,000 + 20 + 8

Ⓑ 5,000 + 200 + 8

Ⓒ 50,000 + 20 + 8

Ⓓ 50,000 + 200 + 8

2 What is the value of 757 rounded to the nearest ten?

Ⓐ 700

Ⓑ 750

Ⓒ 760

Ⓓ 800

3 Which of these is represented by the shaded area of the grid?

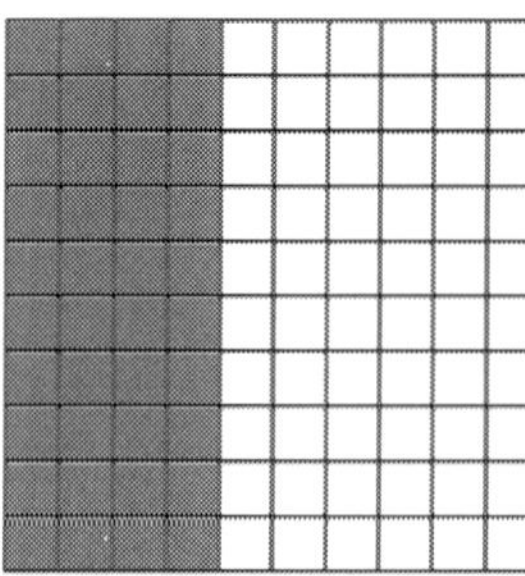

Ⓐ 4 ones

Ⓑ 4 tens

Ⓒ 4 hundreds

Ⓓ 4 thousands

4 Place the numbers listed below in order. Write one number on each blank line.

187 169 178 196

__________ < __________ < __________ < __________

5 Sawyer plots a number represented by J on the number line below.

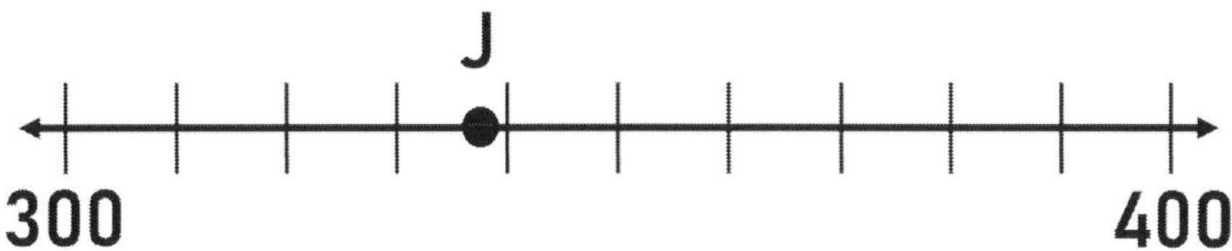

Which of these numbers could Sawyer have plotted?

Ⓐ 304

Ⓑ 328

Ⓒ 337

Ⓓ 340

6 What is the number below in standard form? Write your answer on the line below.

9,000 + 500 + 30

Answer ____________

7 Select **all** the statements that are correct.

☐ 5,230 > 5,320

☐ 5,021 > 5,721

☐ 3,700 > 3,070

☐ 2,615 < 2,611

☐ 6,124 < 6,724

☐ 6,445 < 6,405

8 Complete the missing numbers to represent 6,800 in three different ways.

_______ thousands and _______ hundreds

_______ hundreds

_______ tens

9 Complete the missing numbers to show the number represented below.

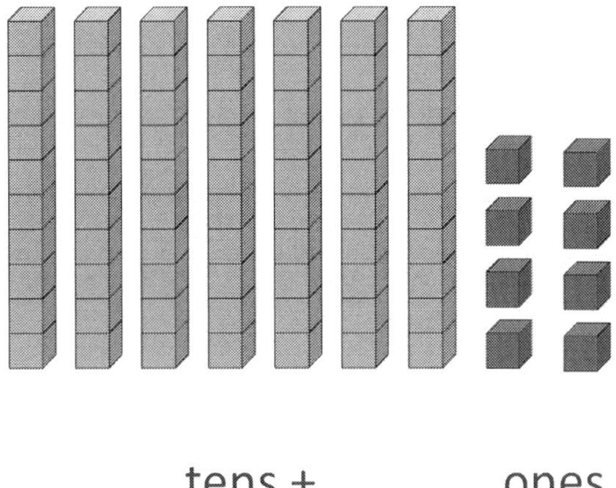

______ tens + ______ ones

What number is represented? Write your answer on the line below.

Answer ___________

10 Tick the correct box to show the value of each number rounded to the nearest hundred.

	300	**400**	**500**
411	☐	☐	☐
356	☐	☐	☐
475	☐	☐	☐

Place Value – Practice Set 3

1 Which of these shows the number two hundred and fifty thousand?

Ⓐ 250

Ⓑ 2,500

Ⓒ 250,000

Ⓓ 2,500,000

2 Which of these is the same as 6,040?

Ⓐ 6 hundreds + 4 ones

Ⓑ 6 hundreds + 4 tens

Ⓒ 6 thousands + 4 ones

Ⓓ 6 thousands + 4 tens

3 Carey plotted a number on a number line, as shown below.

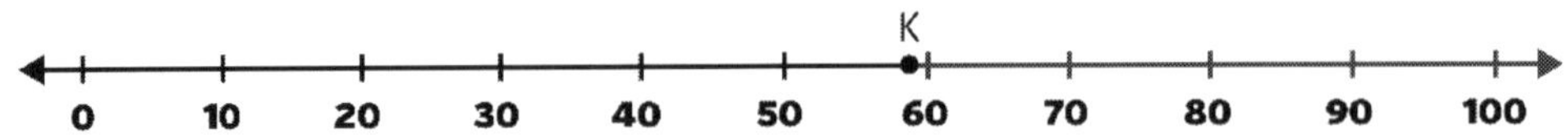

Which number could Carey have plotted?

Ⓐ 55

Ⓑ 58

Ⓒ 61

Ⓓ 69

4 Complete the missing numbers to show 7,603 in expanded form.

________________ + ________________ + ________________

5 The sale price of a guitar is shown below.

What is the sale price rounded to the nearest ten?

Ⓐ $150

Ⓑ $160

Ⓒ $190

Ⓓ $200

6 What number is represented by the shaded number cubes? Write your answer on the line below.

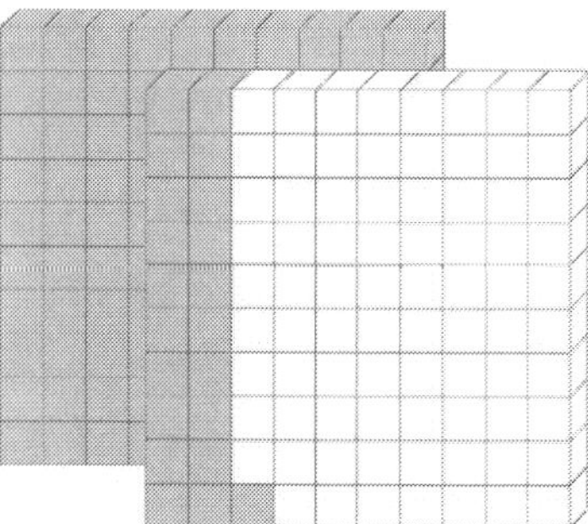

Answer __________

7 Select **all** the numbers that round to 650 when rounded to the nearest ten.

- ☐ 641
- ☐ 645
- ☐ 648
- ☐ 652
- ☐ 656
- ☐ 659

8 Write the symbol < or > in each box to make each statement true.

1,620 ☐ 1,260

4,905 ☐ 4,509

3,114 ☐ 3,014

9 Place the numbers listed below in order. Write one number on each blank line.

2,754 2,812 2,708

____________ < ____________ < ____________

10 Shade the hundreds grid below to represent 6 tens + 3 ones.

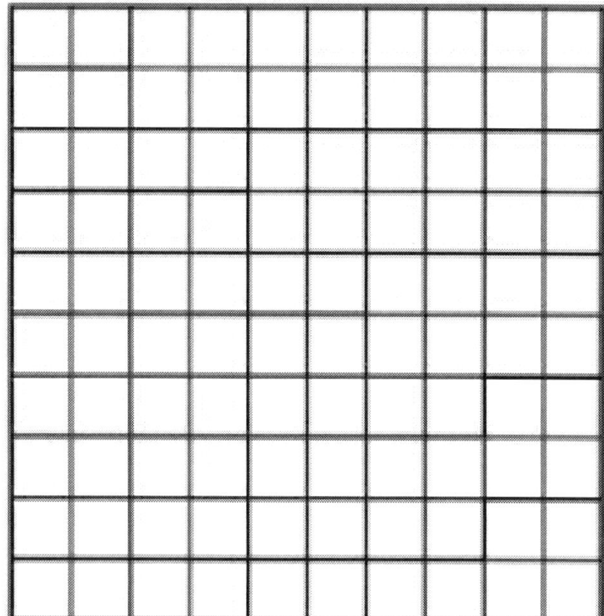

What is the number in standard form? Write your answer on the line below.

Answer ____________

Place Value – Practice Set 4

1 Which expression is the same as 4,089?

Ⓐ 4000 + 80 + 9

Ⓑ 4000 + 80 + 90

Ⓒ 4000 + 800 + 9

Ⓓ 4000 + 800 + 90

2 Which statement correctly compares the numbers?

Ⓐ 3,207 < 3,027

Ⓑ 3,027 > 3,720

Ⓒ 3,207 < 3,702

Ⓓ 3,027 > 3,072

3 The number line shows how much Ellen raised by doing a charity fun run.

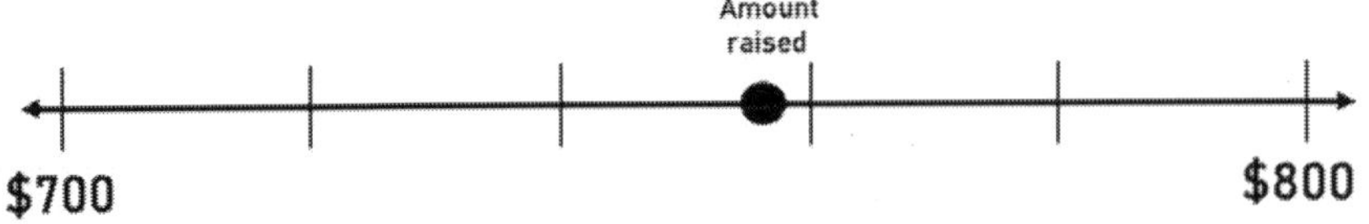

Which of these is the closest estimate of the amount of money raised?

Ⓐ $700

Ⓑ $740

Ⓒ $760

Ⓓ $800

4 Lake Monroe Bridge has a length of 627 feet. What is this length rounded to the nearest ten?

Ⓐ 600 feet

Ⓑ 620 feet

Ⓒ 630 feet

Ⓓ 650 feet

5 What number is represented by the number cubes below?

Ⓐ 114

Ⓑ 141

Ⓒ 1,401

Ⓓ 1,041

6 What is the number below in standard form? Write your answer on the line below.

8,000 + 200 + 7

Answer ____________

7 Select the **two** statements that are correct.

☐ 25,860 > 24,860

☐ 25,860 > 35,860

☐ 25,860 > 25,880

☐ 25,860 > 25,864

☐ 25,860 > 25,960

☐ 25,860 > 25,806

8 Complete the missing numbers to show the number eight thousand three hundred and four in expanded form.

8,000 + ________ + ________

What is the number in standard form? Write your answer on the line below.

Answer ______________

9 Complete the missing numbers to represent 4,700 in three different ways.

_______ thousands and _______ hundreds

_______ hundreds

_______ tens

10 Tick the correct box to show the value of each number rounded to the nearest ten.

	120	**130**	**140**
127	☐	☐	☐
122	☐	☐	☐
136	☐	☐	☐
131	☐	☐	☐

Place Value – Practice Set 5

1 Which number is the same as 63 hundreds?

Ⓐ 603

Ⓑ 630

Ⓒ 6,030

Ⓓ 6,300

2 Olivia's school has three thousand and seventeen students. What is this number in standard form? Write your answer on the line below.

Answer ______________

3 Four students guessed the number of candy canes in a jar.

Student	Guess
Pablo	326
Derek	318
Thomas	370
Mitch	309

Write the guesses on the lines below to order them correctly.

__________ < __________ < __________ < __________

4 Complete the missing numbers to show 6,057 in expanded form.

$$(\_\_\_\_ \times 1{,}000) + (\_\_\_\_ \times 10) + (\_\_\_\_ \times 1)$$

5 Zane used number cubes to model a number.

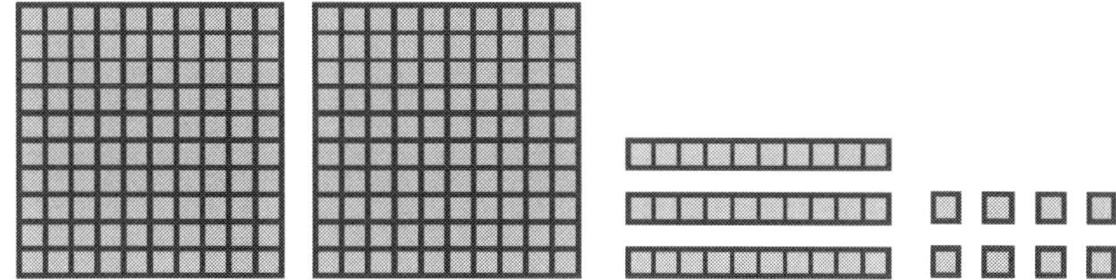

Which number is represented by the model? Write your answer on the line below.

Answer ____________

6 A number represented by M is plotted on the number line below.

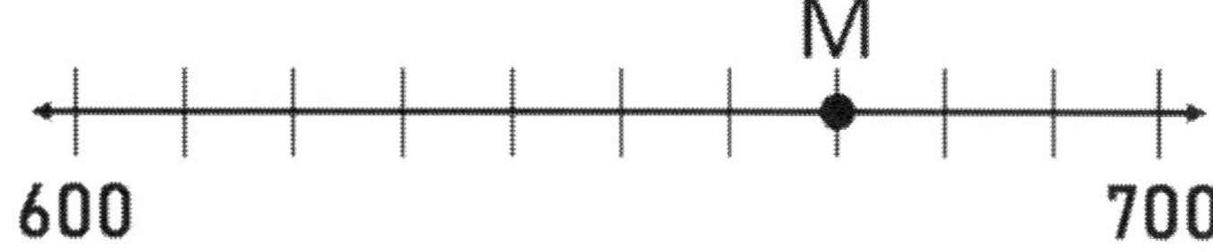

What number is represented by M? Write your answer on the line below.

Answer ____________

7 Which two numbers round to 400 when rounded to the nearest hundred? Select the **two** correct answers.

- ☐ 339
- ☐ 475
- ☐ 412
- ☐ 374
- ☐ 460
- ☐ 308

8 Shade the hundreds grid below to represent the number 23.

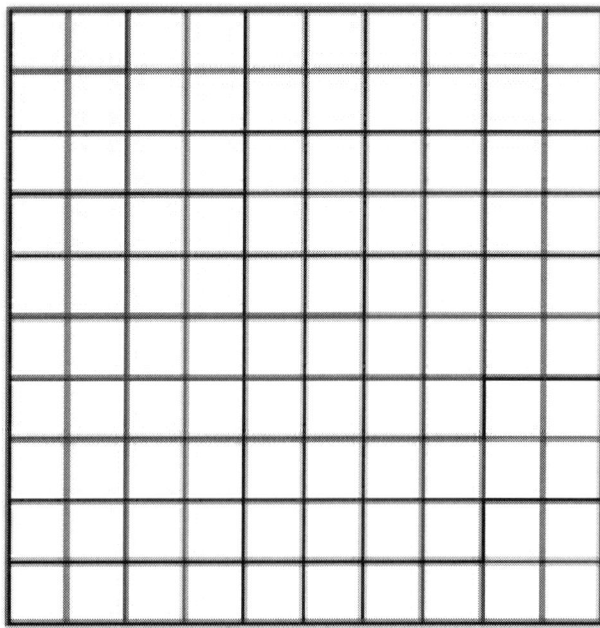

9 Round each number to the nearest ten. Write the rounded numbers on the blank lines.

184	__________	28	__________
73	__________	755	__________
846	__________	622	__________
731	__________	209	__________

10 Write the symbol < or > in each box to make each statement true.

9,705 ☐ 9,605

3,147 ☐ 3,047

2,953 ☐ 2,959

Number Sense and Operations

Addition, Subtraction, Multiplication, and Division

B.E.S.T. Standards

MA.3.NSO.2 Add and subtract multi-digit whole numbers. Build an understanding of multiplication and division operations.

MA.3.NSO.2.1
Add and subtract multi-digit whole numbers including using a standard algorithm with procedural fluency.

MA.3.NSO.2.2
Explore multiplication of two whole numbers with products from 0 to 144, and related division facts.

MA.3.NSO.2.3
Multiply a one-digit whole number by a multiple of 10, up to 90, or a multiple of 100, up to 900, with procedural reliability.

MA.3.NSO.2.4
Multiply two whole numbers from 0 to 12 and divide using related facts with procedural reliability.

Addition, Subtraction, Multiplication, and Division – Practice Set 1

1 Which of these is another way of writing 7 × 4?

Ⓐ 4 + 4 + 4 + 4

Ⓑ 7 + 4 + 7 + 4

Ⓒ 4 + 4 + 4 + 4 + 4 + 4 + 4

Ⓓ 7 + 7 + 7 + 7 + 7 + 7 + 7

2 Which expression could be used to find the missing number below?

□ ÷ 3 = 9

Ⓐ 9 × 3

Ⓑ 9 ÷ 3

Ⓒ 9 + 3

Ⓓ 9 – 3

3 An addition problem is shown below.

$$\begin{array}{r} 167\ + \\ \underline{685} \end{array}$$

What is the sum of the two numbers?

Ⓐ 742

Ⓑ 752

Ⓒ 842

Ⓓ 852

4 Which of these is represented by the diagram?

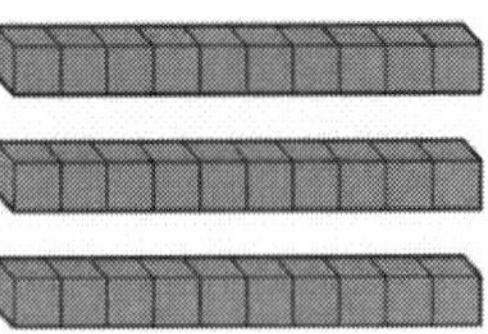

Ⓐ $1 \times 3 = 3$

Ⓑ $10 \times 3 = 30$

Ⓒ $30 \times 3 = 90$

Ⓓ $100 \times 3 = 100$

5 Freya is making fruit bowls. The diagram below represents how she divided apples equally among 5 bowls.

Which expression represents how many apples she had?

Ⓐ $4 + 5$

Ⓑ $4 + 4$

Ⓒ 4×5

Ⓓ 4×4

6 What is the difference of 854 and 127? Write your answer on the line below.

Answer ____________

7 Which two expressions are equal to 160? Select the **two** correct answers.

☐ 80 × 2

☐ 40 × 40

☐ 10 × 6

☐ 20 × 80

☐ 40 × 4

☐ 100 × 6

8 An area model is shown below.

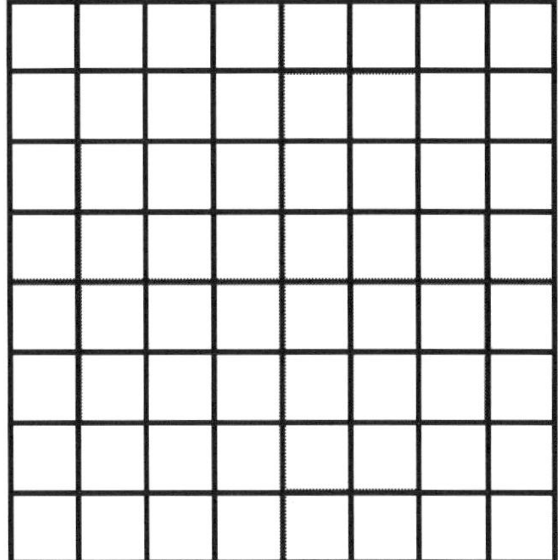

Write the missing numbers to show the product represented by the area model.

_______ × _______ = _______

9 Complete the missing number to show the correct sum for each equation.

$$86 + 10 = \square$$

$$54 + 13 = \square$$

$$91 + 8 = \square$$

$$16 + 41 = \square$$

10 Jacquie buys 6 packets of balloons. There are 12 balloons in each packet. How many balloons does she buy in all?

Show your work.

Answer _______ balloons

Addition, Subtraction, Multiplication, and Division – Practice Set 2

1 What is the product of 8 and 60?

Ⓐ 420

Ⓑ 480

Ⓒ 4,200

Ⓓ 4,800

2 Vinny cycles 4 miles every morning. How far would he cycle in 7 days?

Ⓐ 14 miles

Ⓑ 21 miles

Ⓒ 24 miles

Ⓓ 28 miles

3 Hendrix divided the 15 pencils below into 3 equal groups.

Which expression shows how many pencils would be in each group?

Ⓐ 15 + 3

Ⓑ 15 – 3

Ⓒ 15 ÷ 3

Ⓓ 15 × 3

4 What number makes both equations true? Write your answer on the line below.

$$5 \times \square = 55$$

$$55 \div \square = 5$$

Answer __________

5 A subtraction problem is shown below.

2,708 –
1,954

What is the difference of the two numbers?

Ⓐ 754

Ⓑ 854

Ⓒ 1,054

Ⓓ 1,254

6 Complete the missing numbers to write 4 × 5 as two different addition expressions.

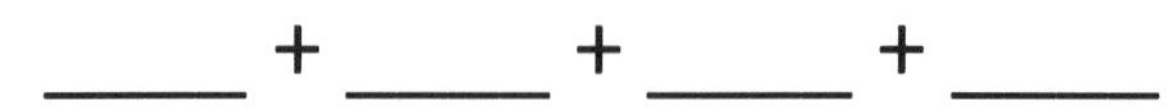

7 Which two sums have a value of 100? Select the **two** correct answers.

☐ 35 + 55

☐ 28 + 72

☐ 53 + 57

☐ 19 + 81

☐ 46 + 64

☐ 22 + 72

8 Write the symbol + or – in each empty box to create a correct equation.

20 ☐ 38 = 58

68 ☐ 20 = 88

46 ☐ 21 = 67

24 ☐ 14 = 10

9 The diagram below represents a sheet of stamps.

Complete the equation to show how many stamps are on a sheet.

________ × ________ = ________

10 Shade the hundreds grid below to represent the product of 4 and 10.

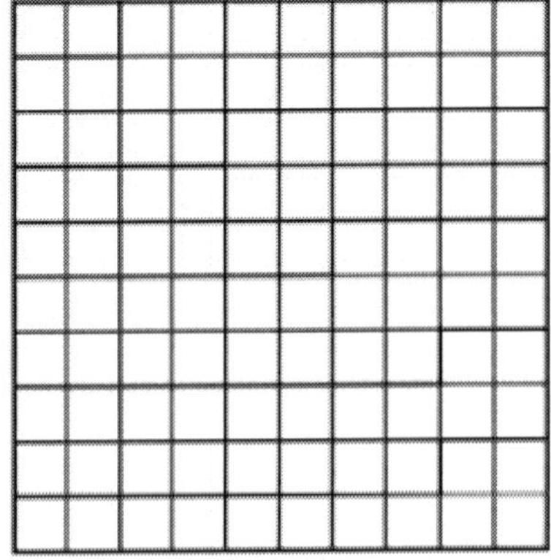

What is the product of 4 and 10? Write your answer on the line below.

Answer ____________

Addition, Subtraction, Multiplication, and Division – Practice Set 3

1 What is the sum of 458 and 242?

Ⓐ 680

Ⓑ 690

Ⓒ 700

Ⓓ 710

2 Which expression is equal to 420?

Ⓐ 7×60

Ⓑ 8×40

Ⓒ 70×60

Ⓓ 80×40

3 The diagram below shows the squares on a chessboard.

Which expression represents the number of squares on a chessboard?

Ⓐ $8 + 8$

Ⓑ 8×8

Ⓒ $8 + 8 + 8$

Ⓓ $8 \times 8 \times 8$

4 Which of these is equal to 64?

Ⓐ 6 × 6

Ⓑ 7 × 7

Ⓒ 8 × 8

Ⓓ 9 × 9

5 Aiden used number cubes to model a multiplication problem.

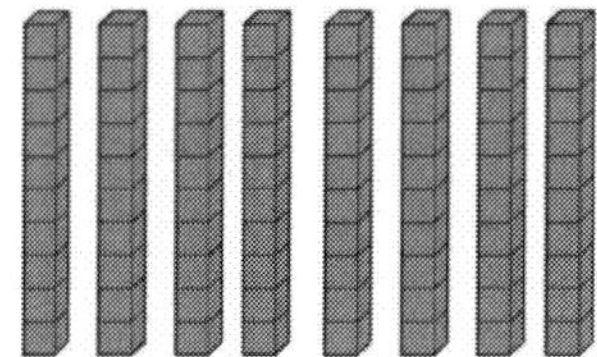

Which problem is modeled?

Ⓐ 1 × 8 = 8

Ⓑ 10 × 8 = 80

Ⓒ 80 × 8 = 640

Ⓓ 100 × 8 = 800

6 A subtraction problem is shown below.

9,854 –
<u>3,603</u>

What is the difference of the numbers? Write your answer on the line below.

Answer ____________________

7 Joan wants to buy 24 notebooks. Which of these is a way of buying exactly 24 notebooks? Select the **two** correct answers.

☐ buy 4 packets of 6 notebooks each

☐ buy 5 packets of 5 notebooks each

☐ buy 7 packets of 3 notebooks each

☐ buy 9 packets of 2 notebooks each

☐ buy 6 packets of 6 notebooks each

☐ buy 8 packets of 3 notebooks each

8 Complete the missing number to show the correct sum or difference for each equation.

$$48 + 30 = \square$$

$$99 - 84 = \square$$

$$82 + 5 = \square$$

$$65 - 44 = \square$$

9 Alex decorated 5 cakes with an equal number of strawberries, as shown below.

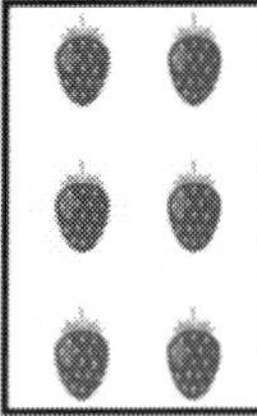 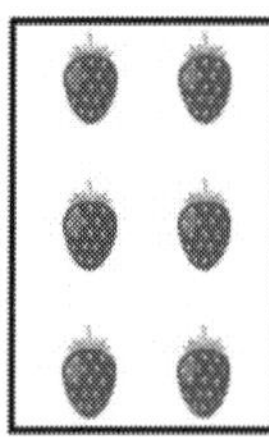  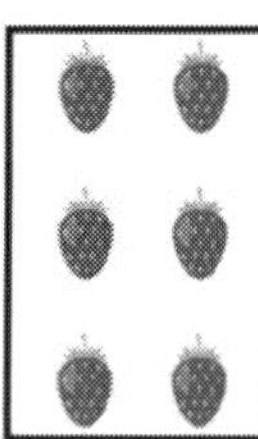 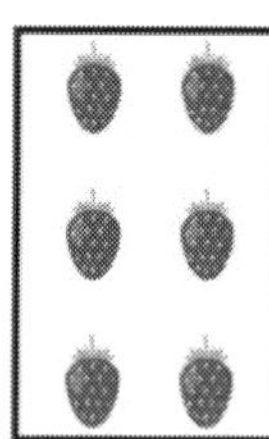

Complete the missing numbers to write an expression representing how many strawberries Alex used.

How many strawberries did Alex use? Write your answer on the line below.

Answer ____________

10 Daniel wants to solve the equation below.

$$\square \div 9 = 6$$

Write a multiplication expression that could be used to find the missing number.

Addition, Subtraction, Multiplication, and Division – Practice Set 4

1 What is the difference of 308 and 49?

Ⓐ 251

Ⓑ 261

Ⓒ 259

Ⓓ 269

2 Which of these is another way to write 900 × 7?

Ⓐ 9 × 7 × 10

Ⓑ 9 × 7 × 100

Ⓒ 90 × 70 × 10

Ⓓ 90 × 70 × 100

3 Miss McKee divided drama students into 6 teams. The diagram represents how many students were on each team.

12	12	12	12	12	12

How many drama students were there?

Ⓐ 24

Ⓑ 36

Ⓒ 72

Ⓓ 84

4 Which question gives one way to find the value of $36 \div 4$?

Ⓐ What number added to 4 equals 36?

Ⓑ What number subtracted from 36 equals 4?

Ⓒ What number multiplied by 4 equals 36?

Ⓓ What number divided by 4 equals 36?

5 The diagram below represents the area of an office.

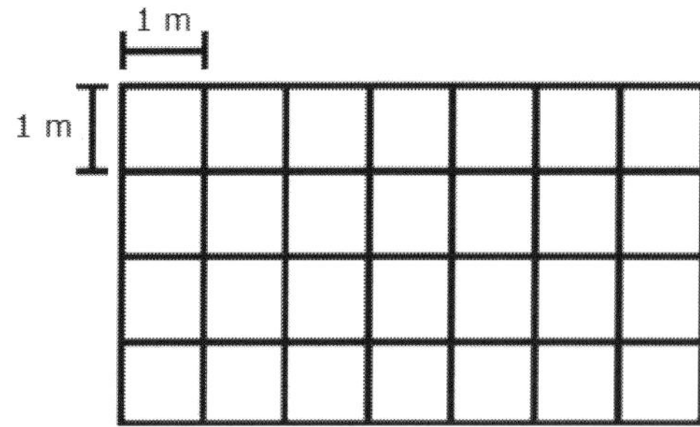

Which equation represents the area of the office, in square meters?

Ⓐ $4 + 7 = 11$

Ⓑ $4 + 4 + 7 + 7 = 22$

Ⓒ $4 \times 7 = 28$

Ⓓ $7 \times 7 = 49$

6 Complete the missing numbers to write 6×3 as two addition expressions.

_____ + _____ + _____

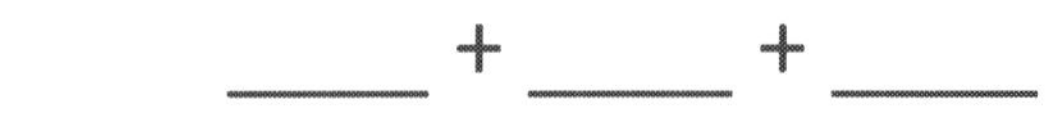

7 Shade the squares for all the sums that equal 10.

3+5	4+6	4+2
6+1	8+2	1+7
1+9	5+5	1+4

8 Write the missing number on the blank line to make equation true.

49 ÷ _____ = 7

54 ÷ _____ = 6

77 ÷ _____ = 7

63 ÷ _____ = 9

9 Complete the missing number to show the correct sum or difference for each equation.

$$53 + 16 = \square$$

$$14 - 6 = \square$$

$$80 - 40 = \square$$

$$29 + 20 = \square$$

10 Sierra orders 3 pizzas. Each pizza is cut into 10 slices.

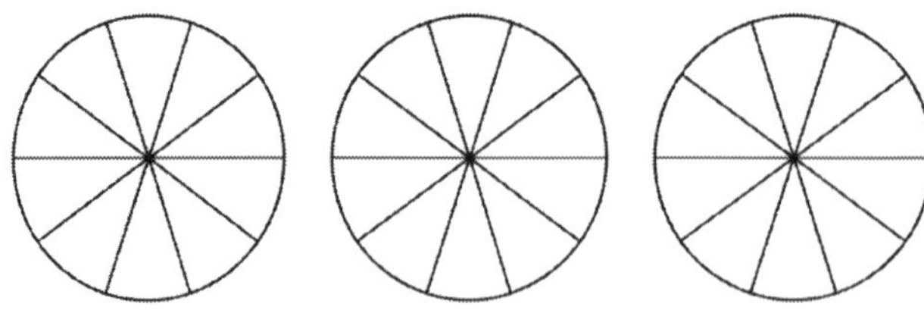

Complete the missing numbers to write an equation representing how many slices of pizza there are in all.

Addition, Subtraction, Multiplication, and Division – Practice Set 5

1 Adam buys 6 packets of golf balls. There are 12 golf balls in each packet. Which of these shows how many golf balls he bought in all?

Ⓐ 12 + 6

Ⓑ 12 – 6

Ⓒ 12 × 6

Ⓓ 12 ÷ 6

2 What is the difference of 954 and 123?

Ⓐ 721

Ⓑ 731

Ⓒ 821

Ⓓ 831

3 What does the array below represent?

Ⓐ 24 ÷ 6 = 4

Ⓑ 24 + 6 = 30

Ⓒ 24 × 6 = 144

Ⓓ 24 – 6 = 18

4 What is the quotient of 72 and 8?

Ⓐ 6

Ⓑ 7

Ⓒ 8

Ⓓ 9

5 All the members of a choir were divided into 8 groups of 3 to practice.

How many members are in the choir?

Ⓐ 11

Ⓑ 16

Ⓒ 24

Ⓓ 32

6 An addition problem is shown below.

$$\begin{array}{r} 2{,}385 + \\ \underline{2{,}465} \end{array}$$

What is the sum of the numbers? Write your answer on the line below.

Answer ________________

7 Which two products are equal to 270? Select the **two** correct answers.

☐ 4×60

☐ 2×70

☐ 60×4

☐ 90×3

☐ 70×2

☐ 3×90

8 There are 12 inches in 1 foot. Complete the table below to show the number of inches in 2, 3, and 4 feet.

Feet	Inches
1	12
2	
3	
4	

9 Complete the missing number that makes each equation true.

$8 \times \_\_\_\_ = 800$

$50 \times \_\_\_\_ = 450$

$200 \times \_\_\_\_ = 1,400$

10 Complete the missing number to show the correct sum or difference for each equation.

18 + 2 = ☐

17 − 7 = ☐

15 + 2 = ☐

Fractions

Understanding Fractions

B.E.S.T. Standards

MA.3.FR.1 Understand fractions as numbers and represent fractions.

MA.3.FR.1.1
Represent and interpret unit fractions in the form $\frac{1}{n}$ as the quantity formed by one part when a whole is partitioned into *n* equal parts.

MA.3.FR.1.2
Represent and interpret fractions, including fractions greater than one, in the form of $\frac{m}{n}$ as the result of adding the unit fraction $\frac{1}{n}$ to itself m times.

MA.3.FR.1.3
Read and write fractions, including fractions greater than one, using standard form, numeral-word form and word form.

Understanding Fractions – Practice Set 1

1 What is the value of $\frac{1}{8}+\frac{1}{8}+\frac{1}{8}+\frac{1}{8}+\frac{1}{8}+\frac{1}{8}$?

Ⓐ $\frac{2}{8}$

Ⓑ $\frac{4}{8}$

Ⓒ $\frac{6}{8}$

Ⓓ $\frac{8}{8}$

2 Which of these is a correct way of writing $\frac{4}{5}$?

Ⓐ 4 fives

Ⓑ 4 fifths

Ⓒ 4 fifteens

Ⓓ 4 fifty

3 Which fraction is represented below?

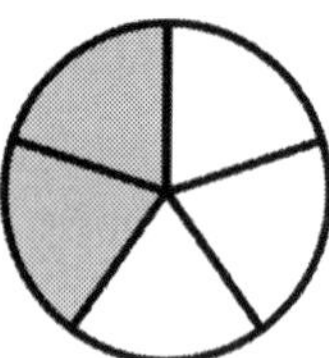

Ⓐ $\frac{1}{5}$

Ⓑ $\frac{2}{5}$

Ⓒ $\frac{3}{2}$

Ⓓ $\frac{2}{3}$

4 How is the fraction represented below written in words?

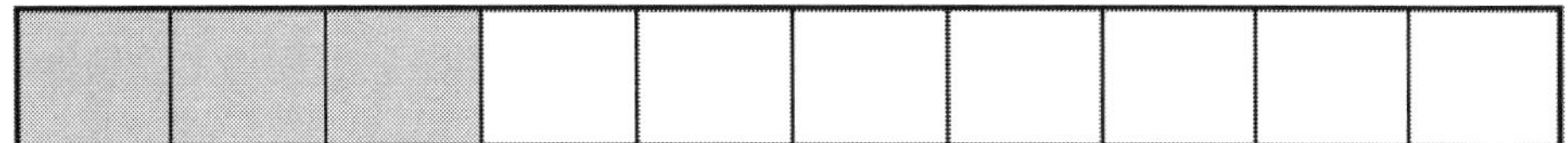

Ⓐ three-tens

Ⓑ three-tenths

Ⓒ ten-threes

Ⓓ ten-thirds

5 A pizza is divided into equal slices, as shown below.

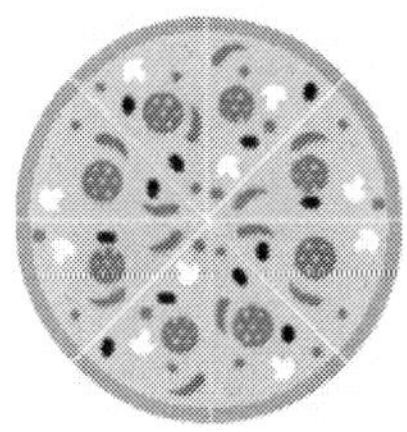

What fraction of the whole pizza is each slice?

Ⓐ $\frac{1}{4}$

Ⓑ $\frac{1}{6}$

Ⓒ $\frac{1}{8}$

Ⓓ $\frac{1}{12}$

6 What is the value of $\frac{1}{3} + \frac{1}{3}$? Write your answer on the line below.

Answer ____________

7 The diagram below represents 30 seconds on a 1-minute timer.

Which of these is 30 seconds? Select the **one** correct answer.

☐ half a minute

☐ one third of a minute

☐ one quarter of a minute

☐ one fifth of a minute

☐ one sixth of a minute

☐ one tenth of a minute

8 Shade the diagram below to represent $\frac{1}{4}+\frac{1}{4}+\frac{1}{4}+\frac{1}{4}+\frac{1}{4}$.

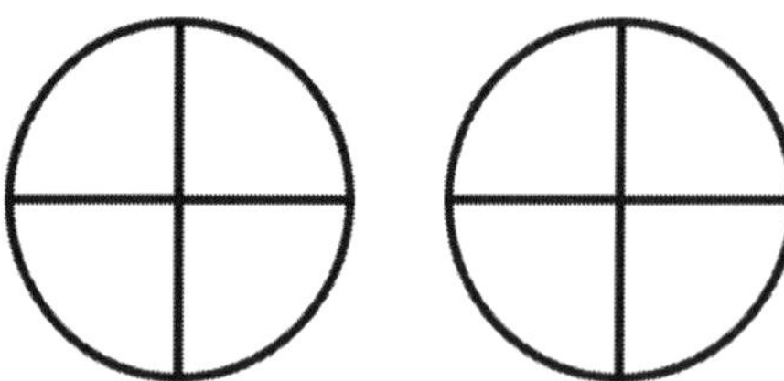

What is the value of $\frac{1}{4}+\frac{1}{4}+\frac{1}{4}+\frac{1}{4}+\frac{1}{4}$? Write your answer on the line below.

Answer __________

9 A carton of eggs is shown below.

What fraction of the whole carton is each egg? Write your answer on the line below.

Answer ____________

10 Plot the fraction $\frac{1}{4}$ on the number line below.

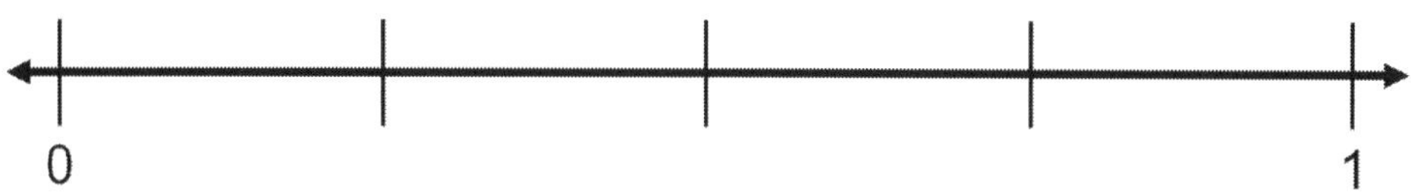

Understanding Fractions – Practice Set 2

1 What is the value of $\frac{1}{4}+\frac{1}{4}+\frac{1}{4}+\frac{1}{4}+\frac{1}{4}$?

Ⓐ $\frac{5}{4}$

Ⓑ $\frac{5}{20}$

Ⓒ $\frac{1}{20}$

Ⓓ $\frac{11}{4}$

2 Which of these is the fraction three-tenths?

Ⓐ $\frac{3}{1}$

Ⓑ $\frac{1}{3}$

Ⓒ $\frac{3}{10}$

Ⓓ $\frac{10}{3}$

3 Phillip has the ties shown below.

What fraction of the ties have stripes? Write your answer on the line.

Answer ___________

4 Which of these is a correct way to write the fraction $\frac{6}{8}$?

Ⓐ 6 eights

Ⓑ 6 eighths

Ⓒ 8 sixes

Ⓓ 8 sixths

5 Leah has 3 red apples and 1 green apple.

What fraction of the apples are green?

Ⓐ $\frac{1}{3}$

Ⓑ $\frac{1}{4}$

Ⓒ $\frac{3}{4}$

Ⓓ $\frac{4}{3}$

6 What fraction is plotted on the number line? Write your answer on the line below.

Answer __________

7 Shade the diagram below to represent $\frac{1}{3}+\frac{1}{3}+\frac{1}{3}+\frac{1}{3}$.

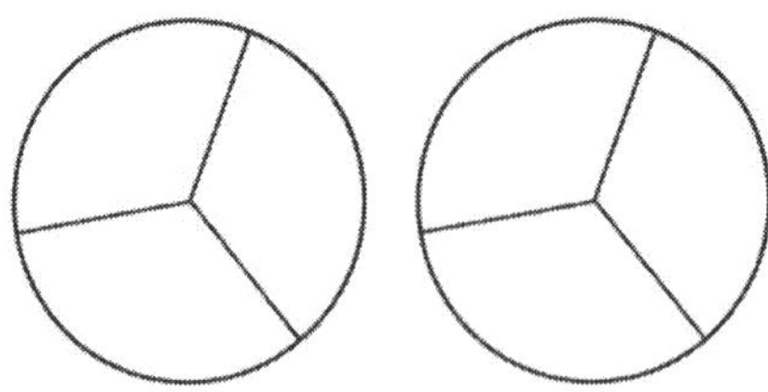

What is the value of $\frac{1}{3}+\frac{1}{3}+\frac{1}{3}+\frac{1}{3}$? Write your answer on the line below.

Answer __________

8 Shade the diagram below to represent the fraction $\frac{1}{12}$.

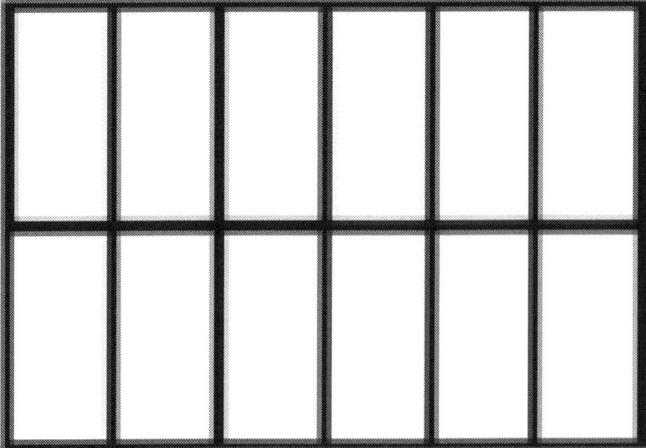

9 Complete the missing numbers to show one way to represent $\frac{2}{3}$.

$$\frac{\_\_\_}{3} + \frac{\_\_\_}{3} = \frac{2}{3}$$

10 Write each fraction in standard form.

six-eighths ____________

nine-thirds ____________

five-sixths ____________

three-tenths ____________

Understanding Fractions – Practice Set 3

1 What is the value of $\frac{1}{2} + \frac{1}{2} + \frac{1}{2}$?

Ⓐ 1

Ⓑ $1\frac{1}{2}$

Ⓒ 2

Ⓓ $2\frac{1}{2}$

2 Which of these is a correct way to write the fraction $\frac{3}{5}$?

Ⓐ 3 fives

Ⓑ 3 fifths

Ⓒ 5 threes

Ⓓ 5 thirds

3 What fraction of the buttons shown below are shaped like circles?

Ⓐ $\frac{1}{2}$

Ⓑ $\frac{1}{4}$

Ⓒ $\frac{1}{5}$

Ⓓ $\frac{1}{10}$

4 Which of these is represented below?

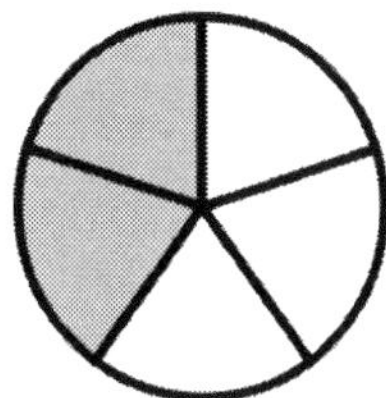

Ⓐ 2 halves

Ⓑ 2 thirds

Ⓒ 2 quarters

Ⓓ 2 fifths

5 An apple is cut into equal slices, as shown below.

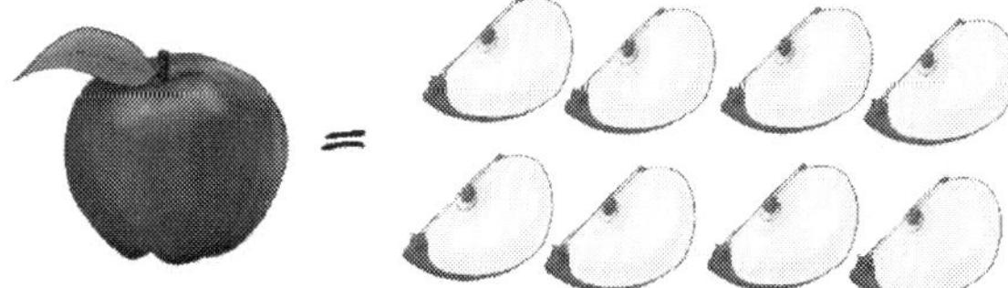

What fraction of the whole apple is each slice?

Ⓐ $\frac{1}{4}$

Ⓑ $\frac{1}{6}$

Ⓒ $\frac{1}{8}$

Ⓓ $\frac{1}{12}$

6 What is the fraction seven-eighths in standard form? Write your answer on the line below.

Answer ____________

7 The number line below shows the point $\frac{6}{10}$. Plot the point on the number line that is $\frac{1}{10}$ more than $\frac{6}{10}$.

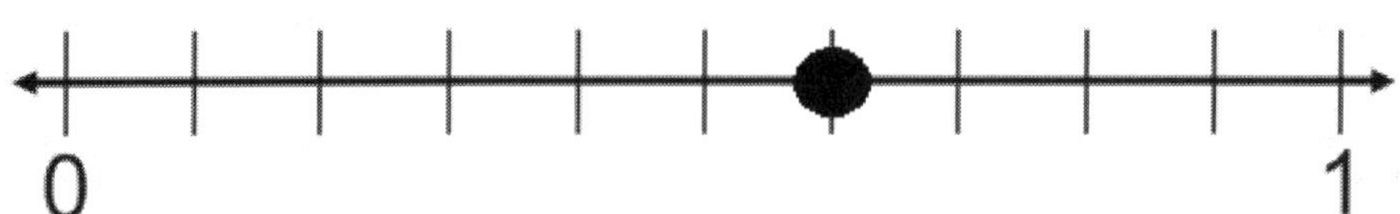

What fraction is $\frac{1}{10}$ more than $\frac{6}{10}$? Write your answer on the line below.

Answer ____________

8 Shade the circle that is divided into sixths.

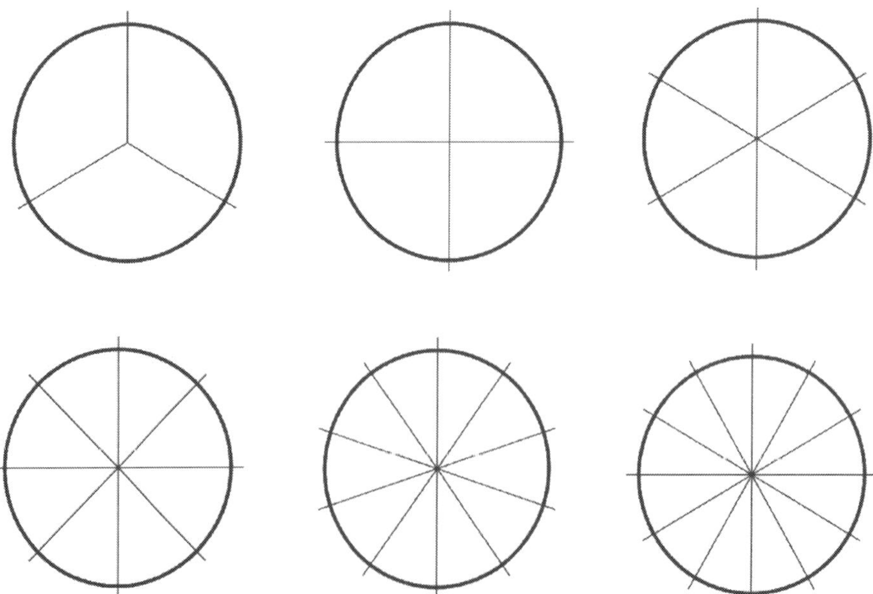

9 Complete the missing numbers to show two ways to represent $\frac{3}{4}$.

$$\frac{\quad}{4} + \frac{\quad}{4} + \frac{\quad}{4} = \frac{3}{4}$$

$$\frac{\quad}{4} + \frac{1}{4} = \frac{3}{4}$$

10 Plot the fraction $\frac{1}{6}$ on the number line below.

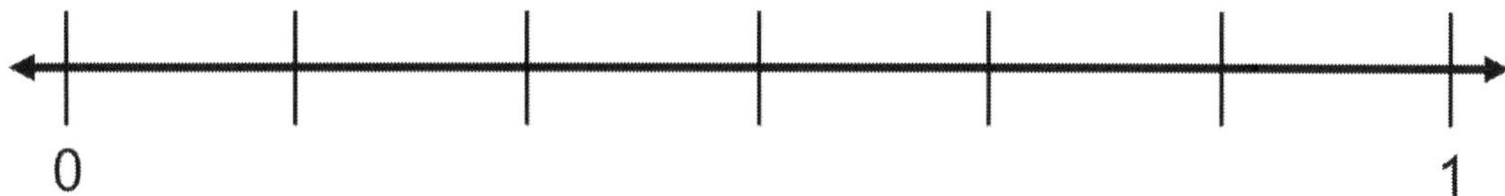

Understanding Fractions – Practice Set 4

1 Which of these shows another way to represent $\frac{2}{3}$?

Ⓐ $\frac{1}{3} + \frac{1}{2}$

Ⓑ $\frac{1}{3} + \frac{1}{3}$

Ⓒ $\frac{1}{3} \times \frac{1}{3}$

Ⓓ $\frac{1}{3} \times \frac{1}{2}$

2 Which of these is a correct way of writing $\frac{3}{4}$?

Ⓐ 3 fours

Ⓑ 3 halves

Ⓒ 3 quarters

Ⓓ 3 forty

3 What fraction is the circle below divided into?

Ⓐ thirds

Ⓑ quarters

Ⓒ sixths

Ⓓ eighths

4 How many strawberries are represented below?

Ⓐ 3

Ⓑ $3\frac{1}{4}$

Ⓒ $3\frac{1}{2}$

Ⓓ 4

5 What fraction of the beanies shown below have stripes?

Ⓐ $\frac{1}{2}$

Ⓑ $\frac{1}{3}$

Ⓒ $\frac{1}{4}$

Ⓓ $\frac{1}{6}$

6 What is the value of $1\frac{1}{3} + \frac{1}{3}$? Write your answer on the line below.

Answer ______________

7 The diagram below represents 15 minutes on a 1 hour clock.

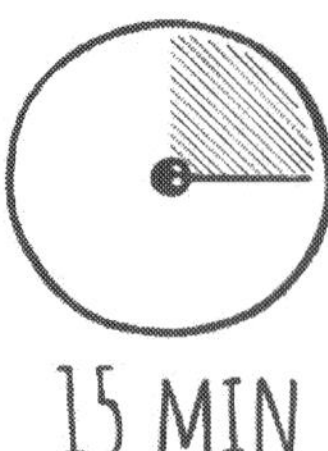

Which of these is 15 minutes? Select the **one** correct answer.

- ☐ half an hour
- ☐ one third of an hour
- ☐ one quarter of an hour
- ☐ one fifth of an hour
- ☐ one sixth of an hour
- ☐ one tenth of an hour

8 Shade the diagram below to show the result of $\frac{2}{5} + \frac{1}{5} + \frac{1}{5}$.

What fraction did you shade? Write your answer on the line below.

Answer __________

9 What fraction is represented by point S on the number line? Write the answer as an improper fraction and a mixed number.

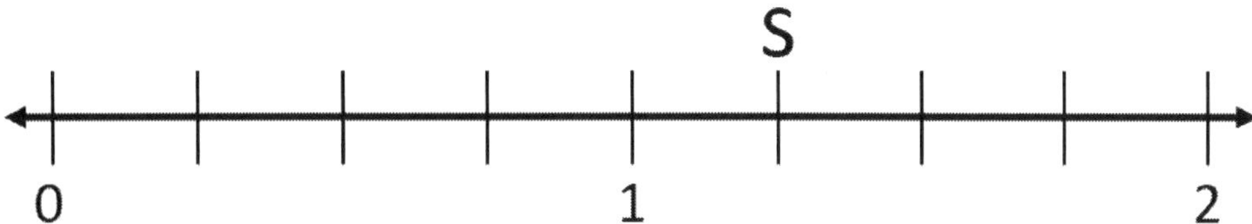

Improper fraction __________

Mixed number __________

10 Shade the diagram below to represent the fraction seven-tenths.

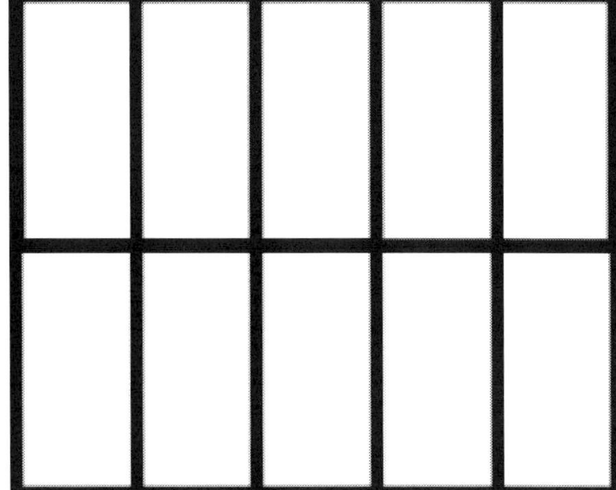

Understanding Fractions – Practice Set 5

1 Which of these is the fraction ten-fourths?

Ⓐ $\frac{4}{1}$

Ⓑ $\frac{1}{4}$

Ⓒ $\frac{4}{10}$

Ⓓ $\frac{10}{4}$

2 What is the value of $2\frac{1}{3} + \frac{1}{3} + \frac{1}{3}$?

Ⓐ $3\frac{1}{3}$

Ⓑ 3

Ⓒ $4\frac{1}{3}$

Ⓓ 4

3 Which letter represents the fraction $\frac{1}{4}$?

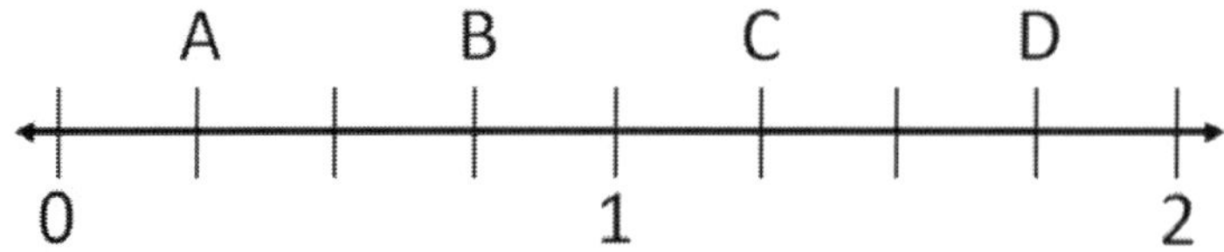

Ⓐ A

Ⓑ B

Ⓒ C

Ⓓ D

4 How is the fraction $\frac{5}{4}$ written in words?

Ⓐ five-fourths

Ⓑ five-fours

Ⓒ four-fives

Ⓓ four-fifths

5 Jacob cut a log into equal pieces, as shown below.

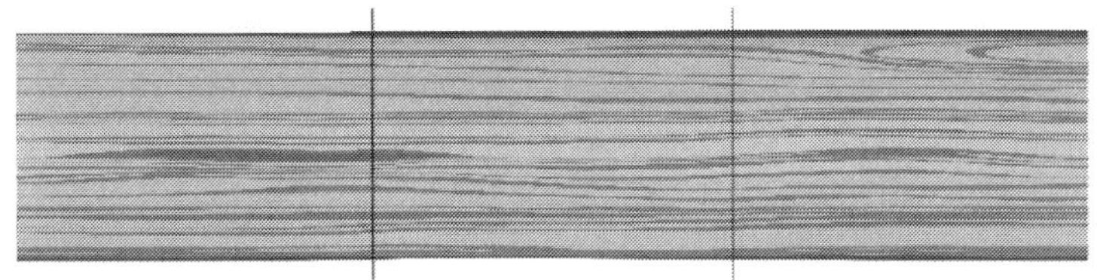

What fraction of the whole log is each piece?

Ⓐ a half

Ⓑ a third

Ⓒ a quarter

Ⓓ a sixth

6 Ava has the flip flops shown below.

What fraction of the flip flops have stripes? Write your answer on the line below.

Answer ____________

7 Which fractions are equivalent to $\frac{1}{5}+\frac{1}{5}+\frac{1}{5}+\frac{1}{5}+\frac{1}{5}+\frac{1}{5}+\frac{1}{5}+\frac{1}{5}$? Select the **two** correct answers.

- ☐ $\frac{1}{40}$
- ☐ $\frac{8}{5}$
- ☐ $\frac{8}{40}$
- ☐ $1\frac{3}{5}$
- ☐ $1\frac{1}{5}$
- ☐ $5\frac{3}{5}$

8 Plot the result of $\frac{1}{6}+\frac{1}{6}+\frac{1}{6}+\frac{1}{6}+\frac{1}{6}$ on the number line.

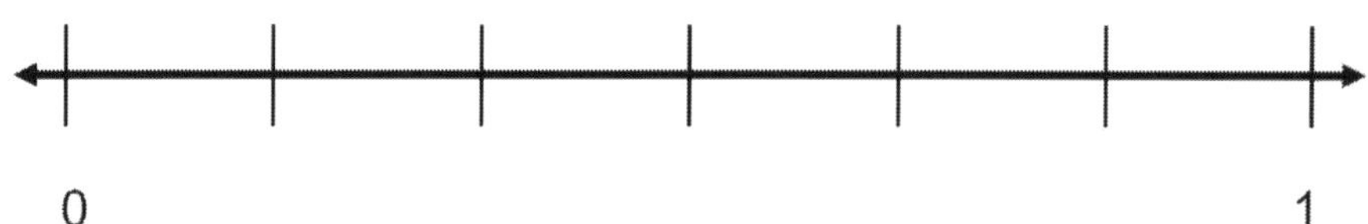

What fraction did you plot? Write your answer on the line below.

Answer __________

9 Write each fraction in standard form.

five-thirds ____________

three-fourths ____________

two-tenths ____________

seven-fifths ____________

10 Shade the square and the rectangle that are divided into parts that are $\frac{1}{8}$ of the shape.

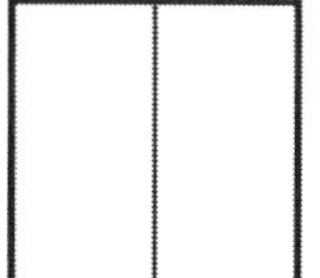 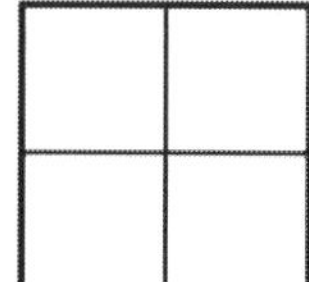 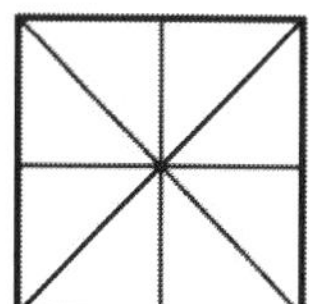 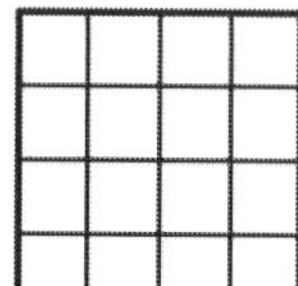

 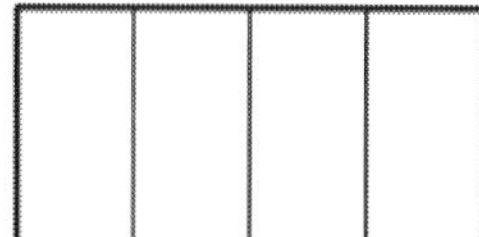 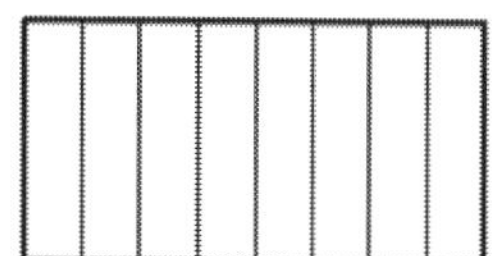 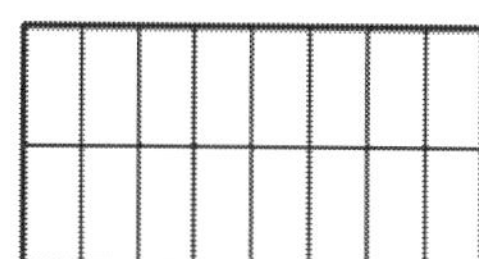

Fractions

Comparing and Ordering Fractions

B.E.S.T. Standards

MA.3.FR.2 Order and compare fractions and identify equivalent fractions.

MA.3.FR.2.1
Plot, order and compare fractional numbers with the same numerator or the same denominator.

MA.3.FR.2.2
Identify equivalent fractions and explain why they are equivalent.

Comparing and Ordering Fractions – Practice Set 1

1 Based on the diagram, what fraction is equivalent to $\frac{2}{3}$? Write your answer on the line below.

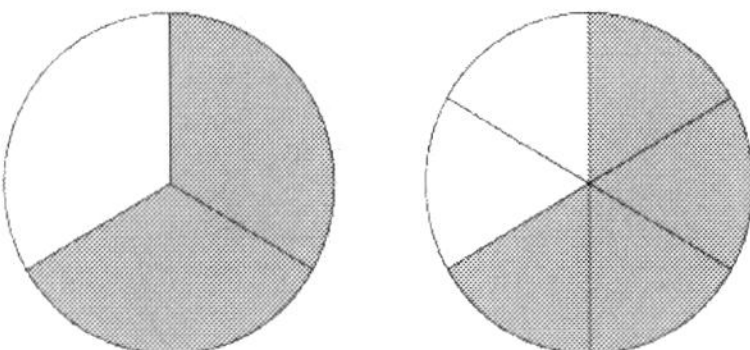

Answer ___________

2 Which fraction is the smallest?

Ⓐ $\frac{1}{4}$

Ⓑ $\frac{1}{2}$

Ⓒ $\frac{1}{12}$

Ⓓ $\frac{1}{10}$

3 Based on the number line, which fraction is less than $\frac{1}{2}$?

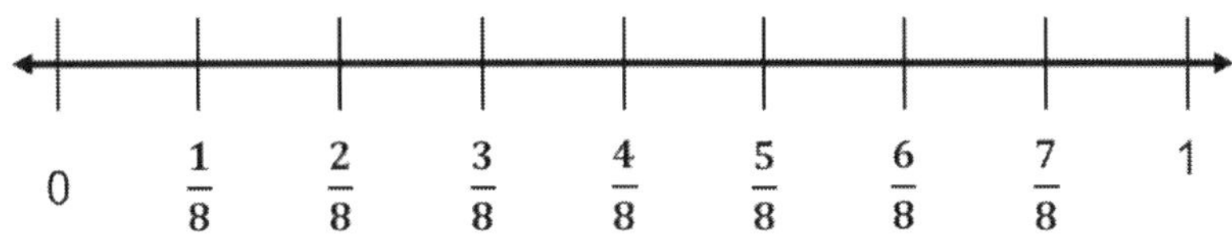

Ⓐ $\frac{2}{8}$

Ⓑ $\frac{4}{8}$

Ⓒ $\frac{6}{8}$

Ⓓ $\frac{7}{8}$

4 Circle the two fractions that are equivalent.

$$\frac{1}{2} \qquad \frac{3}{6} \qquad \frac{6}{4} \qquad \frac{4}{6}$$

5 Plot the fraction $4\frac{3}{4}$ on the number line below.

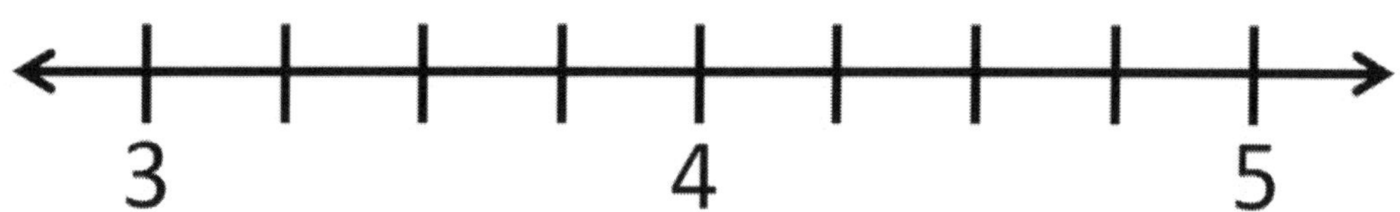

6 The diagram below represents the length of an eraser.

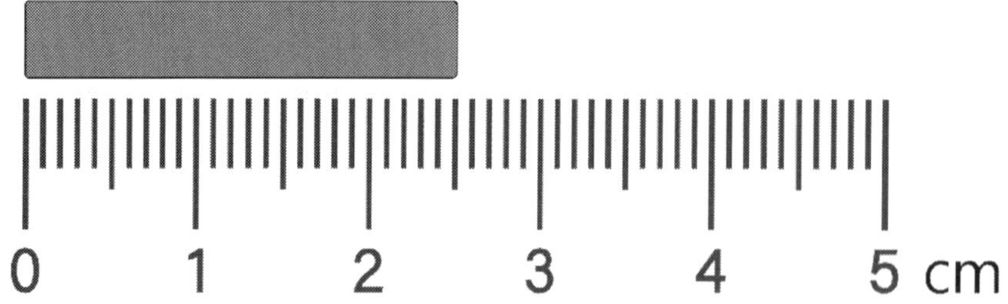

What is the length of the eraser? Write your answer as a fraction on the line below.

Answer ___________ cm

7 Select the two diagrams that represent equivalent fractions.

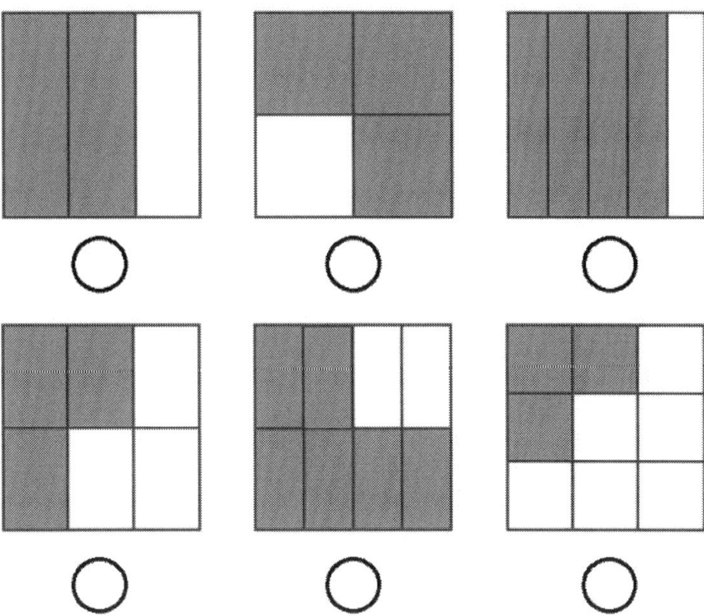

8 Plot the fraction $\frac{1}{3}$ on the number line below.

Plot a fraction equivalent to $\frac{1}{3}$ on the number line below.

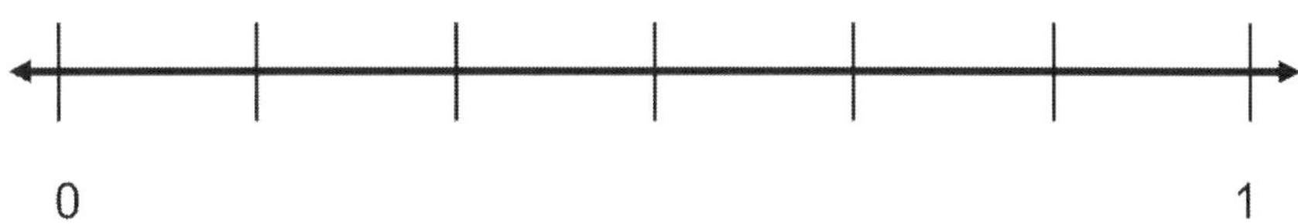

What fraction did you plot? Write your answer on the line below.

Answer ___________

9 Shade the diagrams below to represent the fractions given. Then write <, <, or = in the empty box to compare the fractions.

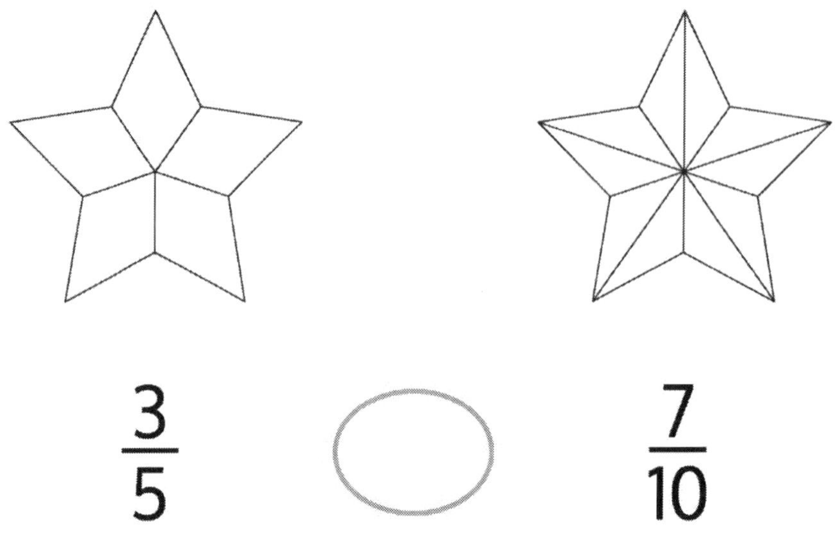

10 Write the missing number in the blank space to complete each pair of equivalent fractions. You can use the number line below to help you find the answers.

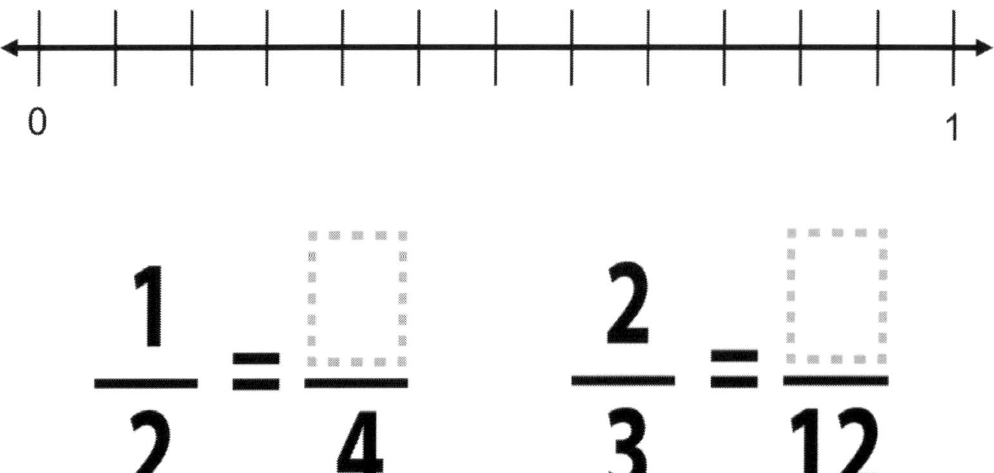

Comparing and Ordering Fractions – Practice Set 2

1 Which point on the line below represents $2\frac{3}{4}$ inches?

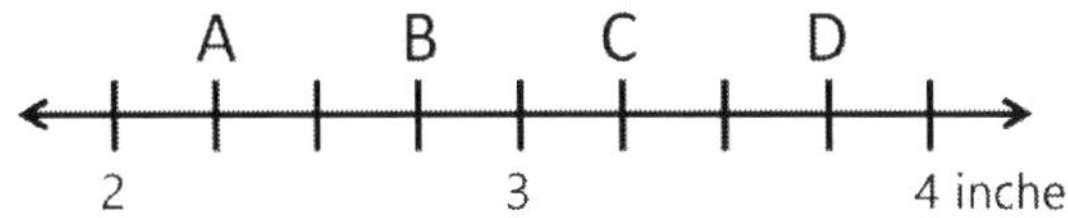

Ⓐ Point A

Ⓑ Point B

Ⓒ Point C

Ⓓ Point D

2 Circle the fraction that is equivalent to the fraction shown in the diagram.

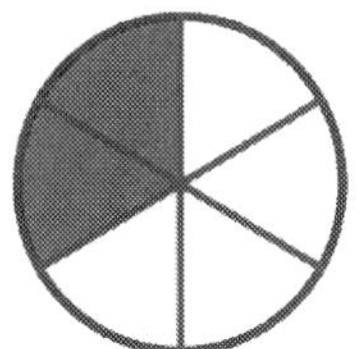

$\frac{2}{3}$ $\frac{2}{8}$ $\frac{3}{4}$ $\frac{1}{3}$

3 Which fraction is plotted on the number line below?

Ⓐ $\frac{2}{3}$

Ⓑ $\frac{2}{5}$

Ⓒ $\frac{3}{5}$

Ⓓ $\frac{3}{2}$

4 Which fraction is equivalent to $\frac{6}{10}$? Circle the letter of the correct fraction.

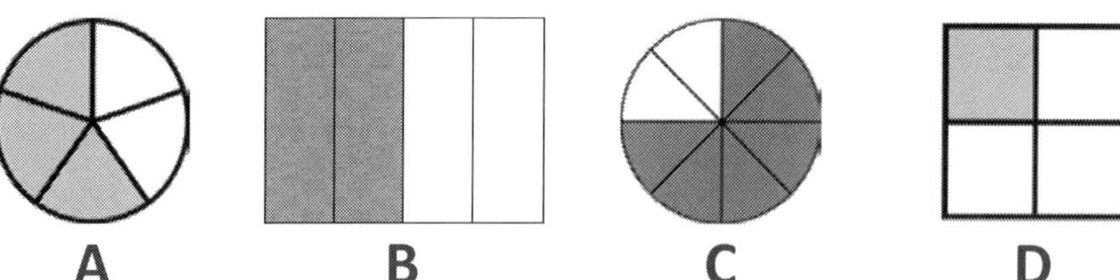

5 Based on the number line, which fractions is $\frac{7}{8}$ between?

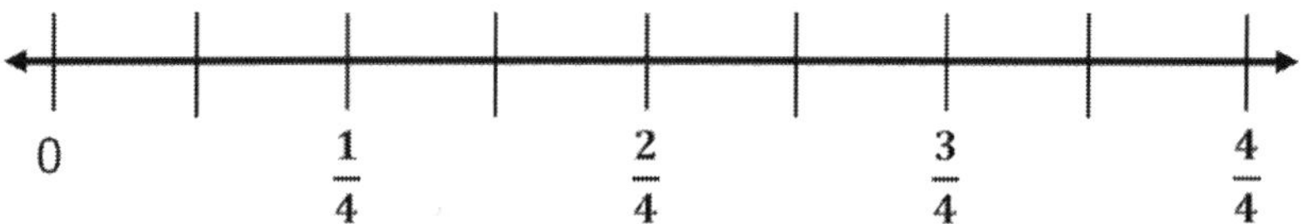

Ⓐ 0 and $\frac{1}{4}$

Ⓑ $\frac{1}{4}$ and $\frac{2}{4}$

Ⓒ $\frac{2}{4}$ and $\frac{3}{4}$

Ⓓ $\frac{3}{4}$ and $\frac{4}{4}$

6 Which fraction is twice the size of $\frac{1}{4}$? Write your answer on the line below.

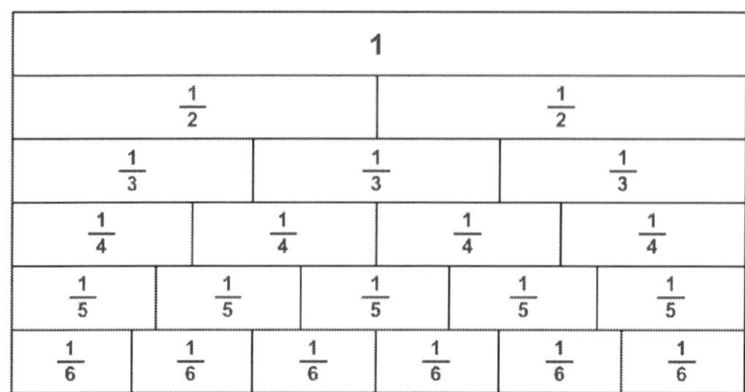

Answer ____________

7 Plot the fraction $\frac{2}{3}$ on the number line below.

Plot a fraction equivalent to $\frac{2}{3}$ on the number line below.

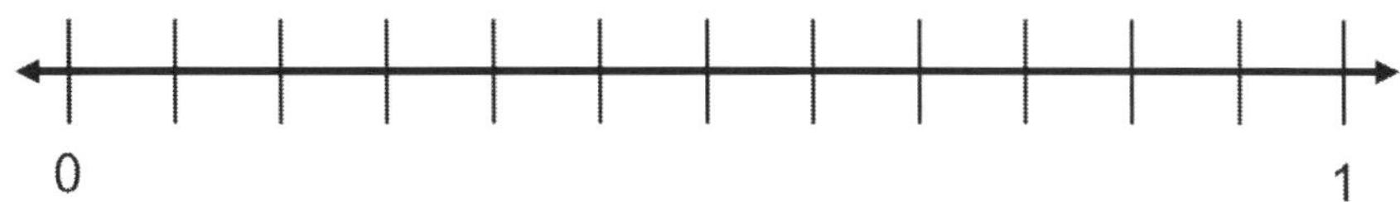

What fraction did you plot? Write your answer on the line below.

Answer ___________

8 Write the fractions shown below under each diagram. Then write <, <, or = in the empty box to compare the fractions.

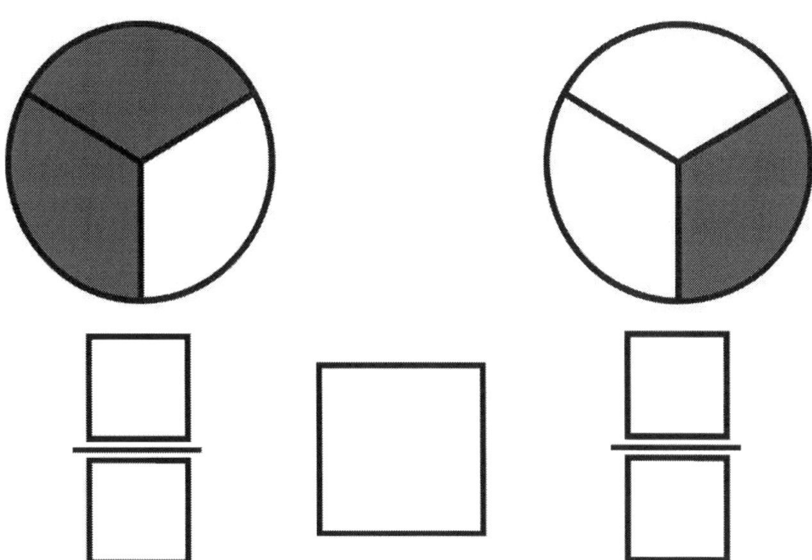

9 Shade the diagrams below to show that $\frac{1}{4}$ and $\frac{3}{12}$ are equivalent.

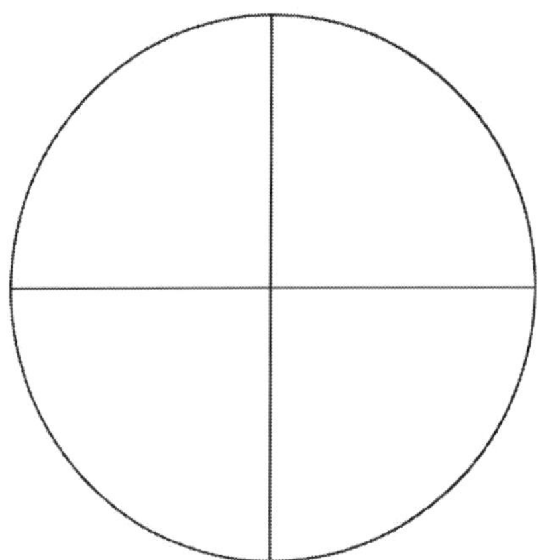
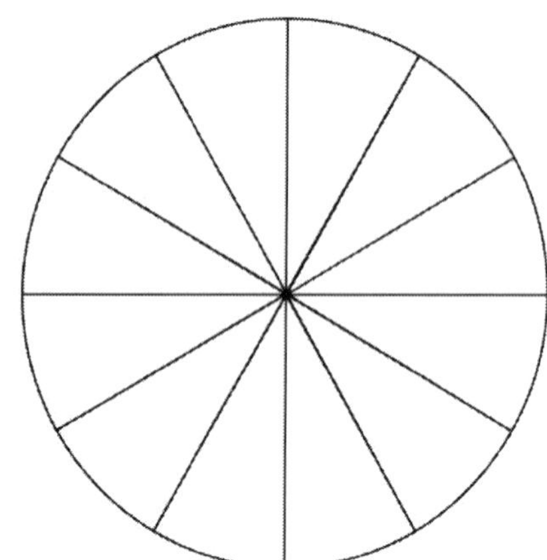

10 What two equivalent fractions are represented below? Write your answers on the blank lines.

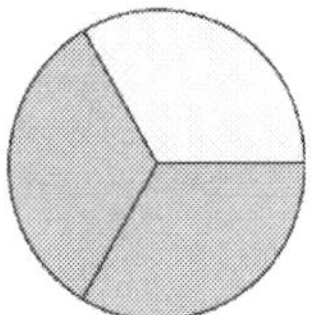
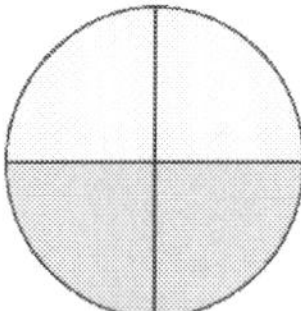
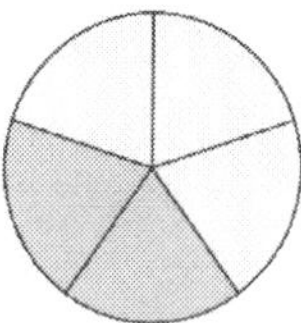
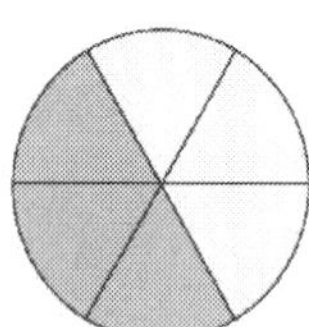
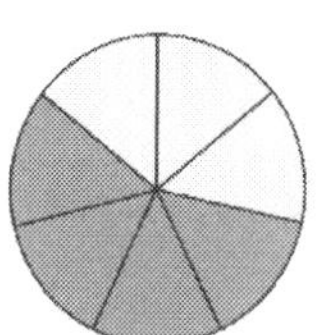

Answer _______ and _______

Comparing and Ordering Fractions – Practice Set 3

1 Based on the diagram, how many fifths are equivalent to $\frac{4}{10}$?

<table>
<tr><td colspan="2">$\frac{1}{5}$</td><td colspan="2">$\frac{1}{5}$</td><td colspan="2">$\frac{1}{5}$</td><td colspan="2">$\frac{1}{5}$</td><td colspan="2">$\frac{1}{5}$</td></tr>
<tr><td>$\frac{1}{10}$</td><td>$\frac{1}{10}$</td><td>$\frac{1}{10}$</td><td>$\frac{1}{10}$</td><td>$\frac{1}{10}$</td><td>$\frac{1}{10}$</td><td>$\frac{1}{10}$</td><td>$\frac{1}{10}$</td><td>$\frac{1}{10}$</td><td>$\frac{1}{10}$</td></tr>
</table>

Ⓐ 2

Ⓑ 6

Ⓒ 8

Ⓓ 10

2 Which fraction is the greatest?

Ⓐ $\frac{9}{10}$

Ⓑ $\frac{1}{10}$

Ⓒ $\frac{3}{10}$

Ⓓ $\frac{7}{10}$

3 Based on the diagram below, which fraction is the greatest?

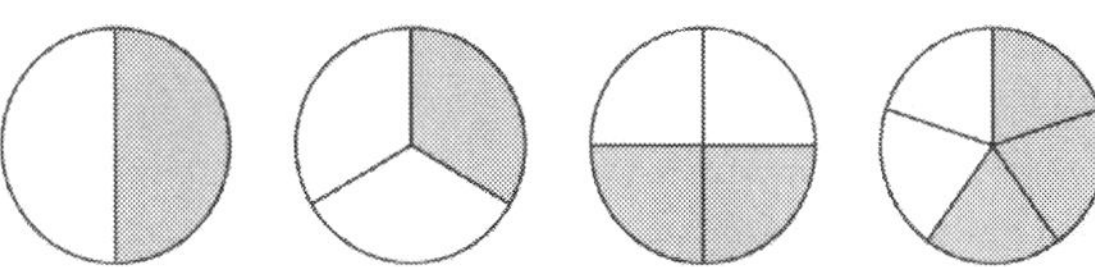

Ⓐ $\frac{1}{2}$

Ⓑ $\frac{1}{3}$

Ⓒ $\frac{2}{4}$

Ⓓ $\frac{3}{5}$

4 Circle the **two** fractions that are equivalent.

$\frac{1}{3}$ $\frac{3}{1}$ $\frac{2}{3}$ $\frac{4}{1}$

$\frac{4}{6}$ $\frac{5}{4}$ $\frac{3}{5}$ $\frac{5}{3}$

5 Based on the number line, which fraction is closest to $\frac{1}{2}$?

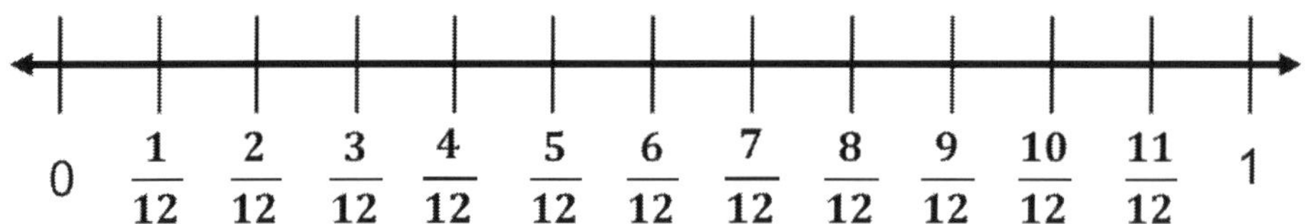

Ⓐ $\frac{2}{12}$

Ⓑ $\frac{5}{12}$

Ⓒ $\frac{8}{12}$

Ⓓ $\frac{11}{12}$

6 Which length is represented by the point on the line below? Write your answer as a fraction on the line below.

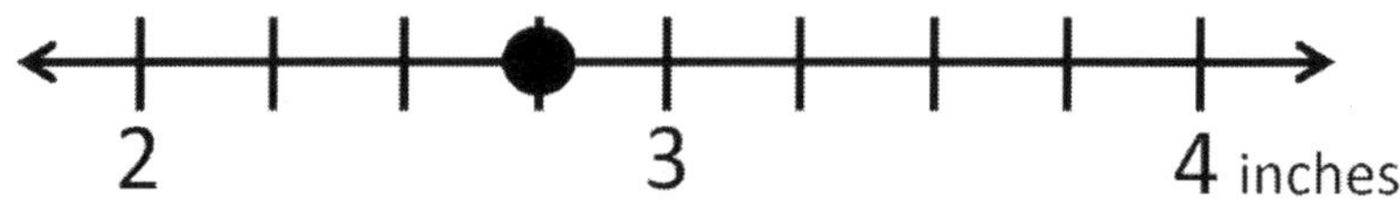

Answer __________ inches

7 Plot the fraction $4\frac{3}{10}$ on the number line below.

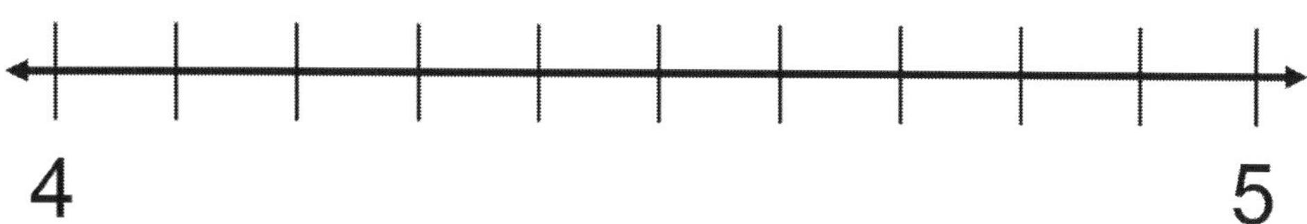

8 Shade the diagrams below to show that $\frac{2}{5}$ and $\frac{4}{10}$ are equivalent.

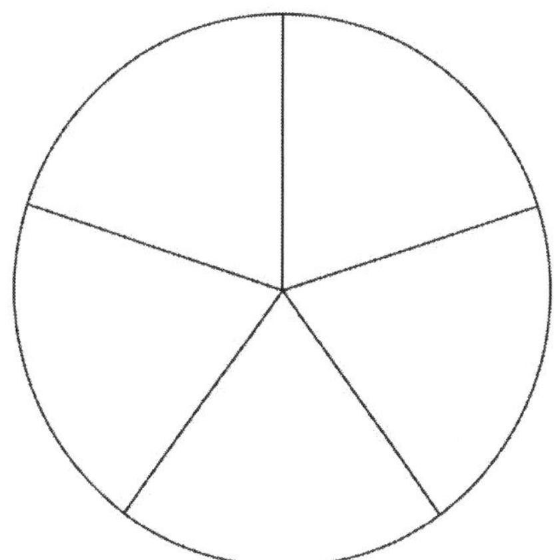

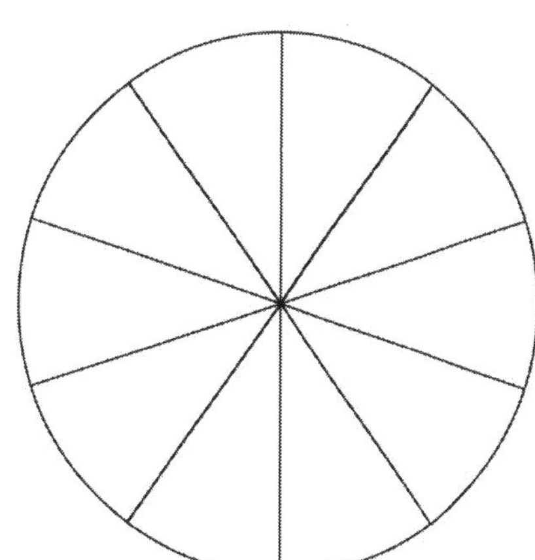

9 Write the fractions in the empty space to show the two equivalent fractions represented.

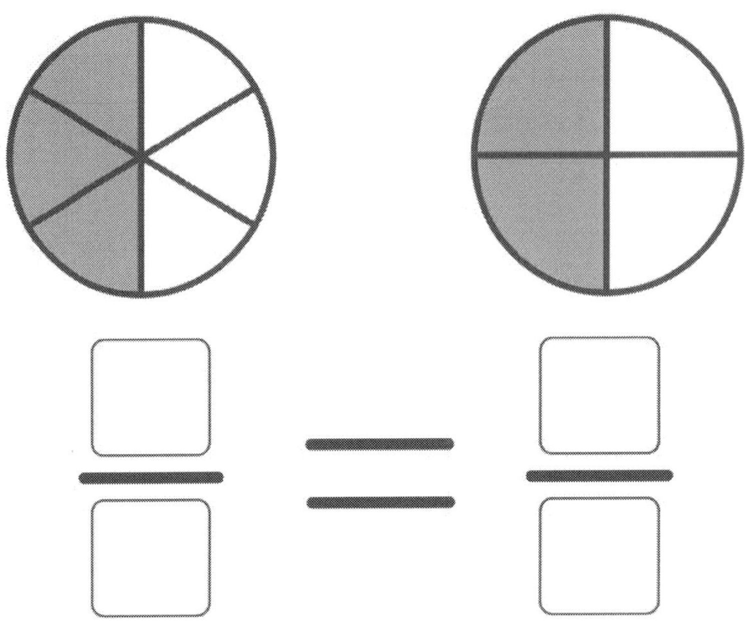

10 Circle the letter of the shape that represents a fraction equivalent to $\frac{2}{3}$.

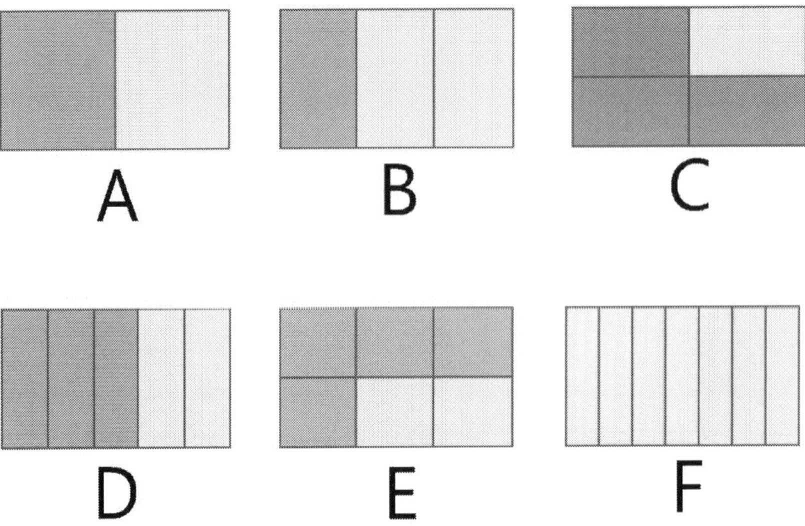

Comparing and Ordering Fractions – Practice Set 4

1 Which fraction is equivalent to $\frac{6}{10}$?

Ⓐ $\frac{1}{6}$

Ⓑ $\frac{2}{5}$

Ⓒ $\frac{3}{5}$

Ⓓ $\frac{2}{6}$

2 Circle the letter of the diagram representing a fraction equivalent to $\frac{3}{4}$.

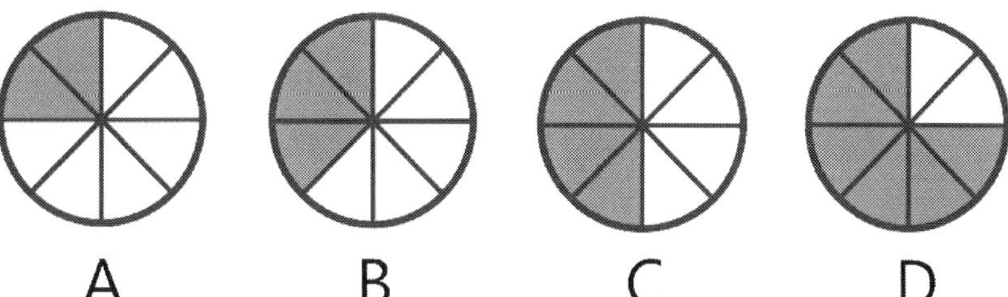

3 Based on the number line, which fraction is closest to 1?

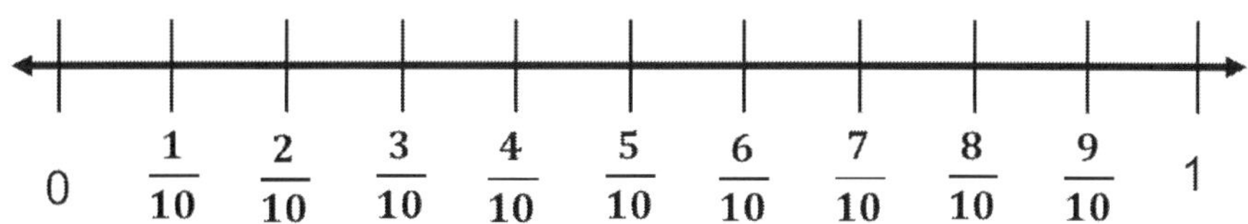

Ⓐ $\frac{1}{10}$

Ⓑ $\frac{2}{10}$

Ⓒ $\frac{5}{10}$

Ⓓ $\frac{9}{10}$

4 Based on the diagram below, which fraction is equivalent to $\frac{2}{3}$?

$\frac{1}{3}$		$\frac{1}{3}$		$\frac{1}{3}$	
$\frac{1}{6}$	$\frac{1}{6}$	$\frac{1}{6}$	$\frac{1}{6}$	$\frac{1}{6}$	$\frac{1}{6}$

Ⓐ $\frac{1}{6}$

Ⓑ $\frac{2}{6}$

Ⓒ $\frac{3}{6}$

Ⓓ $\frac{4}{6}$

5 Which measurement is represented below?

Ⓐ $1\frac{1}{3}$ cm

Ⓑ $1\frac{1}{6}$ cm

Ⓒ $1\frac{3}{10}$ cm

Ⓓ $1\frac{6}{10}$ cm

6 Which fraction is represented by point V? Write your answer on the line.

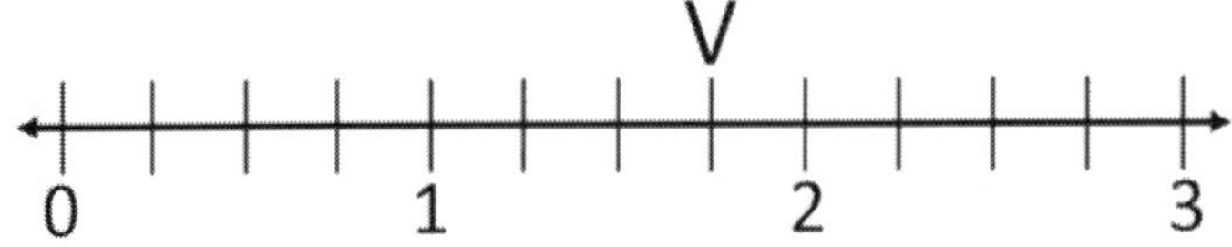

Answer ___________

7 Shade the diagrams below to represent the fractions given. Then write <, <, or = in the empty box to compare the fractions.

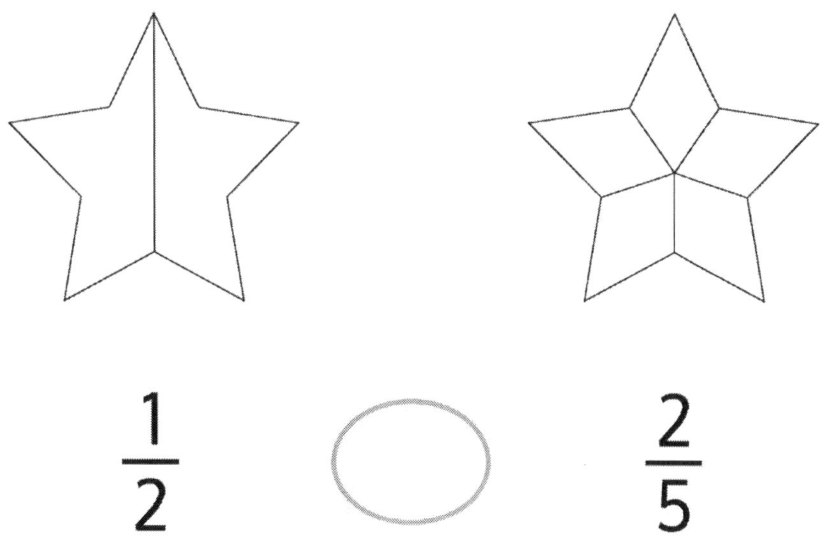

8 Circle the fraction below that is the smallest.

$\frac{1}{4}$ $\frac{1}{3}$ $\frac{1}{5}$ $\frac{1}{6}$ $\frac{1}{2}$ $\frac{1}{10}$ $\frac{1}{12}$ $\frac{1}{8}$

9 Shade the diagram on the right to show a fraction equivalent to the shaded diagram on the left. Then write the equivalent fractions in the blank spaces.

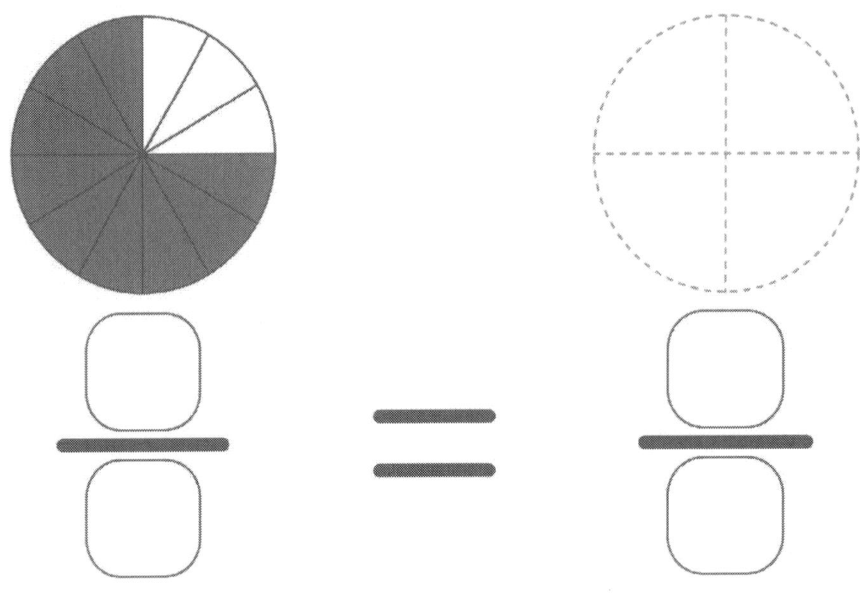

10 The point $\frac{4}{5}$ is plotted below.

Plot an equivalent fraction on the number line below.

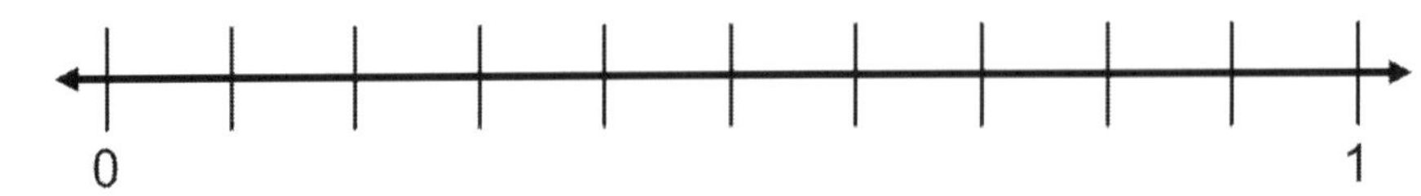

What fraction did you plot? Write your answer on the line below.

Answer ____________

Comparing and Ordering Fractions – Practice Set 5

1 Which statement is true?

Ⓐ $\frac{1}{3} > \frac{2}{3}$

Ⓑ $\frac{1}{8} < \frac{1}{4}$

Ⓒ $\frac{7}{10} > \frac{9}{10}$

Ⓓ $\frac{8}{12} < \frac{4}{12}$

2 Based on the diagram below, how many twelfths are equivalent to $\frac{1}{3}$?

$\frac{1}{3}$				$\frac{1}{3}$				$\frac{1}{3}$			
$\frac{1}{12}$	$\frac{1}{12}$	$\frac{1}{12}$	$\frac{1}{12}$	$\frac{1}{12}$	$\frac{1}{12}$	$\frac{1}{12}$	$\frac{1}{12}$	$\frac{1}{12}$	$\frac{1}{12}$	$\frac{1}{12}$	$\frac{1}{12}$

Ⓐ 2

Ⓑ 3

Ⓒ 4

Ⓓ 6

3 Based on the diagram below, which fraction is the greatest?

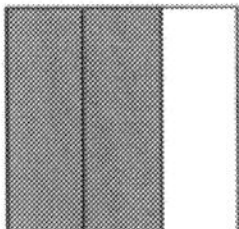 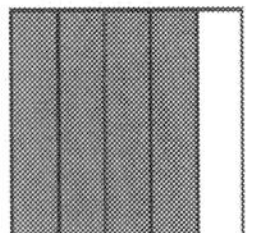 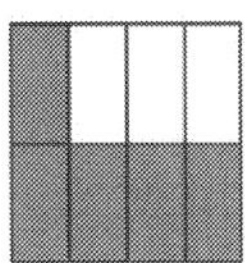 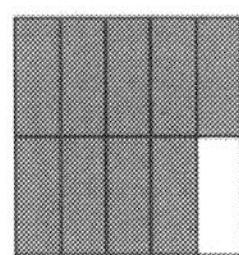

Ⓐ $\frac{2}{3}$

Ⓑ $\frac{4}{5}$

Ⓒ $\frac{5}{8}$

Ⓓ $\frac{9}{10}$

4 Which of these has an equivalent of $\frac{2}{12}$ of the rectangle shaded?

Ⓐ 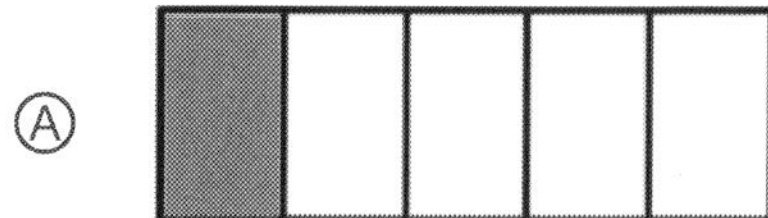

Ⓒ 

Ⓑ 

Ⓓ 

5 The length of a label is shown below.

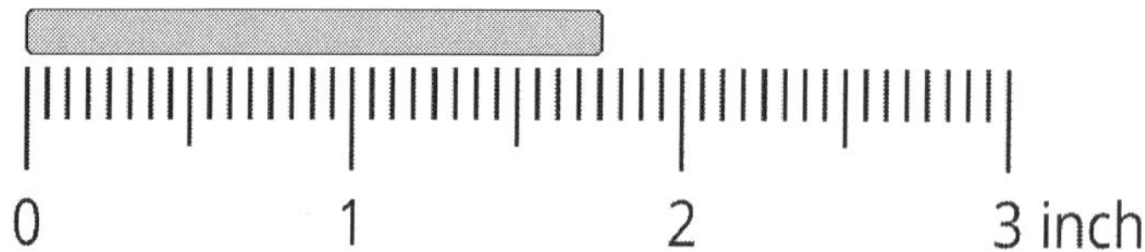

What is the length of the label?

Ⓐ $1\frac{1}{2}$ inches

Ⓑ $1\frac{2}{3}$ inches

Ⓒ $1\frac{3}{4}$ inches

Ⓓ $1\frac{7}{8}$ inches

6 Which fraction is plotted on the number line below? Write your answer on the line below.

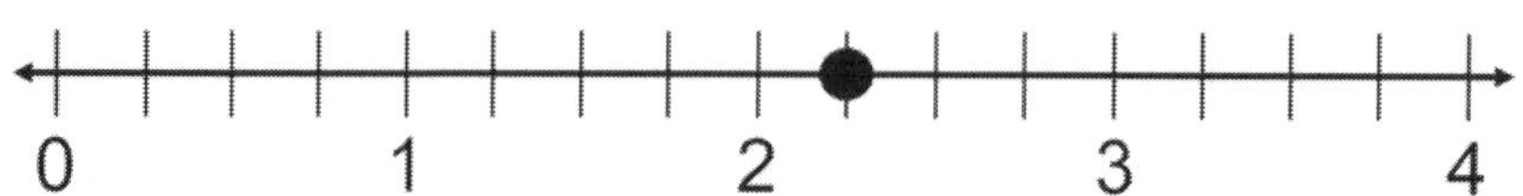

Answer ______________

7 Shade the diagram on the right to show a fraction equivalent to the shaded diagram on the left. Then write the equivalent fractions in the blank spaces.

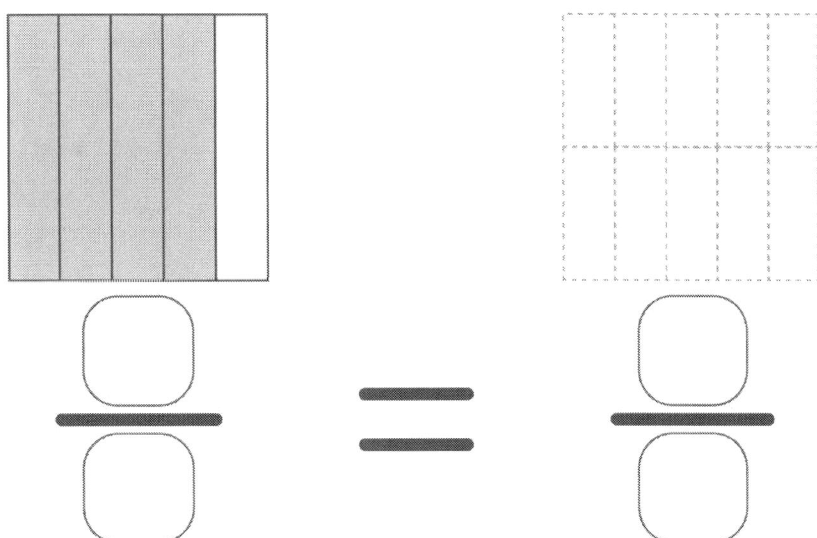

8 Plot the fractions listed below on the number line.

$$\frac{7}{12} \qquad \frac{1}{2} \qquad \frac{3}{4}$$

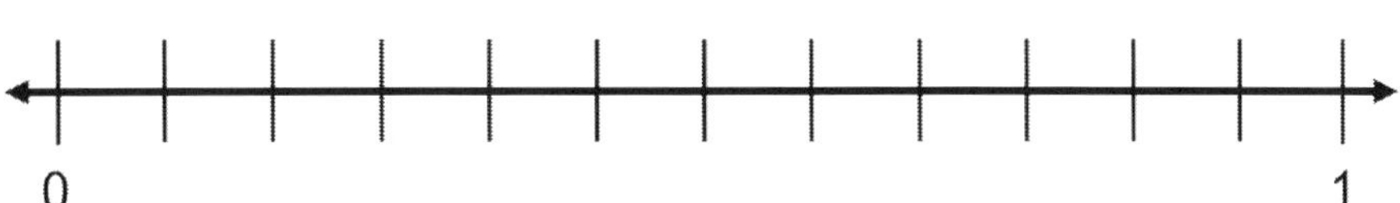

Which fraction is the greatest? Write your answer on the line below.

Answer ___________

9 Write the missing number in the blank space to complete each pair of equivalent fractions. You can use the number line below to help you find the answers.

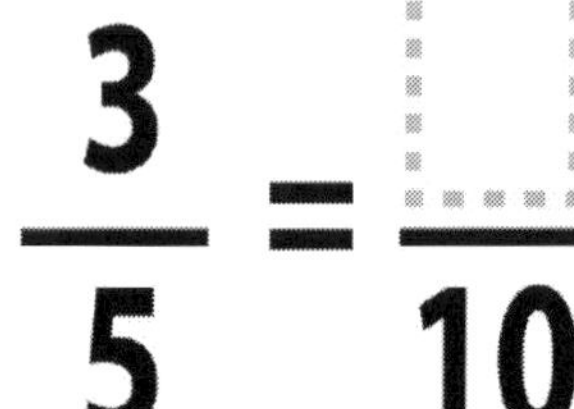

$$\frac{4}{5} = \frac{\square}{10}$$

10 Plot the fraction $\frac{3}{4}$ on the number line below.

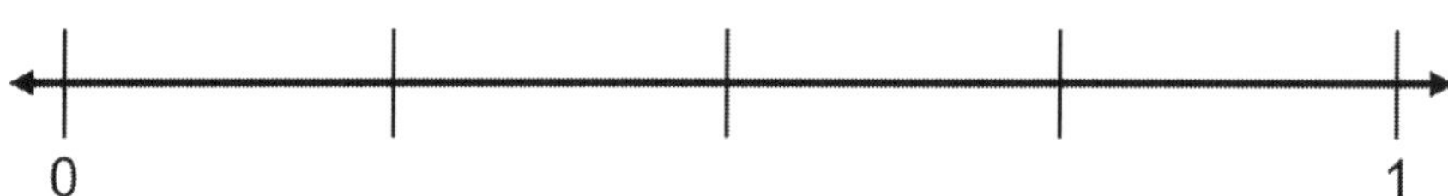

Plot a fraction equivalent to $\frac{3}{4}$ on the number line below.

What fraction did you plot? Write your answer on the line below.

Answer ___________

Algebraic Reasoning

Multiplication and Division Problems

B.E.S.T. Standards

MA.3.AR.1 Solve multiplication and division problems.

MA.3.AR.1.1
Apply the distributive property to multiply a one-digit number and two-digit number. Apply properties of multiplication to find a product of one-digit whole numbers.

MA.3.AR.1.2
Solve one- and two-step real-world problems involving any of four operations with whole numbers.

Multiplication and Division Problems – Practice Set 1

1 Leah made 8 bouquets of 6 roses each. She had 5 roses left over. How many roses did she have in all?

Ⓐ 43

Ⓑ 47

Ⓒ 48

Ⓓ 53

2 Which property is shown below?

$$6 \times (4 + 9) = (6 \times 4) + (6 \times 9)$$

Ⓐ associative property of multiplication

Ⓑ commutative property of multiplication

Ⓒ distributive property of multiplication

Ⓓ zero property of multiplication

3 Which number goes on the blank line to make the equation true?

$$4 \times 28 = 4 \times (\_\_\_\_ + 8)$$

Ⓐ 2

Ⓑ 8

Ⓒ 20

Ⓓ 28

4 Circle the **two** expressions that have the same value.

$25 - 5$	$25 \div 5$	25×5
5×25	$5 + 25$	$5 \div 25$

5 A café sells 12 different types of pie.

The café has 4 slices of each type of pie on display. How many pieces of pie are on display?

Ⓐ 3

Ⓑ 16

Ⓒ 36

Ⓓ 48

6 Rebekah saves $35 every month. How much would she save in 6 months? Write your answer on the line below.

Answer $__________

7 Which two expressions have the same value? Select the **two** expressions.

- ☐ $8 \times 9 \times 4$
- ☐ $8 \times 9 + 4$
- ☐ $8 + 9 \times 4$
- ☐ $8 \times 4 \times 9$
- ☐ $8 \times 4 + 9$
- ☐ $8 + 4 + 9$

8 Draw lines to match each multiplication property to the example shown.

Property	**Example**
associative property	$32 \times 5 = (30 \times 5) + (2 \times 5)$
distributive property	$9 \times 3 = 3 \times 9$
commutative property	$4 \times (7 \times 5) = (4 \times 7) \times 5$

9 The picture below shows the price of hosting a website per month.

Complete the table by listing how much it would cost in all for 1, 3, and 6 months for each plan.

	Starter	**Basic**	**Premium**
1 month	\$12		
3 months	\$36		
6 months	\$72		

10 Allen buys 4 tires for \$55 each. He is also charged a fitting fee of \$30. How much does he pay in all?

Show your work.

Answer \$____________

Multiplication and Division Problems – Practice Set 2

1 A museum tour charges \$8 per person. One tour made a total of \$72. How many people were on the tour?

Ⓐ 6

Ⓑ 7

Ⓒ 8

Ⓓ 9

2 Which of these shows the distributive property of multiplication?

Ⓐ $8 \times (4 + 6) = (8 \times 4) + (8 \times 6)$

Ⓑ $8 \times 10 = 10 \times 8$

Ⓒ $(8 \times 5) \times 2 = (8 \times 2) \times 5$

Ⓓ $8 \times 10 = (4 + 4) \times (5 + 5)$

3 Which number goes on the blank line to make the equation true?

$$8(7 \times 3) = (8 \times 7) + (\_\_\_\_ \times 3)$$

Ⓐ 3

Ⓑ 7

Ⓒ 8

Ⓓ 11

4 A pallet can hold 12 boxes, as shown below.

How many pallets would be needed to hold 96 boxes?

Ⓐ 6

Ⓑ 7

Ⓒ 8

Ⓓ 9

5 Complete the multiplication calculations below.

$$\begin{array}{r} 8 \\ \times 4 \\ \hline \end{array} \qquad \begin{array}{r} 7 \\ \times 6 \\ \hline \end{array} \qquad \begin{array}{r} 5 \\ \times 6 \\ \hline \end{array}$$

6 An indoor soccer match was played for 4 quarters of 15 minutes each, plus 6 minutes of extra time. How long was the match in all? Write your answer on the line below.

Answer ____________ minutes

7 Three waiters receive $9 per hour. The table below shows how many hours each waiter worked on Saturday and how much they earned in tips. Complete the table with total amount earned.

Waiter	Hours Worked	Tips	Total Amount Earned
Hamid	6	$21	
Allysa	8	$35	
Kieran	5	$28	

8 Use the distributive property to complete the calculation below.

$$2(7 \times 8) = (2 \times \_\_\_\_) + (2 \times \_\_\_\_)$$

$$= \_\_\_\_ + \_\_\_\_$$

$$= \_\_\_\_$$

9 Use the commutative property to write each expression in another way.

12×27 ______ × ______

9×42 ______ × ______

45×10 ______ × ______

36×8 ______ × ______

10 Mr. Jefferson is a golf tutor. He buys 5 packets of 12 golf balls each. He gives 3 golf balls to each of the students he tutors. How many students does he tutor?

Show your work.

Answer ____________

Multiplication and Division Problems – Practice Set 3

1 Which property is shown below?

$$15 \times 7 = 7 \times 15$$

Ⓐ associative property of multiplication

Ⓑ commutative property of multiplication

Ⓒ distributive property of multiplication

Ⓓ zero property of multiplication

2 A sheet of stamps has 12 stamps. How many stamps would be on 6 sheets?

Ⓐ 64

Ⓑ 72

Ⓒ 78

Ⓓ 96

3 Mila bought 8 herb pots for $4 each.

How much would she have left over from $50? Write your answer on the line below.

Answer $____________

4 Anna gives her 3 dogs 4 treats each every day. How long would a packet of 60 treats last?

Ⓐ 4 days

Ⓑ 5 days

Ⓒ 15 days

Ⓓ 20 days

5 Complete the multiplication calculations below.

$$\begin{array}{r} 9 \\ \times\ 6 \\ \hline \end{array} \qquad \begin{array}{r} 2 \\ \times\ 4 \\ \hline \end{array} \qquad \begin{array}{r} 4 \\ \times\ 4 \\ \hline \end{array}$$

6 Leanna bought 6 packets of 3 tennis balls and 6 packets of 5 tennis balls.

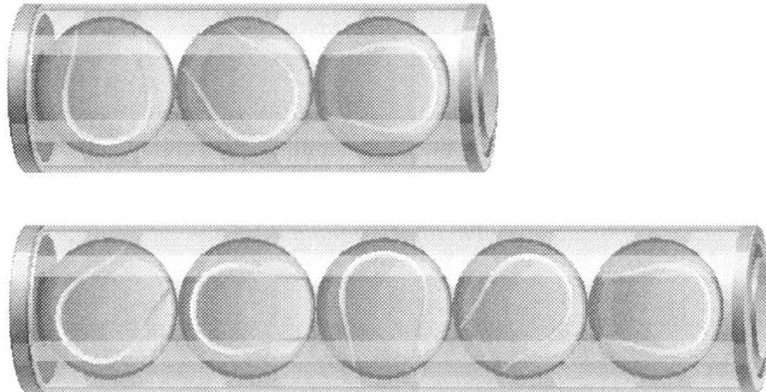

How many tennis balls did she buy in all? Write your answer on the line below.

Answer ___________

7 Which expressions are the same as 6 × 93? Select the **two** correct answers.

- ☐ 6 × (9 + 3)
- ☐ 6 × (90 + 3)
- ☐ (6 × 90) + 3
- ☐ (6 × 3) + 90
- ☐ 6 × (3 + 90)
- ☐ 6 × (30 + 90)

8 Circle the **two** expressions that have the same value.

18 – 3	18 ÷ 3	18 × 3
3 × 18	3 + 18	3 ÷ 18

9 Write the missing numbers on the blank lines to show the distributive property. Then complete the steps in the calculation.

$$5(4 \times 9) = (5 \times \_\_\_\_) + (5 \times \_\_\_\_)$$

$$= (\_\_\_\_) + (\_\_\_\_)$$

$$= \_\_\_\_$$

10 The layout of the seats in a cinema is shown below.

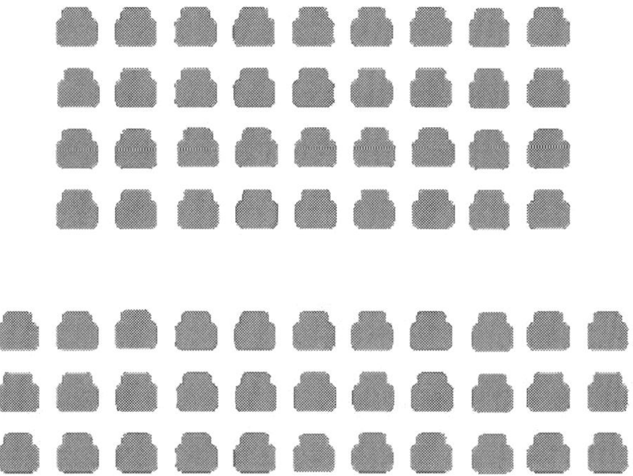

How many seats are in the cinema?

Show your work.

Answer ____________

Multiplication and Division Problems – Practice Set 4

1 Which of these shows the commutative property of multiplication?

Ⓐ $3 \times 17 = 17 + 17 + 17$

Ⓑ $3 \times 17 = 17 \times 3$

Ⓒ $3 \times 17 = (3 \times 10) + (3 \times 7)$

Ⓓ $3 \times 17 = (3 \times 17) \times 1$

2 Hoy bought 4 shirts online. He paid $6 each, plus postage of $7. How much did he pay in all?

Ⓐ $17

Ⓑ $25

Ⓒ $31

Ⓓ $39

3 A chocolate block is shown below.

Moira gives 6 squares of chocolate to 4 friends. How many squares of chocolate would be left over?

Ⓐ 1

Ⓑ 2

Ⓒ 3

Ⓓ 4

4 Complete the multiplication calculations below.

$$\begin{array}{r} 7 \\ \times\, 7 \\ \hline \end{array} \qquad \begin{array}{r} 5 \\ \times\, 7 \\ \hline \end{array} \qquad \begin{array}{r} 4 \\ \times\, 8 \\ \hline \end{array}$$

5 The picture below shows the prices of large stuffed toys.

Which of these would cost exactly $40?

Ⓐ 2 birds and 2 cats

Ⓑ 1 pig and 3 fish

Ⓒ 2 dogs and 1 hamster

Ⓓ 2 fish and 2 hamsters

6 Lana sells homemade candles for $9 each. She had an order of $54. How many candles was the order for? Write your answer on the line below.

Answer ____________

7 Which two expressions have the same value? Select the **two** expressions.

☐ 16×4

☐ $16 \div 4$

☐ $16 - 4$

☐ 4×16

☐ $4 + 16$

☐ $4 \div 16$

8 Use the commutative property to complete the table with equal expressions.

Expression 1	Expression 2
9×1	1×9
2×4	
3×8	
9×7	

9 Use the distributive property to complete the calculation below.

$$4(9 \times 3) = (4 \times \_\_\_\_) + (4 \times \_\_\_\_)$$

$$= \_\_\_\_ + \_\_\_\_$$

$$= \_\_\_\_$$

10 Kendra is choosing a phone plan. She can pay $12 per month or $105 for the whole year. How much would she save by paying for the whole year?

Show your work.

Answer $____________

Multiplication and Division Problems – Practice Set 5

1 Matthew bought 4 packets of 12 folders. How many folders did he buy?

Ⓐ 36

Ⓑ 42

Ⓒ 48

Ⓓ 56

2 Ed bought 6 packets of 5 croissants. He ate 3 croissants and froze the rest.

How many croissants did he freeze?

Ⓐ 22

Ⓑ 27

Ⓒ 28

Ⓓ 33

3 Write the missing numbers on the blank lines to show the distributive property.

$$8(3 \times 6) = (8 \times \_\_\_\_) + (8 \times \_\_\_\_)$$

4 Which property is shown below?

$$(9 \times 7) \times 4 = 9 \times (7 \times 4)$$

Ⓐ associative property of multiplication

Ⓑ commutative property of multiplication

Ⓒ distributive property of multiplication

Ⓓ identity property of multiplication

5 Kyra makes 3 sets of 9 balloons and 3 sets of 3 balloons to put on the tables at a party. How many balloons are there in all?

Ⓐ 27

Ⓑ 30

Ⓒ 33

Ⓓ 36

6 Kylie made apple pies to sell at a local market.

- She sold 28 apple pies before lunch.
- She sold another 19 apple pies after lunch.
- She sold each apple pie for $4.

How much did she make in all? Write your answer on the line below.

Answer $________

7 Which two expressions have the same value? Select the **two** expressions.

☐ $5 \times 3 \times 7$

☐ $5 \times 3 + 7$

☐ $5 + 3 \times 7$

☐ $5 \times 7 \times 3$

☐ $5 \times 7 + 3$

☐ $5 + 7 + 3$

8 Draw lines to match each multiplication property to the example shown.

Property	**Example**
associative property	$24 \times 9 = (20 \times 9) + (4 \times 9)$
distributive property	$5 \times 8 = 8 \times 5$
commutative property	$7 \times (3 \times 8) = (7 \times 3) \times 8$

9 Use the commutative property to write each expression in another way.

17×6 ______ × ______

53×5 ______ × ______

87×11 ______ × ______

64×22 ______ × ______

10 A bakery had 752 loaves of bread at the start of the day. The bakery sold 719 loaves of bread by 4 p.m. The remaining bread was put on sale for $2 per loaf. How much would the remaining bread sell for in all?

Show your work.

Answer $____________

Algebraic Reasoning

Understanding and Using Equations

B.E.S.T. Standards

MA.3.AR.2 Develop an understanding of equality and multiplication and division.

MA.3.AR.2.1
Restate a division problem as a missing factor problem using the relationship between multiplication and division.

MA.3.AR.2.2
Determine and explain whether an equation involving multiplication or division is true or false.

MA.3.AR.2.3
Determine the unknown whole number in a multiplication or division equation, relating three whole numbers, with the unknown in any position.

Understanding and Using Equations – Practice Set 1

1 What value of p makes the equation below true?

$$42 \div p = 7$$

Ⓐ 5

Ⓑ 6

Ⓒ 8

Ⓓ 9

2 Which equation is true?

Ⓐ $4 \times 5 = 20 \div 2$

Ⓑ $3 \times 7 = 8 \times 4$

Ⓒ $24 \div 6 = 12 \div 3$

Ⓓ $16 \div 2 = 4 \times 4$

3 What number does the butterfly represent to create a correct equation?

Ⓐ 3

Ⓑ 4

Ⓒ 7

Ⓓ 9

4 Which expression could be used to find the value of $40 \div 5$?

Ⓐ 5×6

Ⓑ 5×7

Ⓒ 5×8

Ⓓ 5×9

5 The diagram below represents a balanced equation.

What number goes in the blank space to create a balanced equation?

Ⓐ 4

Ⓑ 5

Ⓒ 6

Ⓓ 7

6 What number makes both equations true? Write your answer on the line.

$$8 \times \square = 40$$

$$40 \div \square = 8$$

Answer ____________

7 Which two equations are true? Select the **two** correct answers.

☐ $8 \times 1 = 32 \div 4$

☐ $4 \times 5 = 40 \div 10$

☐ $3 \times 2 = 24 \div 6$

☐ $9 \times 3 = 45 \div 9$

☐ $3 \times 3 = 36 \div 4$

☐ $5 \times 2 = 25 \div 5$

8 Complete the missing number in the equations below.

9 Draw lines to match the value on the left with the same value on the right.

3 x 2 ○ ○ **12**

5 x 3 ○ ○ **6**

8 x 2 ○ ○ **16**

10 Edison wants to solve the equation below.

$$\square \div 7 = 7$$

Write a multiplication expression that could be used to find the missing number.

$$\square \times \square$$

Understanding and Using Equations – Practice Set 2

1 Martine is finding the quotient 12 ÷ 3. Which statement correctly describes the answer?

Ⓐ The answer is 9 because 12 – 3 = 9.

Ⓑ The answer is 4 because 4 × 3 = 12.

Ⓒ The answer is 15 because 12 + 3 = 15.

Ⓓ The answer is 36 because 12 × 3 = 36.

2 Which equation is true?

Ⓐ 3 × 4 = 48 ÷ 4

Ⓑ 5 × 2 = 40 × 8

Ⓒ 45 ÷ 9 = 20 ÷ 5

Ⓓ 18 ÷ 2 = 3 × 4

3 What number does the apple represent to create a correct equation?

Ⓐ 6

Ⓑ 7

Ⓒ 8

Ⓓ 9

4 What value of t makes the equation below true?

$$t \div 4 = 8$$

Ⓐ 24

Ⓑ 32

Ⓒ 36

Ⓓ 48

5 The diagram below represents a balanced equation.

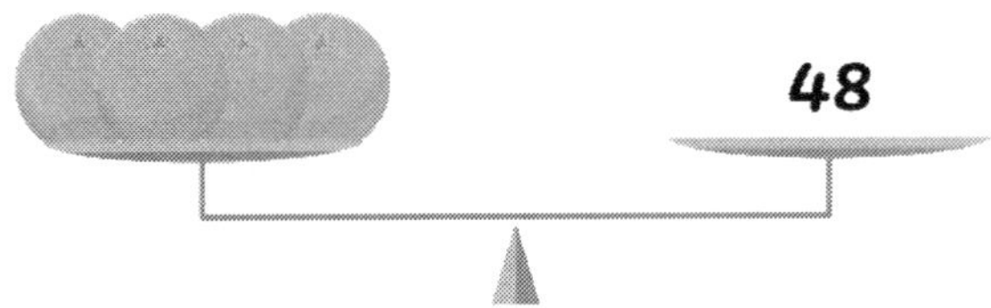

Which expression is represented on the left side?

Ⓐ 4×8

Ⓑ 4×9

Ⓒ 4×11

Ⓓ 4×12

6 The number 36 divided by what number equals 3? Write your answer on the line below.

Answer ___________

7 Joshua is finding the quotient below.

$$54 \div 6$$

Which two expressions would help him find the quotient? Select the **two** correct answers.

☐ $24 \div 3$

☐ 54×6

☐ $6 + 54$

☐ 6×9

☐ $54 - 6$

☐ 9×6

8 Complete the missing number in the equations below.

$$5 \times 3 = \square$$

$$7 \times 4 = \square$$

$$5 \times 8 = \square$$

$$9 \times 3 = \square$$

9 The scales below represent a balanced equation. Write the numbers listed below in the empty spaces to create a balanced equation.

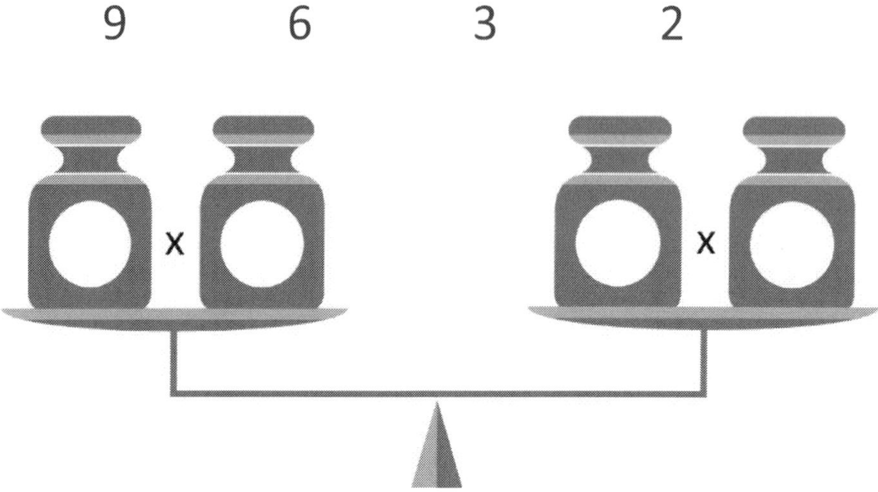

10 Complete the missing number in the equations below.

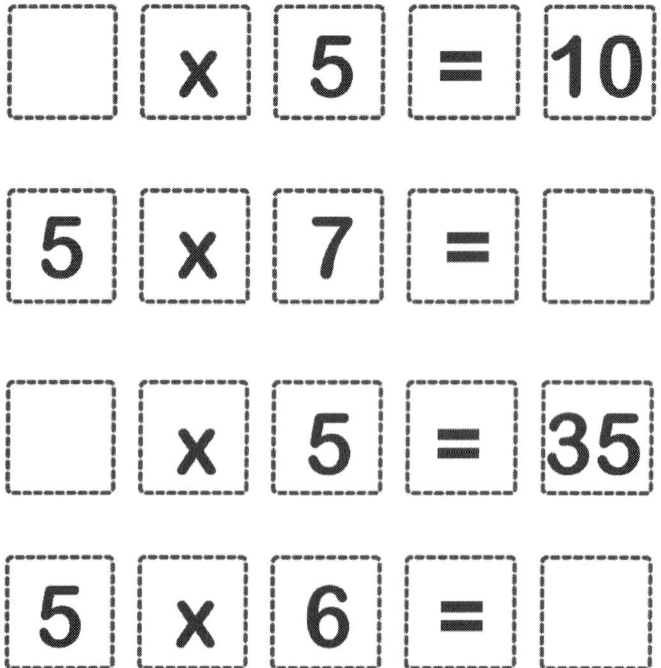

Understanding and Using Equations – Practice Set 3

1 Which number makes the equation below true?

$$4 \times \_\_\_ = 36 \div 3$$

Ⓐ 2

Ⓑ 3

Ⓒ 4

Ⓓ 6

2 The number 48 divided by what number equals 8?

Ⓐ 4

Ⓑ 6

Ⓒ 8

Ⓓ 9

3 The diagram below represents a balanced equation.

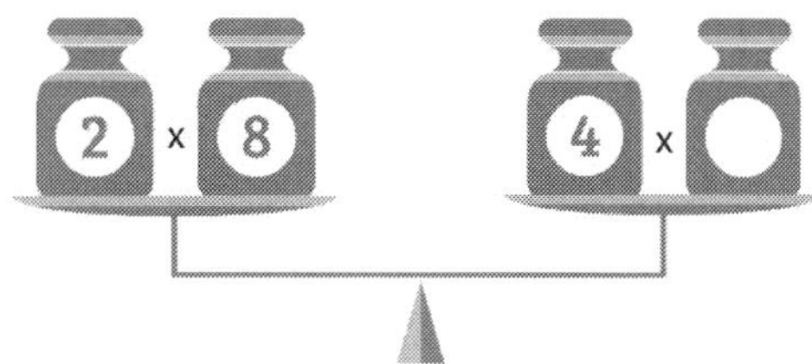

What number goes in the blank space to create a balanced equation?

Ⓐ 3

Ⓑ 4

Ⓒ 5

Ⓓ 6

4 In which of these does m have the same value as in the equation below?

$$18 \div 6 = m$$

Ⓐ $18 \times m = 6$

Ⓑ $6 \times m = 18$

Ⓒ $6 \div m = 18$

Ⓓ $6 \div 18 = m$

5 What number does the fish represent to create a correct equation?

Ⓐ 6

Ⓑ 7

Ⓒ 8

Ⓓ 9

6 What value of k makes the equation below true? Write your answer on the line below.

$$72 \div k = 9$$

Answer ________

7 Draw lines to match the value on the left with the same value on the right.

6 x 4 ○	○ **18**
10 x 0 ○	○ **7**
3 x 6 ○	○ **0**
1 x 7 ○	○ **24**

8 Write T or F on the line to show whether each equation is true or false.

______ $1 \times 7 = 49 \div 7$

______ $3 \times 2 = 63 \div 9$

______ $36 \div 6 = 4 \times 2$

______ $60 \div 5 = 2 \times 6$

9 Complete the missing number in the equations below.

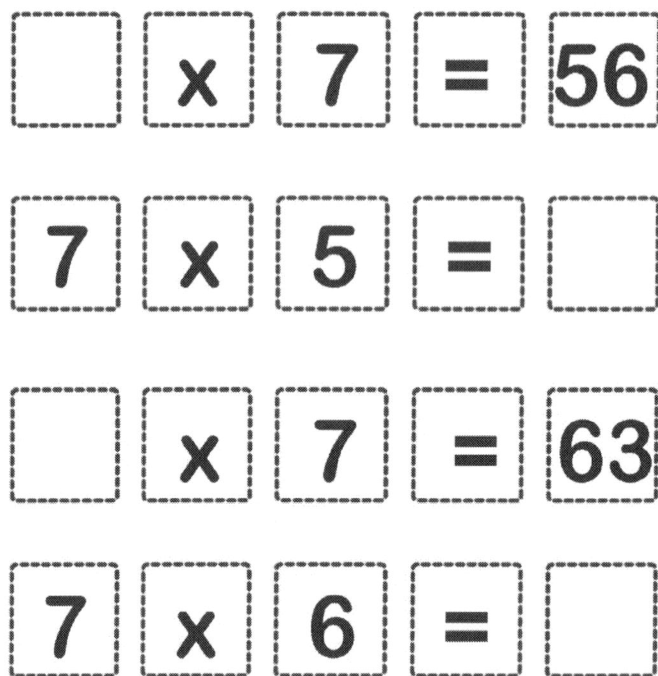

10 Sophie wants to solve the equation below.

$$\square \div 11 = 6$$

Write a multiplication expression that could be used to find the missing number.

Understanding and Using Equations – Practice Set 4

1 What value of *q* makes the equation below true?

$$35 \div k = 5$$

Ⓐ 5

Ⓑ 6

Ⓒ 7

Ⓓ 8

2 Which expression could be used to find the value of 36 ÷ 6?

Ⓐ 6 × 3

Ⓑ 6 × 4

Ⓒ 6 × 6

Ⓓ 6 × 8

3 The diagram below represents a balanced equation.

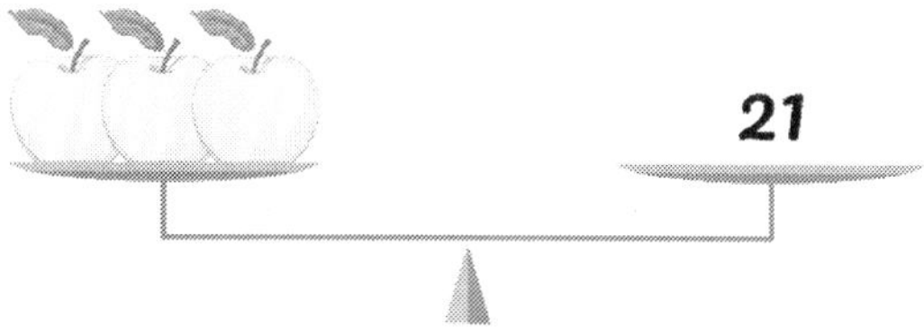

Which expression is represented on the left side?

Ⓐ 3 × 5

Ⓑ 3 × 6

Ⓒ 3 × 7

Ⓓ 3 × 8

4 What number makes both equations true? Write your answer on the line.

$$8 \times \square = 56$$

$$56 \div \square = 8$$

Answer __________

5 Which number makes the equation below true?

$$2 \times \_\_\_ = 144 \div 12$$

Ⓐ 3

Ⓑ 4

Ⓒ 6

Ⓓ 8

6 What number does the panda represent to create a correct equation? Write your answer on the line below.

Answer __________

7 Lani is finding the quotient below.

$$40 \div 8$$

Which two expressions would help her find the quotient? Select the **two** correct answers.

☐ $8 \div 40$

☐ 40×8

☐ $8 + 40$

☐ 8×5

☐ $40 - 8$

☐ 5×8

8 Complete the missing number in the equations below.

8 x 6 = ☐

9 The scales below represent a balanced equation. Write the numbers listed below in the empty spaces to create a balanced equation.

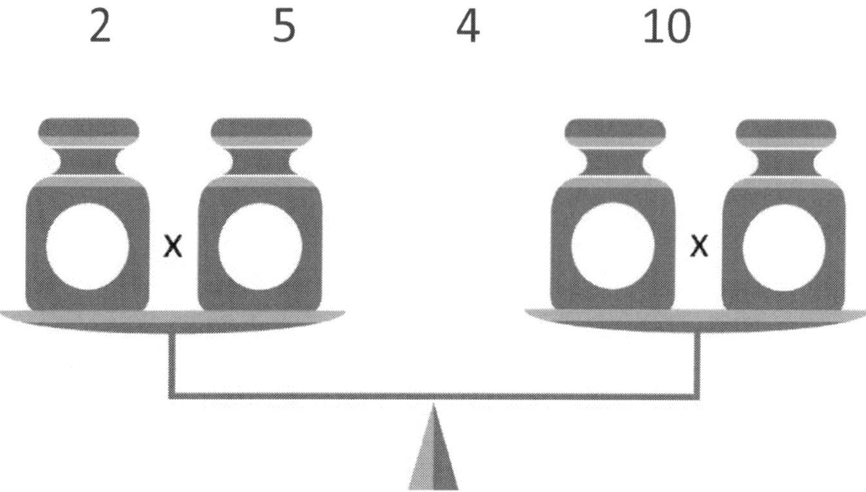

10 Complete the missing number in the equations below.

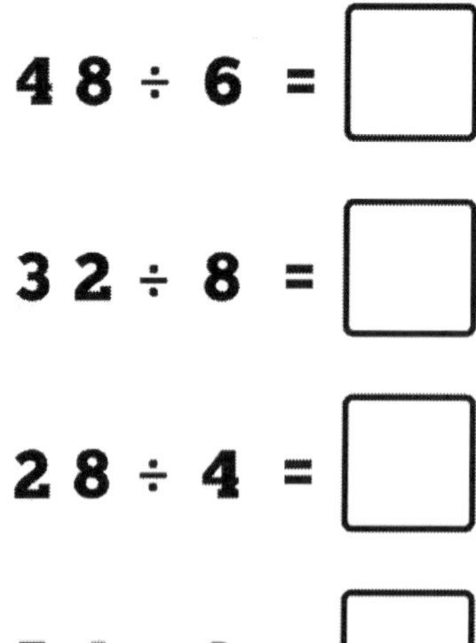

Understanding and Using Equations – Practice Set 5

1 In which of these does *y* have the same value as in the equation below?

$$36 \div 9 = y$$

Ⓐ $36 \times y = 9$

Ⓑ $9 \times y = 36$

Ⓒ $9 \div y = 36$

Ⓓ $9 \div 36 = y$

2 Which equation is true?

Ⓐ $4 \times 2 = 40 \div 8$

Ⓑ $3 \times 3 = 54 \div 6$

Ⓒ $35 \div 7 = 9 \div 3$

Ⓓ $8 \times 7 = 6 \times 9$

3 What number does the fish represent to create a correct equation?

$$36 \div \quad = 6$$

Ⓐ 6

Ⓑ 7

Ⓒ 8

Ⓓ 9

4 Angelo is finding the quotient $24 \div 3$. Which statement correctly describes the answer?

Ⓐ The answer is 21 because $24 - 3 = 21$.

Ⓑ The answer is 8 because $8 \times 3 = 24$.

Ⓒ The answer is 27 because $24 + 3 = 27$.

Ⓓ The answer is 72 because $24 \times 3 = 72$.

5 The diagram below represents a balanced equation.

What number goes in the blank space to create a balanced equation?

Ⓐ 3

Ⓑ 4

Ⓒ 5

Ⓓ 6

6 Which number makes the equation below true? Write your answer on the line below.

$$2 \times 6 = 96 \div \_\_\_$$

Answer __________

7 Complete the missing number in the equations below.

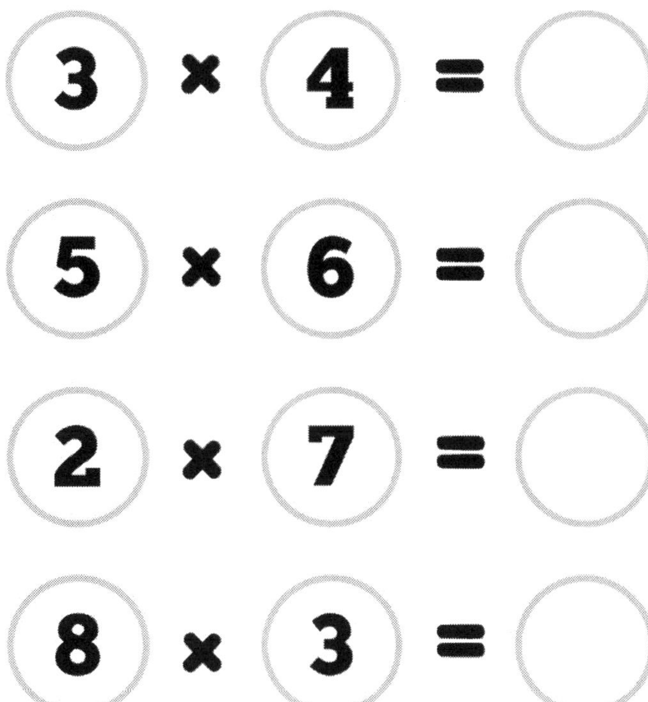

8 Draw lines to match the value on the left with the same value on the right.

6 x 3 ○	○ 10
1 x 10 ○	○ 18
3 x 3 ○	○ 9
1 x 11 ○	○ 11

9 Briana wants to solve the equation below.

$$\square \div 81 = 9$$

Write a multiplication expression that could be used to find the missing number.

10 Complete the missing number in the equations below.

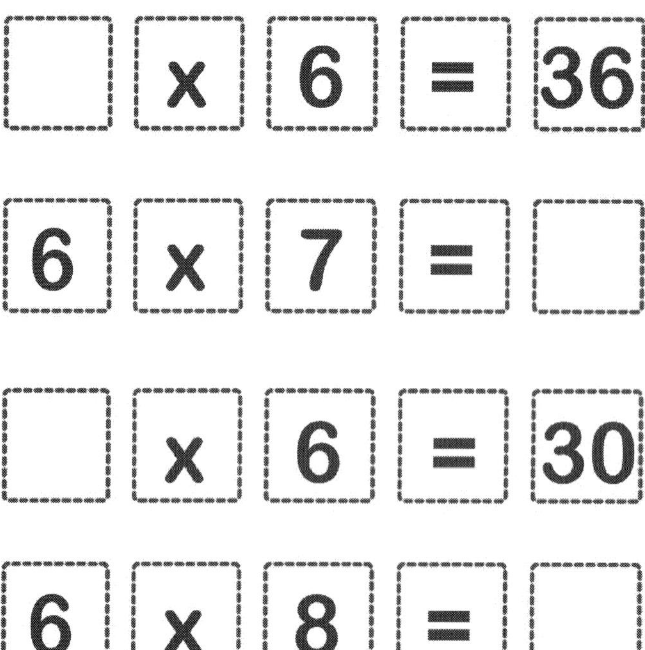

Algebraic Reasoning

Number Patterns

B.E.S.T. Standards

MA.3.AR.3 Identify numerical patterns, including multiplicative patterns.

MA.3.AR.3.1
Determine and explain whether a whole number from 1 to 1,000 is even or odd.

MA.3.AR.3.2
Determine whether a whole number from 1 to 144 is a multiple of a given one-digit number.

MA.3.AR.3.3
Identify, create and extend numerical patterns.

Number Patterns – Practice Set 1

1 Which digit in the number 5,368 tells whether the number is even or odd?

Ⓐ 5

Ⓑ 3

Ⓒ 6

Ⓓ 8

2 Which equation shows that 35 is a multiple of 5?

Ⓐ $5 + 30 = 35$

Ⓑ $5 \times 7 = 35$

Ⓒ $35 \times 5 = 175$

Ⓓ $40 - 35 = 5$

3 A number is represented by the number cubes below.

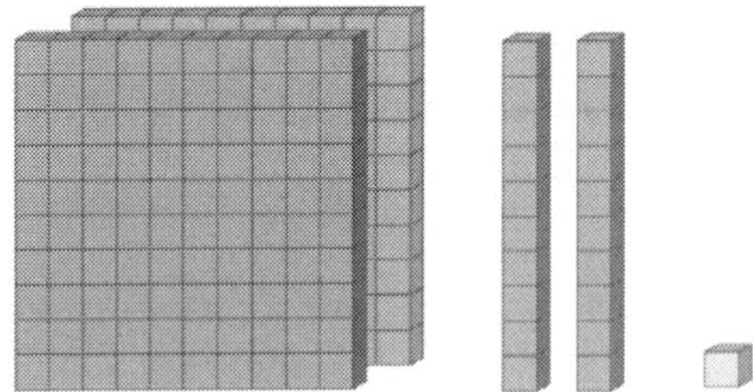

Which statement explains how to tell whether the number is even or odd?

Ⓐ There is an odd number of places.

Ⓑ There is an odd number in the ones place.

Ⓒ There is an even number in the tens place.

Ⓓ There is an even number in the hundreds place.

4 Circle **all** the numbers that are multiples of 6.

22 24 26 28 30 34

5 The first 4 terms of a number pattern are shown below.

40	50	60	70				

What would be the 8th term in the pattern?

Ⓐ 80

Ⓑ 90

Ⓒ 110

Ⓓ 140

6 Based on the multiplication table, what number is a multiple of both 7 and 8? Write your answer on the line below.

	1	**2**	**3**	**4**	**5**	**6**	**7**	**8**	**9**	**10**
1	**1**	2	3	4	5	6	7	8	9	10
2	2	**4**	6	8	10	12	14	16	18	20
3	3	6	**9**	12	15	18	21	24	27	30
4	4	8	12	**16**	20	24	28	32	36	40
5	5	10	15	20	**25**	30	35	40	45	50
6	6	12	18	24	30	**36**	42	48	54	60
7	7	14	21	28	35	42	**49**	56	63	70
8	8	16	24	32	40	48	56	**64**	72	80
9	9	18	27	36	45	54	63	72	**81**	90
10	10	20	30	40	50	60	70	80	90	**100**

Answer ___________

7 Write O or E next to each set of items to show whether there is an even or an odd number of items.

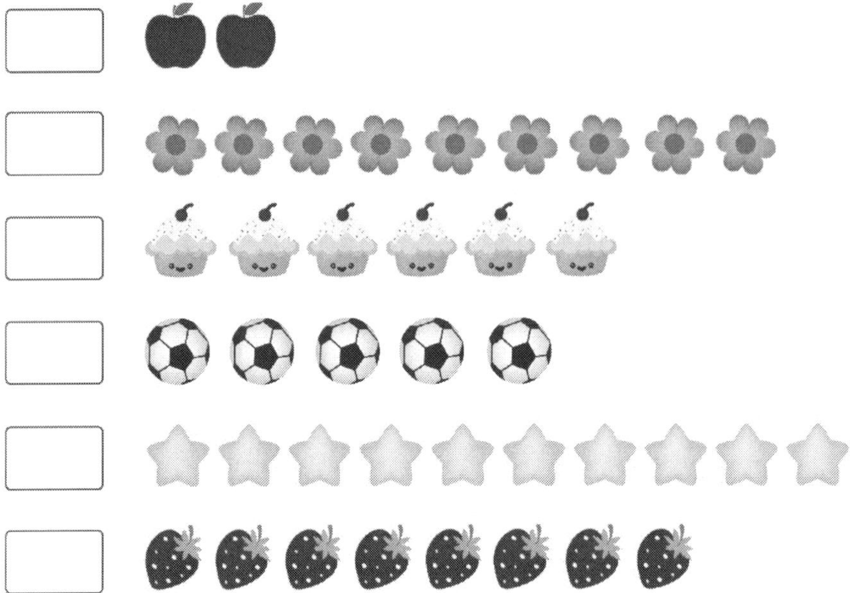

8 Gemma is saving money to purchase a new pair of headphones. She starts with $15 in savings and adds $6 at the end of every week. Complete the table with how much she would have at the start of weeks 2, 3, and 4.

Week	Total Savings
1	$15
2	
3	
4	

9 Complete the next number in each pattern below.

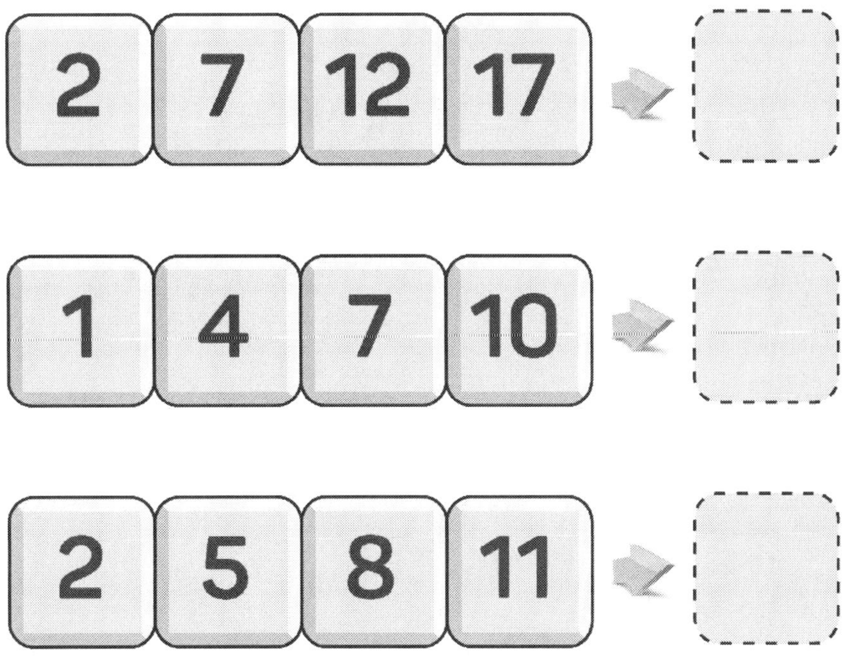

10 A bus arrives at a stop at 10:05 in the morning and then every 9 minutes from 10:05. Leon catches the 4th bus that arrives after 10:00. What time does the bus arrive that Leon catches?

Show your work.

Answer ___________ a.m.

Number Patterns – Practice Set 2

1 Which statement describes how you can tell that 366 is an even number?

Ⓐ The number is a multiple of 3.

Ⓑ There are 3 digits in the number.

Ⓒ The number is greater than 100.

Ⓓ There is no remainder when it is divided by 2.

2 Which pattern contains only numbers that are multiples of 8?

Ⓐ 8, 12, 16, 20, 24, 28

Ⓑ 40, 48, 56, 64, 72, 80

Ⓒ 18, 28, 38, 48, 58, 68

Ⓓ 2, 4, 8, 16, 32, 64

3 The first 4 terms of a number pattern are shown below.

$$3, 6, 12, 24, \ldots$$

What would be the 6th term in the pattern?

Ⓐ 36

Ⓑ 48

Ⓒ 96

Ⓓ 144

4 What is the lowest number that is a multiple of both 5 and 8?

Ⓐ 15

Ⓑ 24

Ⓒ 40

Ⓓ 58

5 Which of these describes all the numbers on the right of the equations?

9 x 1 = 9	9 x 6 = 54
9 x 2 = 18	9 x 7 = 63
9 x 3 = 27	9 x 8 = 72
9 x 4 = 36	9 x 9 = 81
9 x 5 = 45	9 x 10 = 90

Ⓐ odd numbers

Ⓑ even numbers

Ⓒ multiples of 9

Ⓓ factors of 9

6 Complete the next number in each pattern below.

15	20	25	30	

23	26	29	32	

7 Write O or E in the space under each number represented to show whether the number is odd or even.

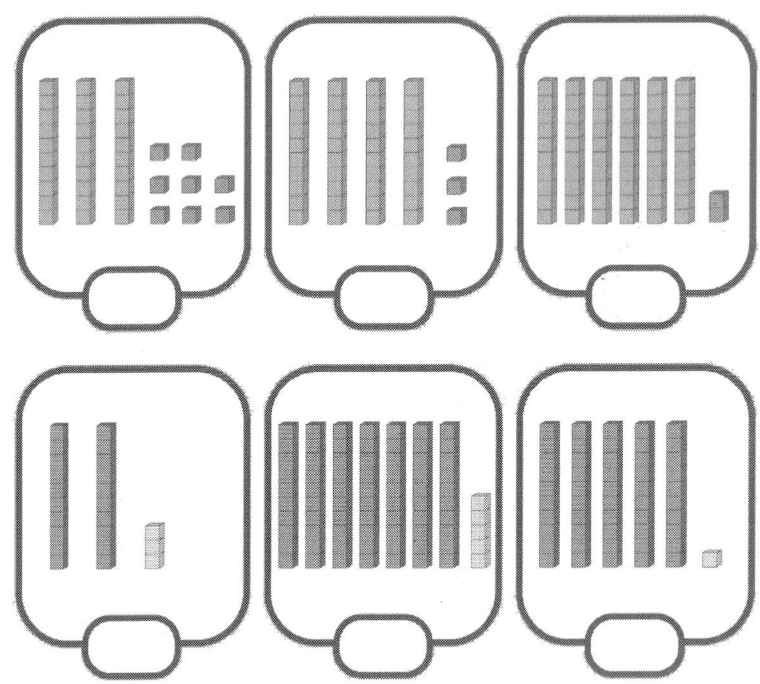

8 Chloe is completing a scrapbook project. She places 5 photos on each page. Complete the missing numbers to show the pattern for how many photos are placed in all from 1 to 8 pages.

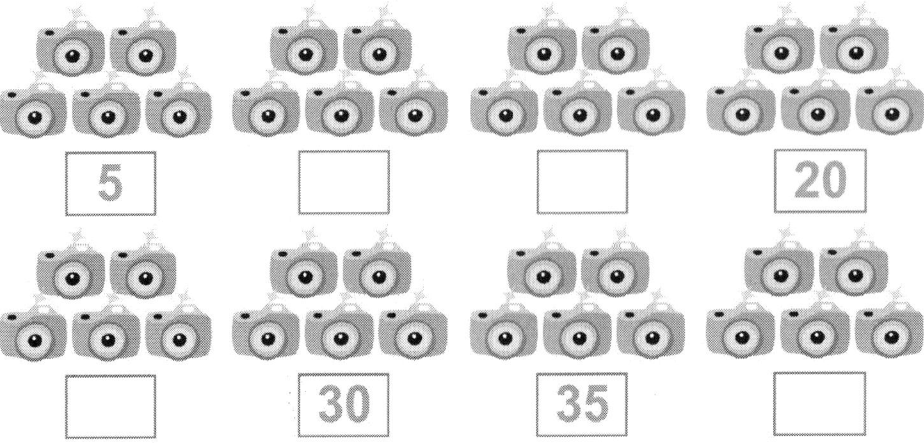

9 The picture below shows the numbers of eight different highways. Shade **all** the numbers that are even numbers.

10 Andrea had 20 pages written in her diary at the start of the week. She then added 4 pages every day. How many pages would she have written after the 5th day?

Show your work.

Answer ________ pages

Number Patterns – Practice Set 3

1 Which of these shows the first four terms of a pattern that is made by multiplying each number by 4?

Ⓐ 4, 8, 16, 32

Ⓑ 1, 4, 16, 64

Ⓒ 10, 14, 18, 22

Ⓓ 40, 36, 32, 28

2 What is the lowest number that is a multiple of both 3 and 8?

Ⓐ 16

Ⓑ 18

Ⓒ 24

Ⓓ 32

3 A number is represented by the number cubes below.

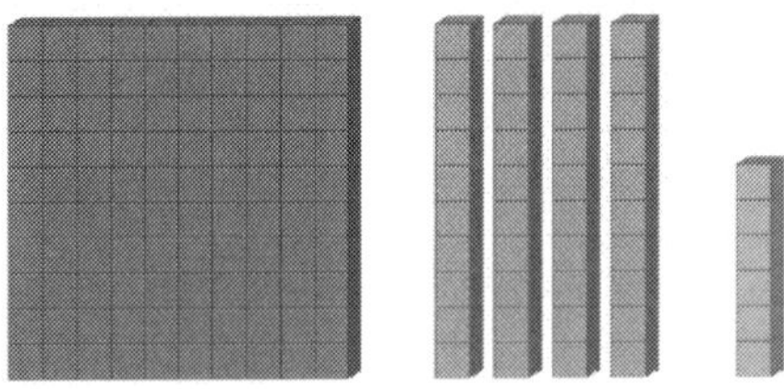

Which statement explains how to tell whether the number is even or odd?

Ⓐ There is an odd number of places.

Ⓑ There is an even number in the ones place.

Ⓒ There is an even number in the tens place.

Ⓓ There is an odd number in the hundreds place.

4 Which equation shows that 15 is a multiple of 3?

Ⓐ $3 + 12 = 15$

Ⓑ $3 \times 5 = 15$

Ⓒ $15 \times 3 = 45$

Ⓓ $18 - 15 = 3$

5 The first 4 terms of a number pattern are shown below.

20, 24, 28, 32, ...

What would be the 6th term in the pattern?

Ⓐ 36

Ⓑ 40

Ⓒ 44

Ⓓ 48

6 Based on the multiplication table, what number is a multiple of both 7 and 9? Write your answer on the line below.

	1	2	3	4	5	6	7	8	9	10
1	**1**	2	3	4	5	6	7	8	9	10
2	2	**4**	6	8	10	12	14	16	18	20
3	3	6	**9**	12	15	18	21	24	27	30
4	4	8	12	**16**	20	24	28	32	36	40
5	5	10	15	20	**25**	30	35	40	45	50
6	6	12	18	24	30	**36**	42	48	54	60
7	7	14	21	28	35	42	**49**	56	63	70
8	8	16	24	32	40	48	56	**64**	72	80
9	9	18	27	36	45	54	63	72	**81**	90
10	10	20	30	40	50	60	70	80	90	**100**

Answer ____________

7 Which numbers below are even numbers? Select the **two** correct answers.

- ☐ 547
- ☐ 280
- ☐ 799
- ☐ 304
- ☐ 885
- ☐ 641

8 Complete the next number in each pattern below.

9 Shade **all** the numbers below that are odd numbers.

34	69	70	75
68	62	67	72
34	57	62	86

10 Maxwell buys 3 novels every month. The pattern below shows how the total number of novels changes each month.

3, 6, 9, 12, ...

How many novels would be in his collection after 9 months?

Show your work.

Answer ________ novels

Number Patterns – Practice Set 4

1 Which of these shows the first four terms of a pattern that is made by multiplying each number by 5?

Ⓐ 5, 10, 15, 20

Ⓑ 1, 5, 25, 125

Ⓒ 15, 30, 60, 120

Ⓓ 50, 45, 40, 35

2 Which of these shows a pattern where all the numbers will be odd?

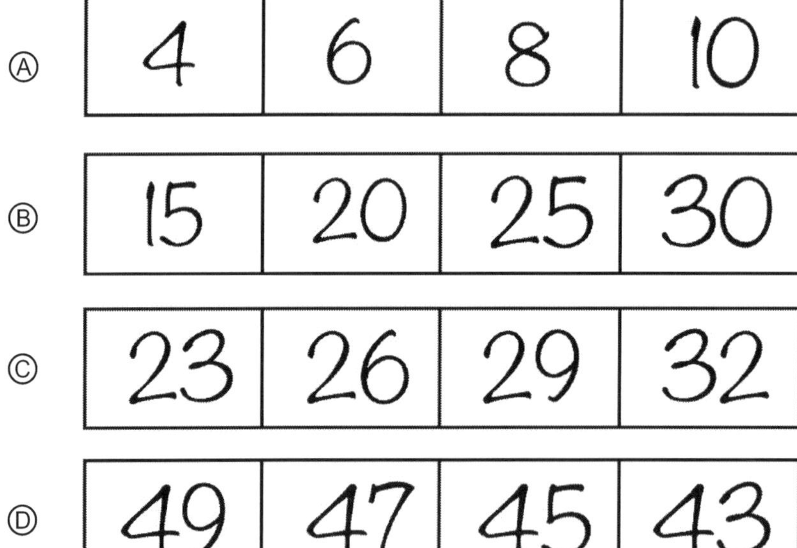

3 Which number is a multiple of 9?

Ⓐ 72

Ⓑ 74

Ⓒ 76

Ⓓ 78

4 Which digit in the number 7,214 tells whether the number is even or odd?

Ⓐ 7

Ⓑ 2

Ⓒ 1

Ⓓ 4

5 Based on the multiplication table, what number is a multiple of both 10 and 9? Write your answer on the line below.

	1	2	3	4	5	6	7	8	9	10
1	**1**	2	3	4	5	6	7	8	9	10
2	2	**4**	6	8	10	12	14	16	18	20
3	3	6	**9**	12	15	18	21	24	27	30
4	4	8	12	**16**	20	24	28	32	36	40
5	5	10	15	20	**25**	30	35	40	45	50
6	6	12	18	24	30	**36**	42	48	54	60
7	7	14	21	28	35	42	**49**	56	63	70
8	8	16	24	32	40	48	56	**64**	72	80
9	9	18	27	36	45	54	63	72	**81**	90
10	10	20	30	40	50	60	70	80	90	**100**

Answer ___________

6 What is the lowest number that is a multiple of both 3 and 4? Write your answer on the line below.

Answer ___________

7 Write O or E next to each set of dots to show whether there is an even or an odd number of dots.

8 Maree is baking pies for a street party. She bakes the pies in batches of 3. Complete the missing numbers to show the pattern for how many pies are baked in all from 1 to 8 batches.

9 Complete the next two numbers in the patterns below.

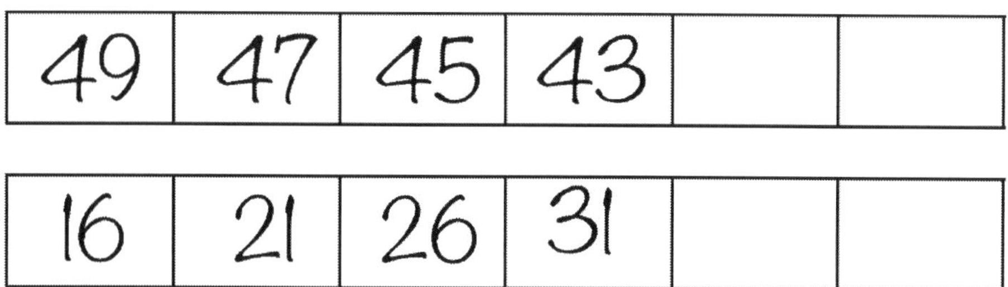

49	47	45	43		
16	21	26	31		

10 Bethany has 60 dog treats in a packet. She gives 5 treats to her dogs every morning. The table below shows how many treats she has left at the end of each day.

Day	0	1	2	3	4
Treats	60	55	50	45	40

How many treats would be left at the end of the 8th day?

Show your work.

Answer ________ treats

Number Patterns – Practice Set 5

1 Which statement describes how to tell that 375 is an odd number?

Ⓐ It has 3 digits.

Ⓑ It has a 3 in the hundreds place.

Ⓒ It has a 7 in the tens place.

Ⓓ It has a 5 in the ones place.

2 Which pattern contains only numbers that are multiples of 6?

Ⓐ 1, 6, 11, 16, 21, 26

Ⓑ 18, 24, 30, 36, 42, 48

Ⓒ 60, 70, 80, 90, 100, 110, 120

Ⓓ 3, 9, 18, 36, 72, 144

3 Which expression shows how to find the next number in the pattern below?

8, 12, 16, 20, ?

Ⓐ 20 – 4

Ⓑ 20 – 16

Ⓒ 20 + 4

Ⓓ 20 + 16

4 Which number is a multiple of 8?

Ⓐ 4

Ⓑ 18

Ⓒ 30

Ⓓ 32

5 Which equation shows that 50 is a multiple of 5?

Ⓐ $5 + 45 = 50$

Ⓑ $5 \times 10 = 50$

Ⓒ $50 \times 5 = 250$

Ⓓ $55 - 5 = 50$

6 Alisa sells paintings that she creates. She sells each painting for $40. Complete the table with how much she would make in total with the sale of 2, 3, and 4 paintings.

Sales	Total Amount
1	$40
2	
3	
4	

7 Complete the next number in each pattern below.

8 Shade **all** the numbers below that are odd numbers.

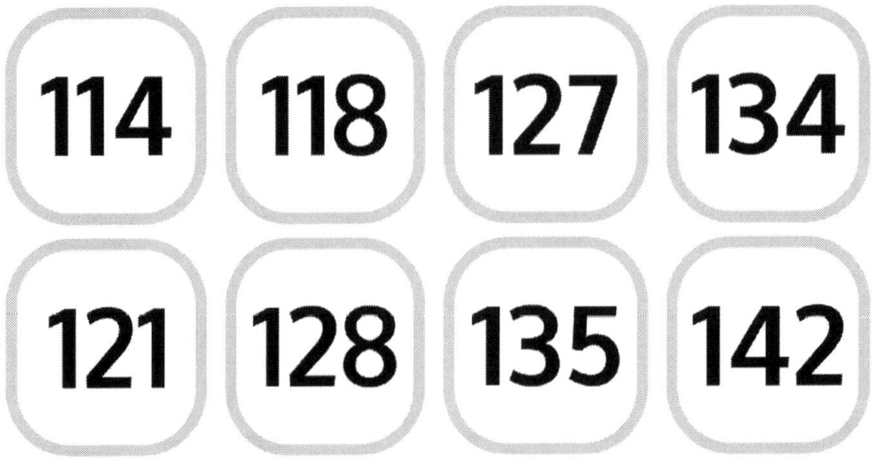

9 Write O or E in the space under each number represented to show whether the number is odd or even.

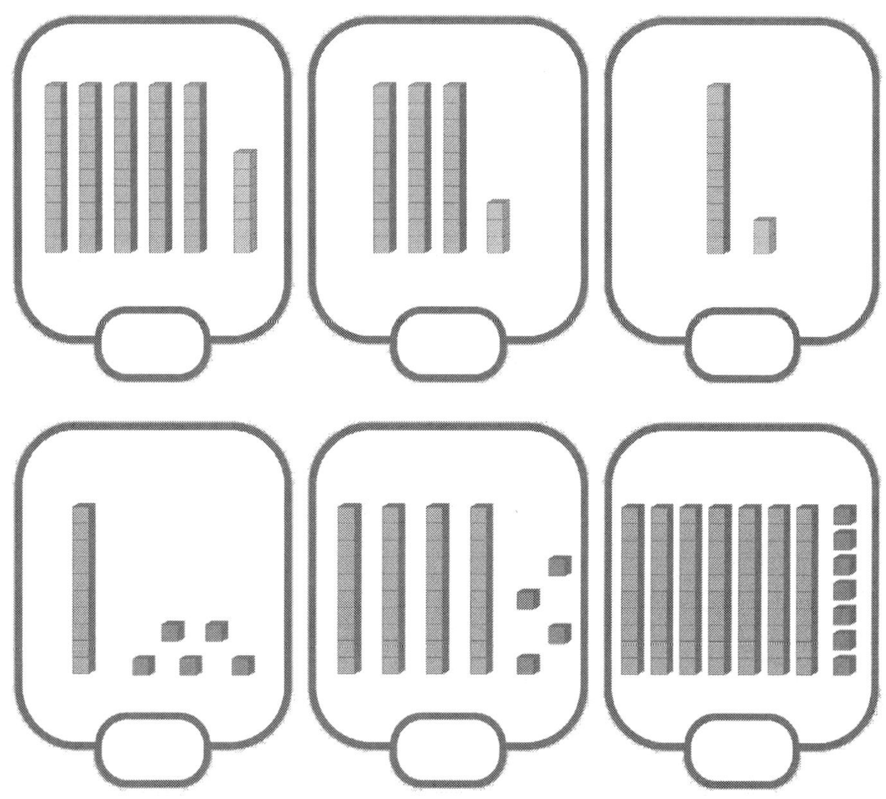

10 Paula has 400 balloons to decorate a party with. She divides the balloons into 2 equal groups. She then divides these groups into 2 more equal groups. She repeats this 4 times in total. Complete the missing numbers to show how many balloons are in each group after each division.

400, _____, _____, _____, _____

How many balloons are in the final group? Write your answer on the line below.

Answer ____________ balloons

Measurement

Use Tools to Measure

B.E.S.T. Standards

MA.3.M.1 Measure attributes of objects and solve problems involving measurement.

MA.3.M.1.1
Select and use appropriate tools to measure the length of an object, the volume of liquid within a beaker and temperature.

Use Tools to Measure – Practice Set 1

1 What length is shown below?

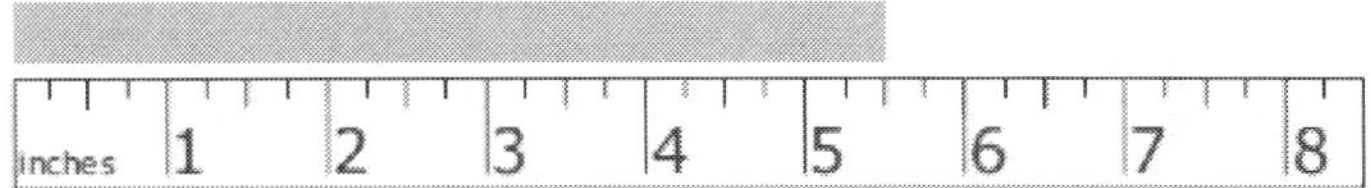

Ⓐ 5 inches

Ⓑ $5\frac{1}{4}$ inches

Ⓒ $5\frac{1}{2}$ inches

Ⓓ $5\frac{3}{4}$ inches

2 Jenna squeezes 20 milliliters of juice from an orange. What does the measurement 20 milliliters tell?

Ⓐ temperature

Ⓑ length

Ⓒ time

Ⓓ volume

3 Which measurement does the reading below give?

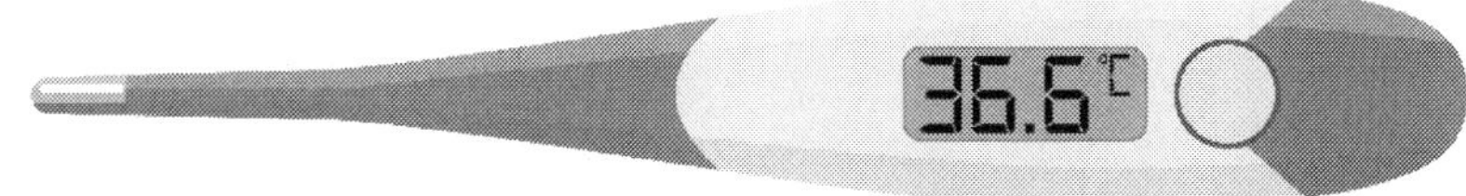

Ⓐ temperature

Ⓑ time

Ⓒ weight

Ⓓ volume

4 Circle the letter of the cup that most likely contains $\frac{1}{4}$ cup of liquid.

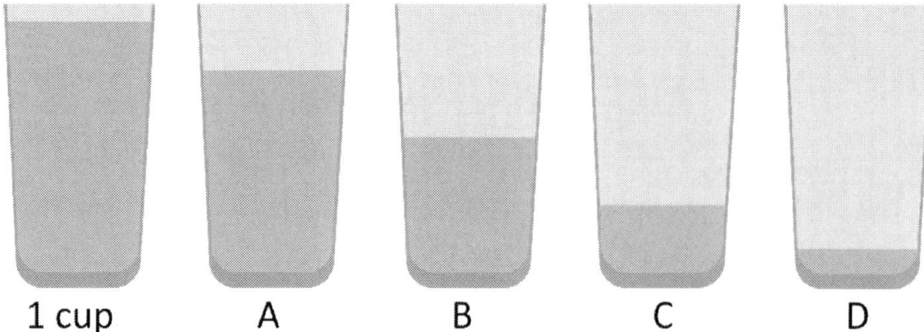

5 What is the length of the comb to the nearest centimeter? Write your answer on the line below.

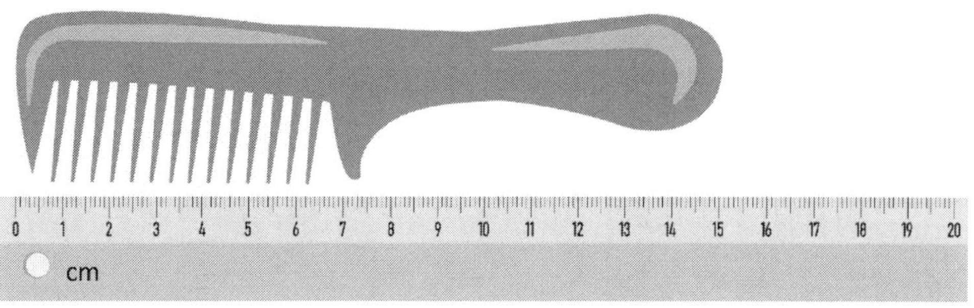

Answer ___________ cm

6 What volume of liquid is in the beaker shown? Write your answer on the line below.

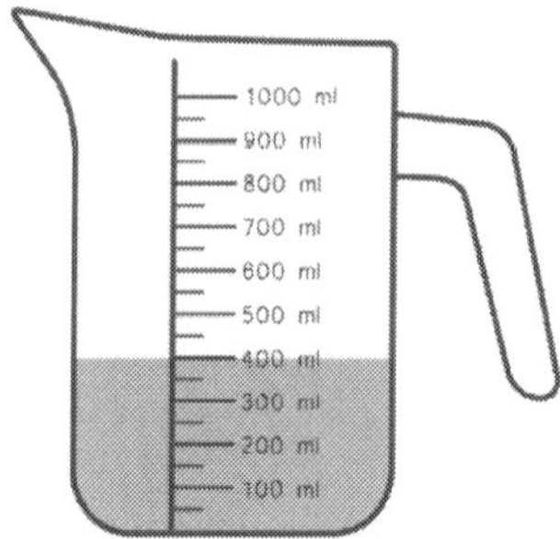

Answer ________ mL

7 What temperature is shown on the thermometer below? Write your answer on the line below.

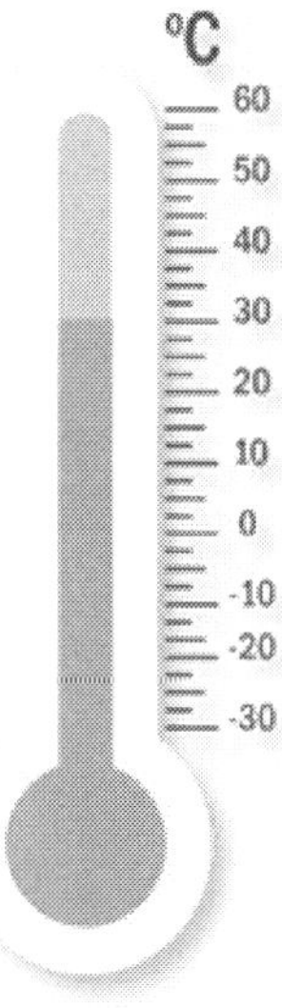

Answer _______ °C

8 Which tools could be used to measure length? Select the **two** correct answers.

☐ meter stick

☐ thermometer

☐ compass

☐ tape measure

☐ measuring cylinder

☐ scales

9 Draw a line below each ruler with the length given.

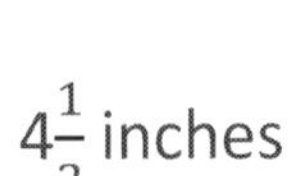

10 A close-up view of the reading on a 100 milliliter measuring cylinder is shown below. What volume is shown?

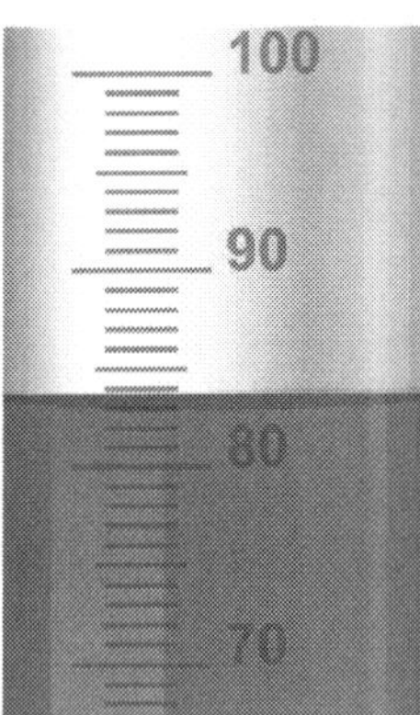

Ⓐ 80 mL

Ⓑ 83 mL

Ⓒ 85 mL

Ⓓ 86 mL

Use Tools to Measure – Practice Set 2

1 What is the tool below used to measure?

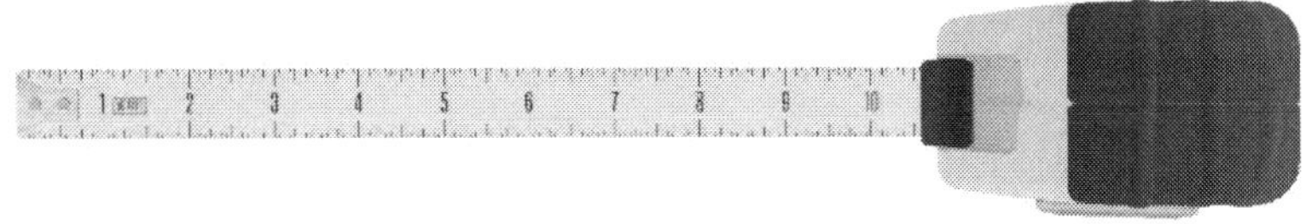

Ⓐ weight

Ⓑ length

Ⓒ time

Ⓓ temperature

2 Kylie places a paintbrush next to a line of ten 1-inch cubes. What is the length of the paintbrush? Write your answer on the line below.

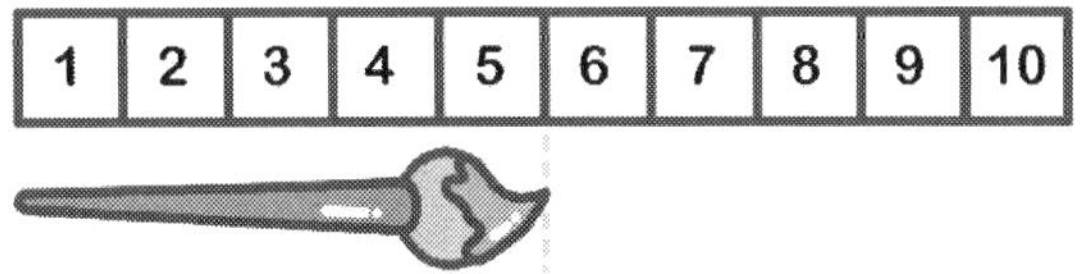

Answer __________ inches

3 What is the length of the pen to the nearest centimeter? Write your answer on the line below.

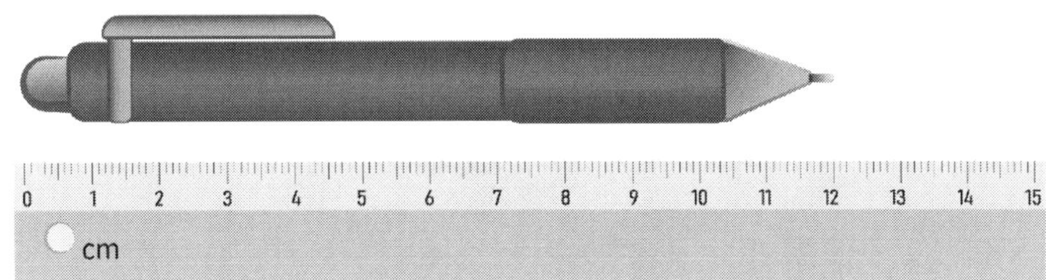

Answer ___________ cm

4 A recipe for a cake states that it should be baked at 375°F. What does this detail tell?

Ⓐ how long the cake should be baked for

Ⓑ what size cake tin will be needed

Ⓒ what temperature the cake should be baked at

Ⓓ how many people the cake will serve

5 Which measurement describes the volume of an object?

Ⓐ 6 pounds

Ⓑ 6 inches

Ⓒ 6 cups

Ⓓ 6 yards

6 What temperature is shown on the thermometer? Write your answer on the line below.

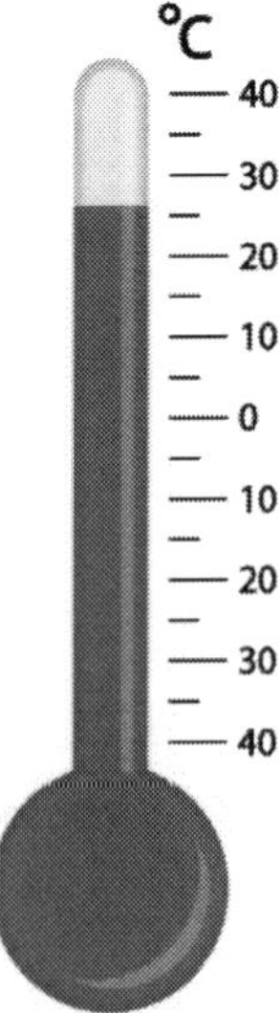

Answer ____________°C

7 What volume of liquid is in the beaker shown? Write your answer on the line below.

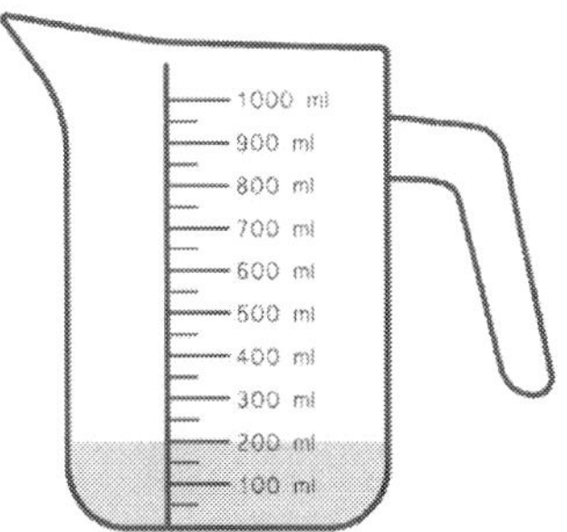

Answer ________ mL

8 Draw a line on each thermometer to represent the given temperature.

°C	°C	°C
50 50	50 50	50 50
40 40	40 40	40 40
30 30	30 30	30 30
20 20	20 20	20 20
10 10	10 10	10 10
0 0	0 0	0 0
25°C	45°C	18°C

9 What is the length of the candle shown below to the nearest inch? Write your answer on the line below.

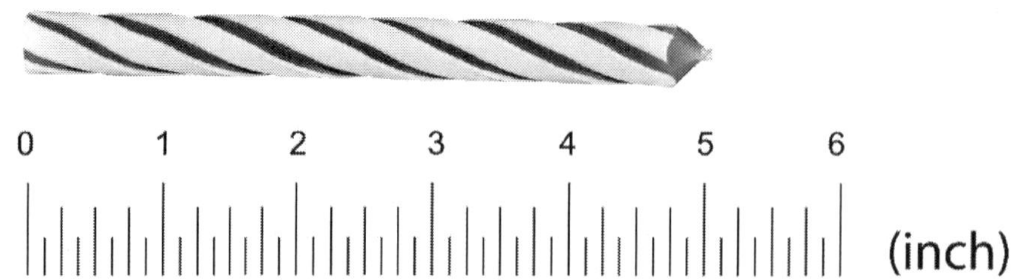

Answer ____________ inches

10 Order the volume of milk shown below from smallest volume to largest volume. Write the numbers 1, 2, 3, 4, and 5 in the empty boxes to show the order.

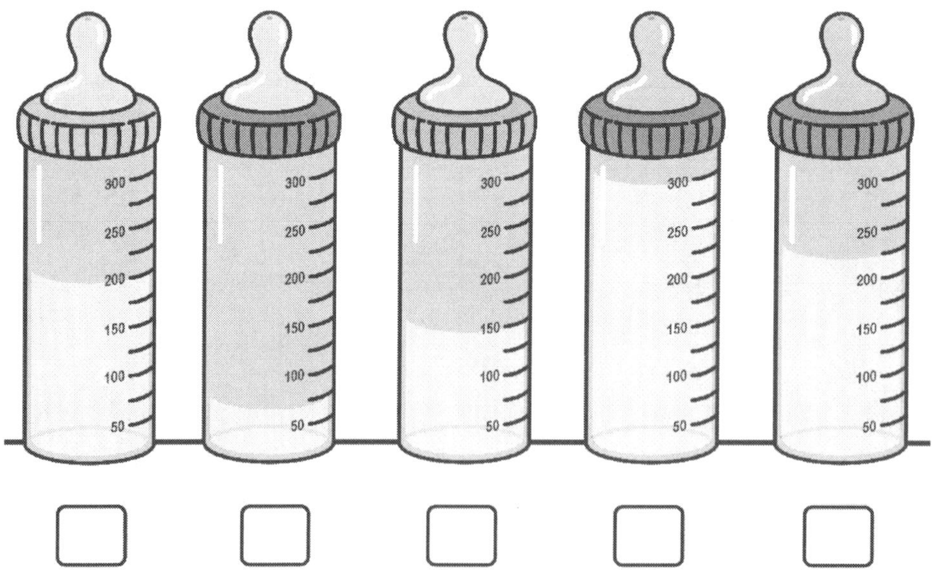

Use Tools to Measure – Practice Set 3

1 Which statement about the weather describes temperature?

Ⓐ There was 2 inches of snowfall.

Ⓑ It was 75 degrees Fahrenheit.

Ⓒ The storm lasted for 25 minutes.

Ⓓ Winds were around 10 miles per hour.

2 What is the object below used to measure?

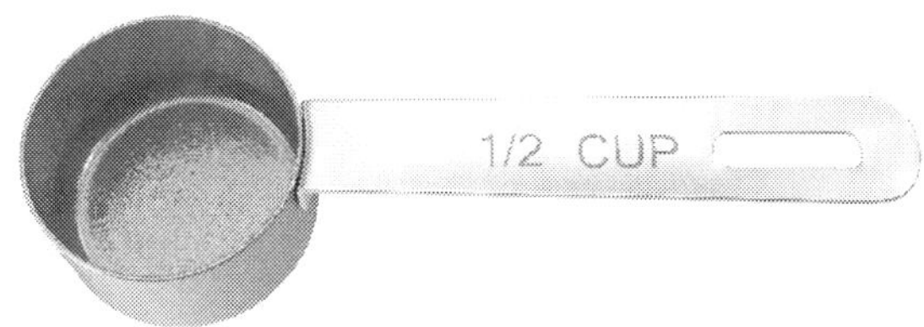

Ⓐ weight

Ⓑ length

Ⓒ volume

Ⓓ temperature

3 What is the length of the screwdriver to the nearest centimeter? Write your answer on the line below.

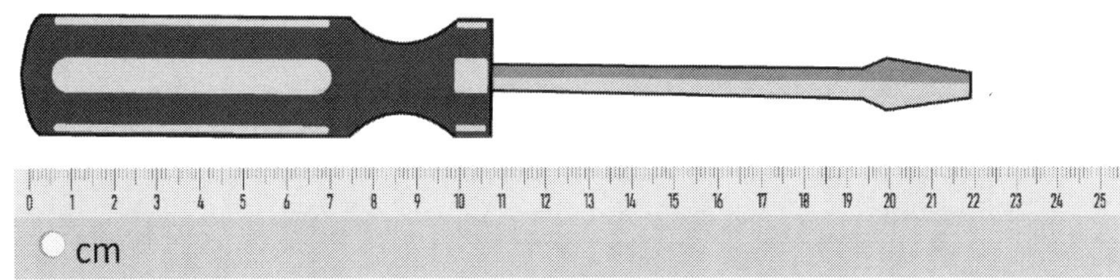

Answer ____________ cm

4 Which measurement describes the length of an object?

Ⓐ 4 grams

Ⓑ 4 meters

Ⓒ 4 liters

Ⓓ 4 hours

5 Jayden took his temperature. The temperature reading is shown by the black line on the thermometer. What was Jayden's temperature?

Ⓐ 36 degrees

Ⓑ 36.6 degrees

Ⓒ 365 degrees

Ⓓ 366 degrees

6 What is the length of the remote control shown below to the nearest half inch? Write your answer on the line below.

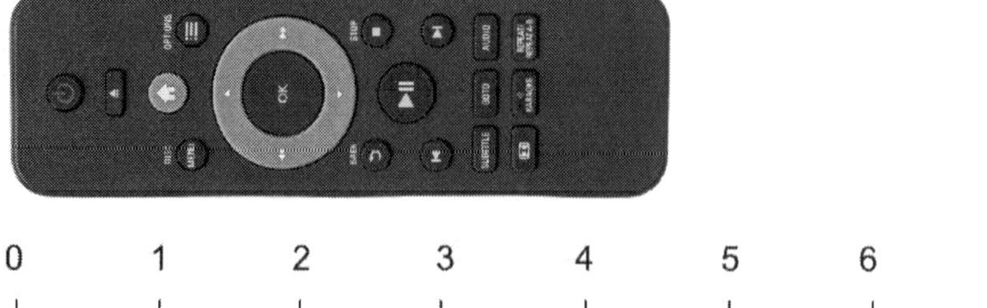

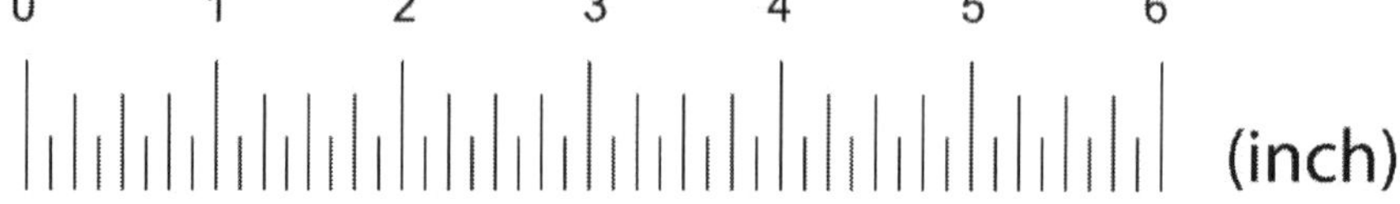

Answer ____________ inches

7 The length of 5 pencils is shown below. Which pencil is closest in length to 4 centimeters? Write the letter of the correct pencil on the line below.

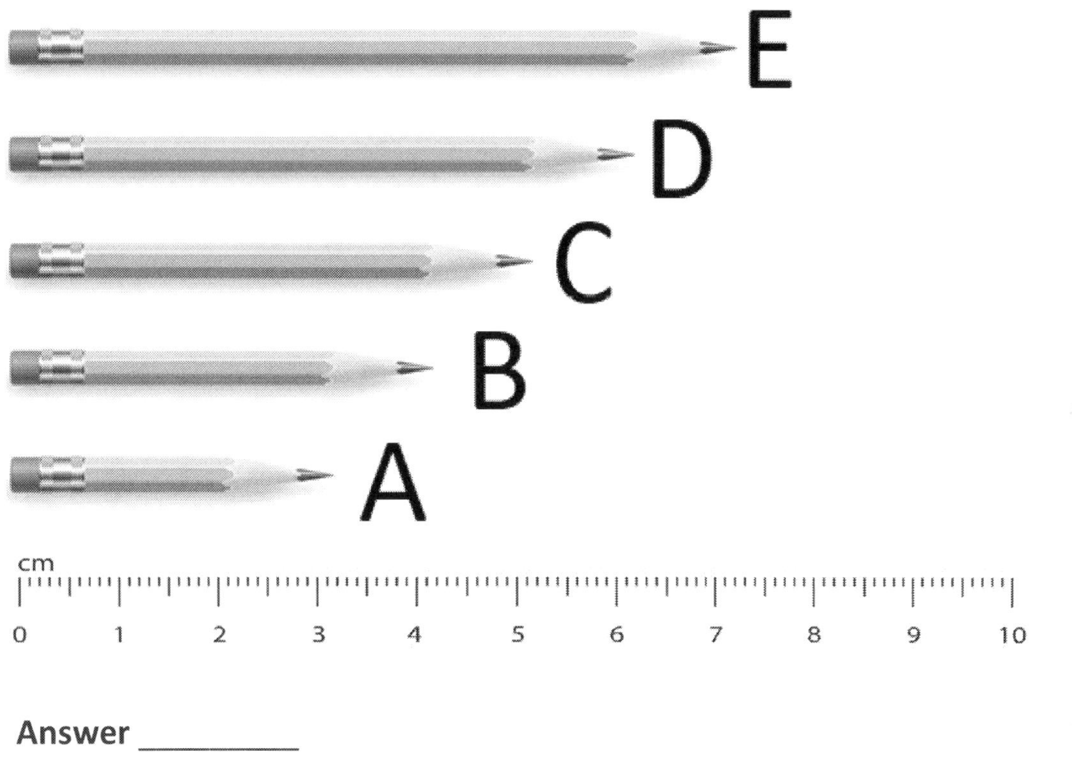

Answer ________

8 The diagram shows the reading on a thermometer in Fahrenheit. What is the temperature? Write your answer on the line below.

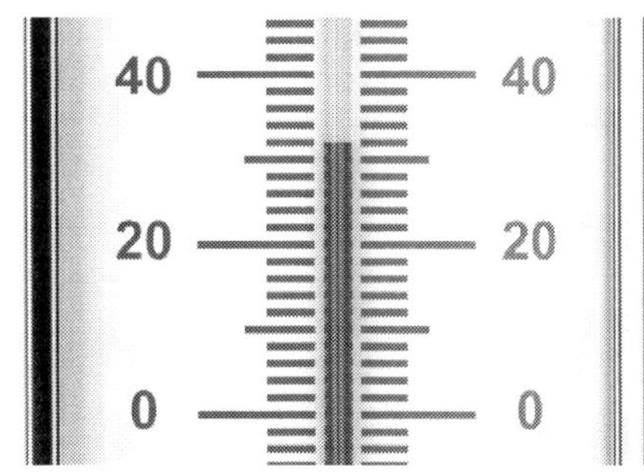

Answer ________°F

9 Draw lines on the beakers to show the measurements given.

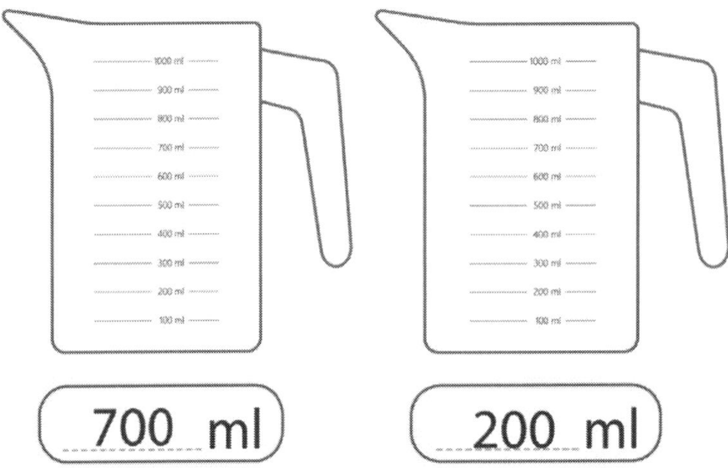

10 The ruler next to each item represents length in inches. Write the length of each item, in inches, in each empty box.

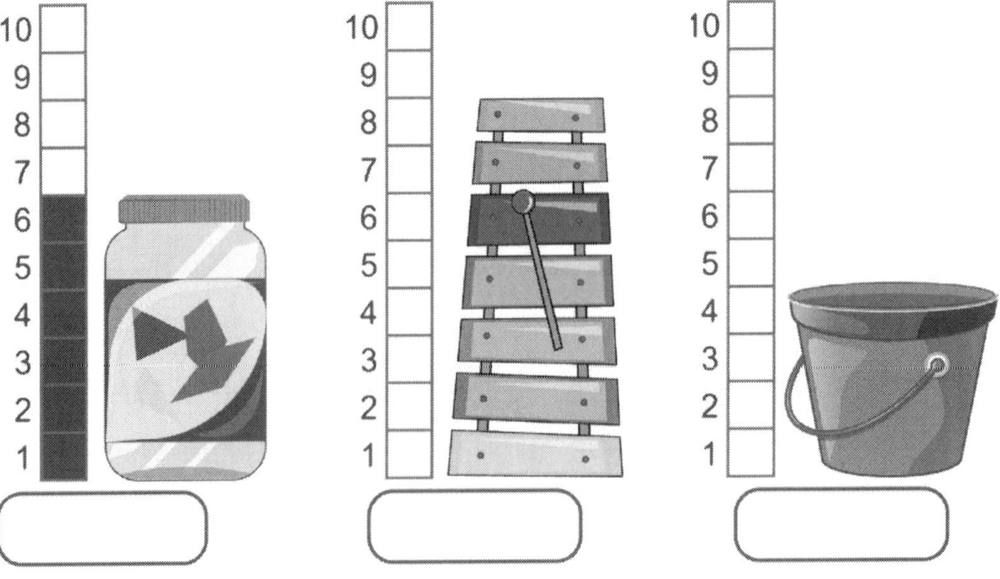

Use Tools to Measure – Practice Set 4

1 Which tool is used to measure temperature?

Ⓐ clock

Ⓑ compass

Ⓒ scales

Ⓓ thermometer

2 A watering can is described as holding 8 liters of liquid. What does this measurement tell?

Ⓐ height

Ⓑ mass

Ⓒ temperature

Ⓓ volume

3 What is the length of the pin to the nearest half centimeter?

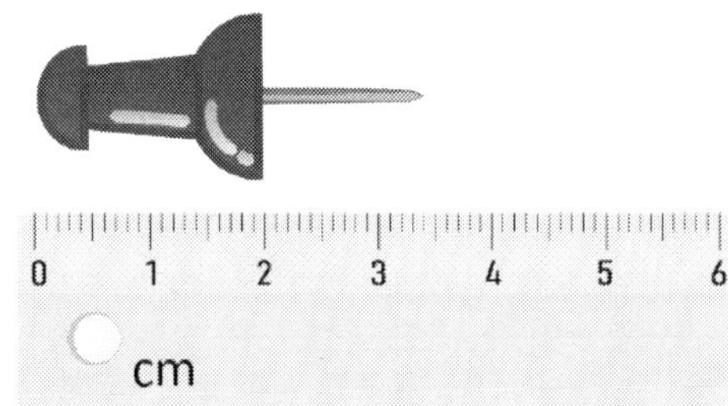

Ⓐ $2\frac{1}{2}$ cm

Ⓑ 3 cm

Ⓒ $3\frac{1}{2}$ cm

Ⓓ 4 cm

4 Which measurement describes the length of an object?

Ⓐ 8 pounds

Ⓑ 8 inches

Ⓒ 8 ounces

Ⓓ 8 cups

5 What temperature is shown on the thermometer below?

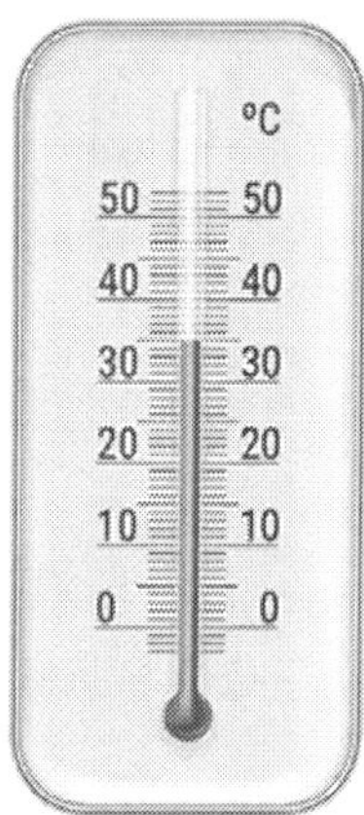

Ⓐ 30°C

Ⓑ 35°C

Ⓒ 40°C

Ⓓ 45°C

6 Kylie places scissors next to a line of ten 1-inch cubes. What is the length of the scissors? Write your answer on the line below.

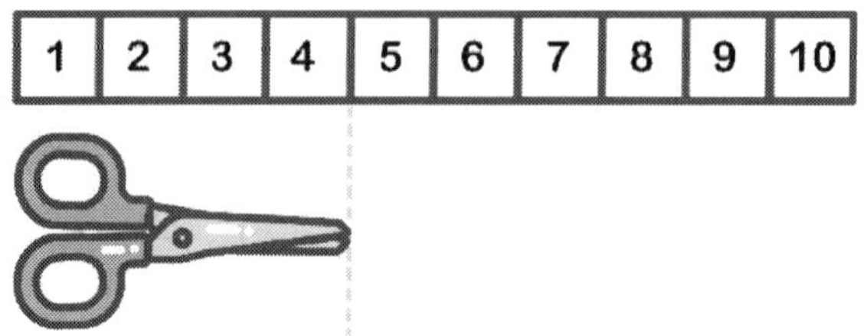

Answer __________ inches

7 The diagram shows the reading on a thermometer in Fahrenheit. What is the temperature? Write your answer on the line below.

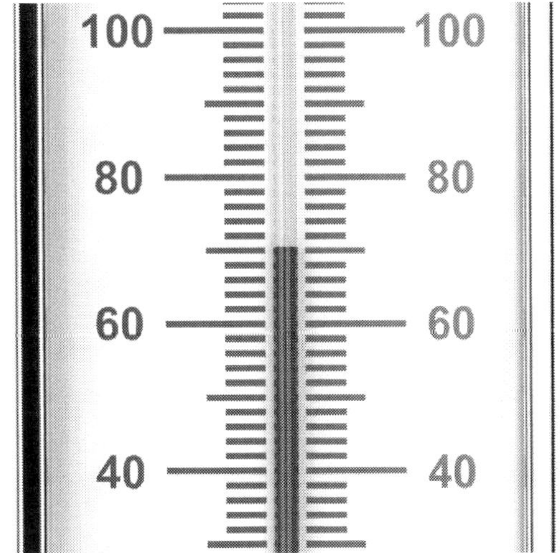

Answer _________°F

8 Draw a line below each ruler with the length given.

$3\frac{1}{2}$ inches

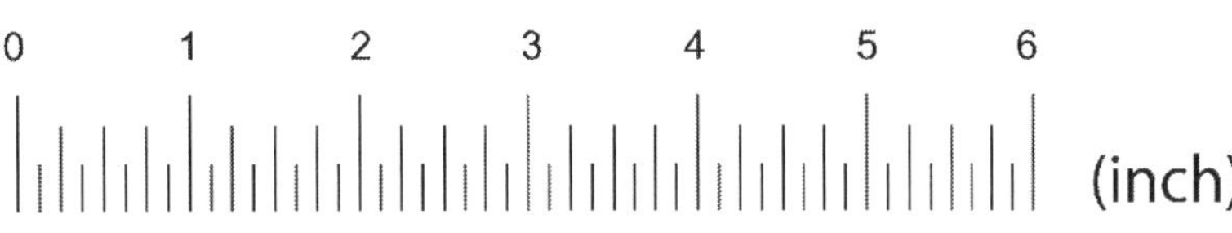

$5\frac{1}{4}$ inches

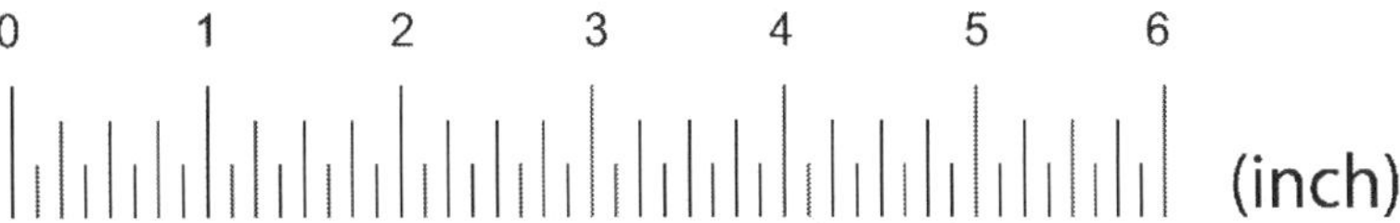

9 What volume of liquid is in the beaker shown? Write your answer on the line below.

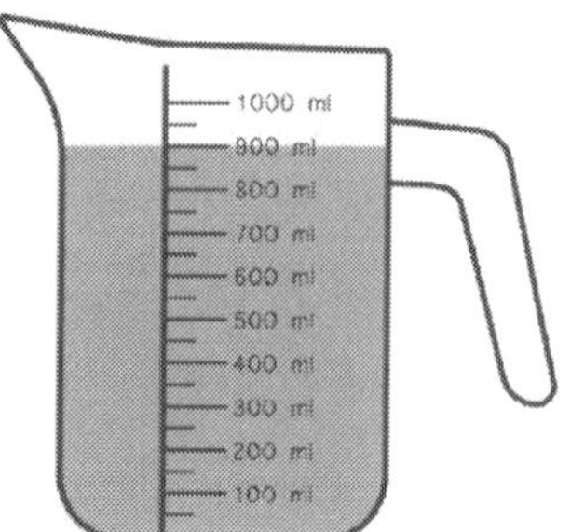

Answer ________ mL

10 Order the liquids shown below from smallest volume to largest volume. Write the numbers 1, 2, 3, 4, 5, and 6 in the empty boxes to show the order.

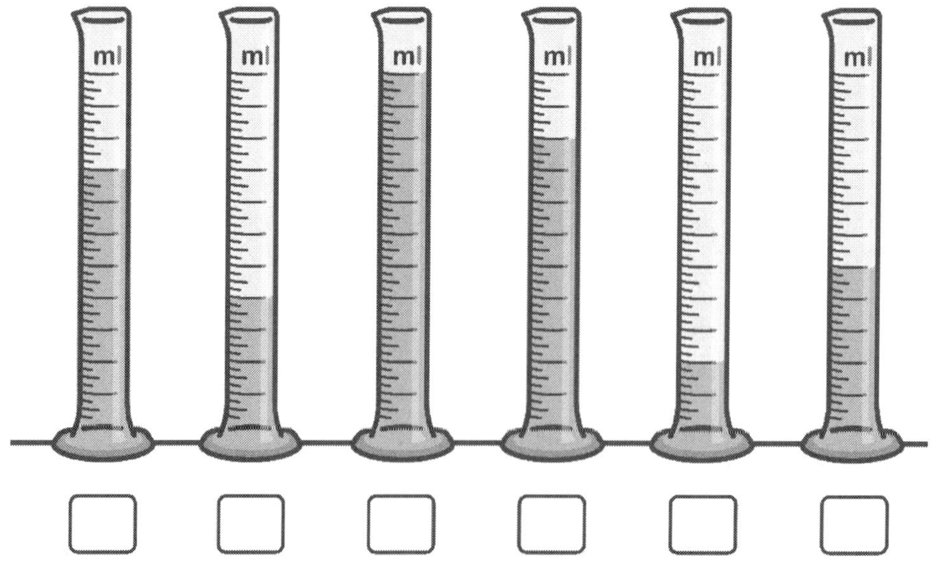

Use Tools to Measure – Practice Set 5

1 Which tool is used to measure length?

Ⓐ beaker

Ⓑ scales

Ⓒ meter stick

Ⓓ stopwatch

2 Which measurement does the diagram below show?

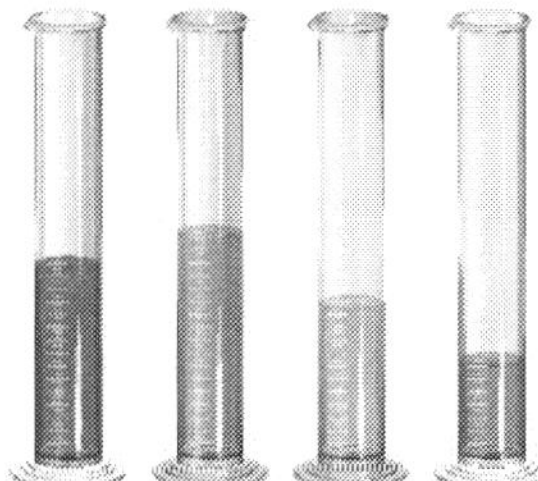

Ⓐ mass

Ⓑ perimeter

Ⓒ temperature

Ⓓ volume

3 What is the length of the toothpaste tube to the nearest centimeter? Write your answer on the line below.

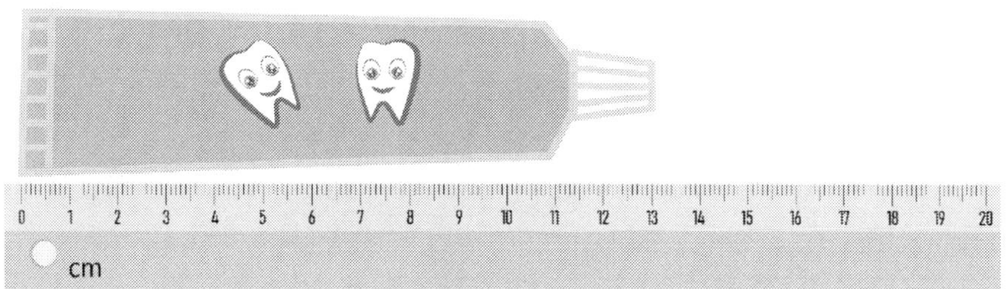

Answer ___________ cm

4 What length is shown below?

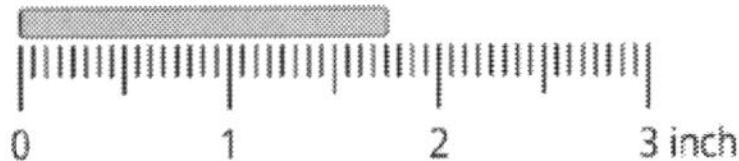

Ⓐ 2 inches

Ⓑ $1\frac{1}{4}$ inches

Ⓒ $1\frac{1}{2}$ inches

Ⓓ $1\frac{3}{4}$ inches

5 What temperature is shown on the thermometer below?

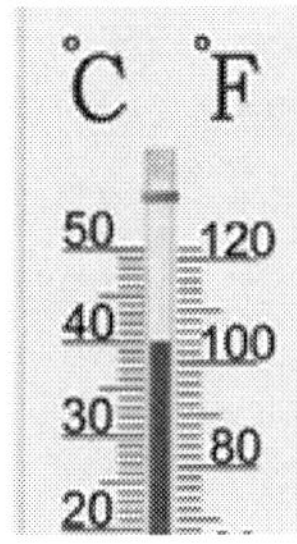

Ⓐ 40°C

Ⓑ 60°C

Ⓒ 105°C

Ⓓ 140°C

6 How much liquid is in the container? Write your answer on the line below.

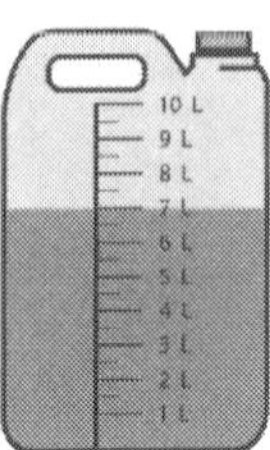

Answer __________ liters

7 What temperature is shown on the thermometer below? Write your answer on the line below.

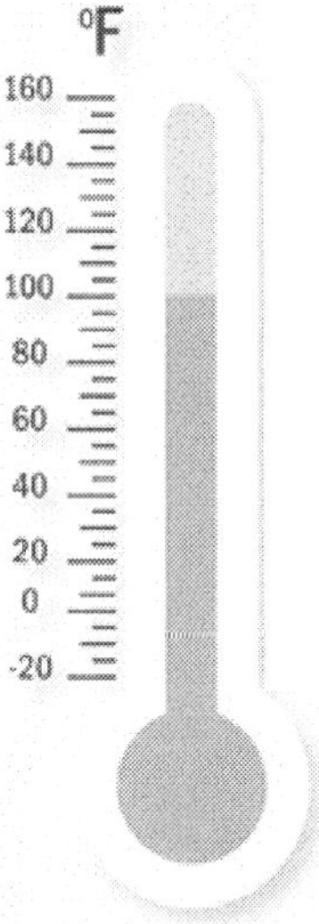

Answer _______ °F

8 What volume of liquid is shown below? Write your answer on the line below.

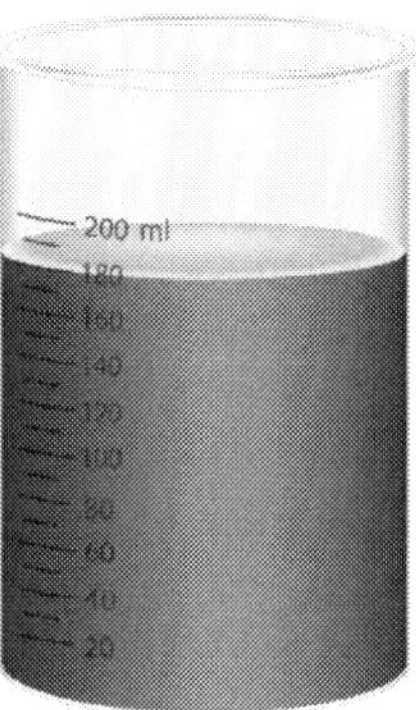

Answer ________ mL

9 Draw lines on the beakers to show the measurements given.

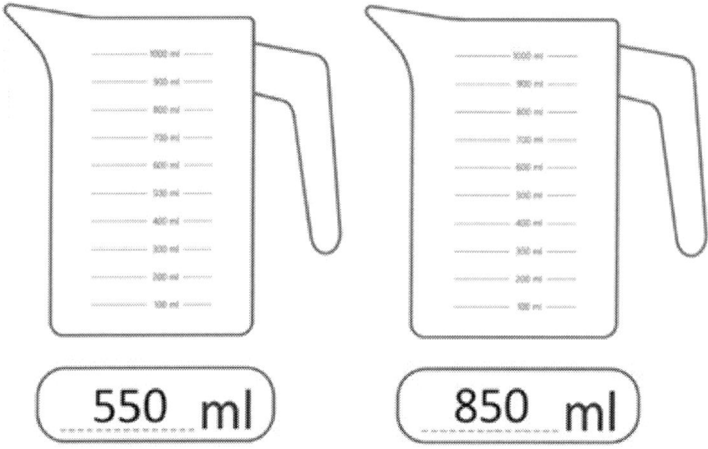

10 The ruler next to each item represents length in inches. Write the length of each item, in inches, in each empty box.

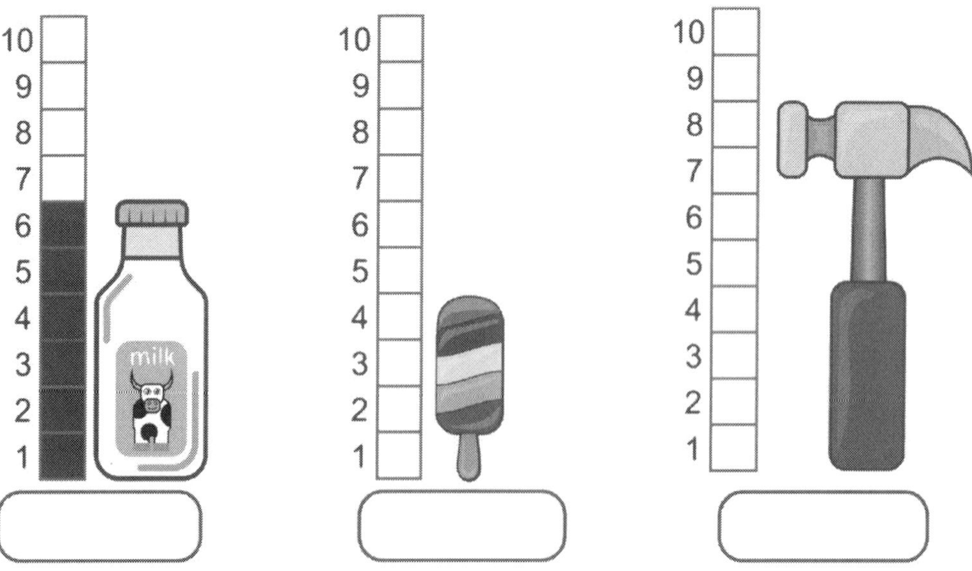

Measurement

Solving Measurement Problems

B.E.S.T. Standards

MA.3.M.1 Measure attributes of objects and solve problems involving measurement.

MA.3.M.1.2
Solve real-world problems involving any of the four operations with whole-number lengths, masses, weights, temperatures or liquid volumes.

Solving Measurement Problems – Practice Set 1

1 A delivery service charges $3 per pound to deliver a parcel. How much would it cost to send a parcel weighing 8 pounds?

Ⓐ $11

Ⓑ $16

Ⓒ $24

Ⓓ $33

2 The temperature was 25°C at noon. It increased by 6°C by 3.p.m. What was the temperature at 3 p.m.?

Ⓐ 19°C

Ⓑ 28°C

Ⓒ 31°C

Ⓓ 33°C

3 The diagram represents a balanced scale with weights in kilograms.

Based on the diagram, what is the weight of the watermelon?

Ⓐ 3 kg

Ⓑ 5 kg

Ⓒ 10 kg

Ⓓ 15 kg

4 A balance has a 10-kilogram weight on one side. How many 2-kilogram weights should be placed on the other side to balance the scale?

Ⓐ 2

Ⓑ 5

Ⓒ 10

Ⓓ 20

5 Hoy placed a lemon and a red pepper on the scales, as shown below.

If the red pepper weighs 140 grams, what does the lemon weigh? Write your answer on the line below.

Answer __________ g

6 Tom buys a 6-pack of water bottles. There is 250 milliliters of water in each bottle. How much water is there in all? Write your answer on the line below.

Answer __________ mL

7 The picture below shows the high and low temperature for five days.

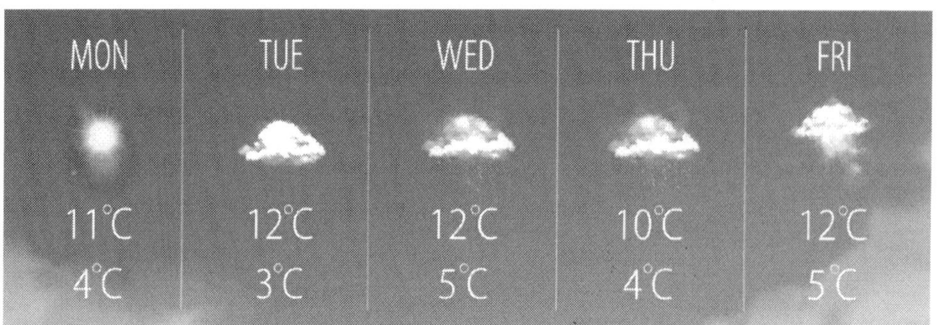

On which day is there 6° difference between the high and low temperature?

☐ Monday

☐ Tuesday

☐ Wednesday

☐ Thursday

☐ Friday

8 A tennis court is shown below.

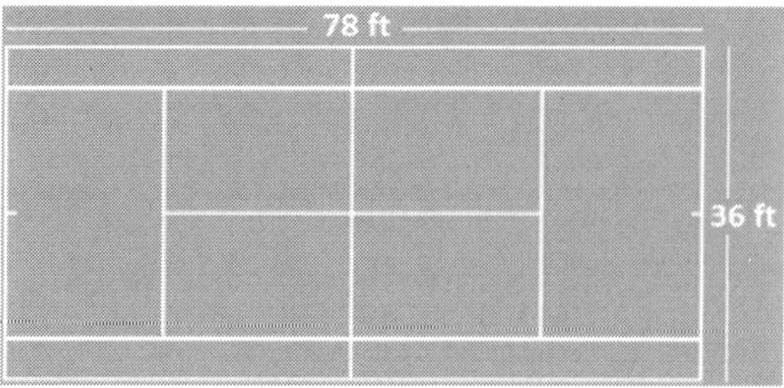

How much greater is the length of the court than the width? Write your answer on the line below.

Answer __________ feet

9 Georgia pours the liquids from the three measuring cylinders into a jug.

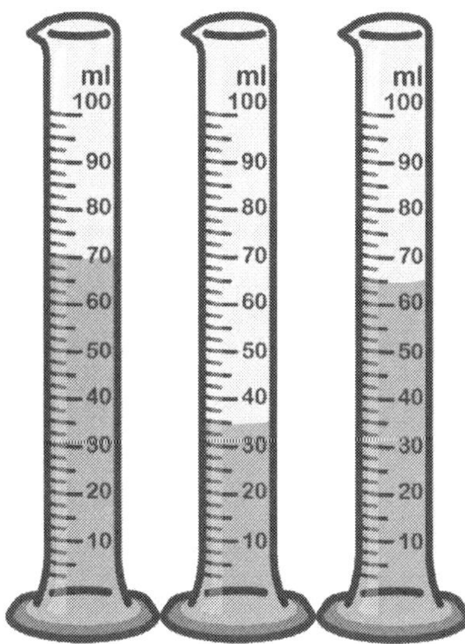

How much liquid would be in the jug? Write your answer on the line below.

Answer __________ mL

10 Mike is making a garden bed. He has blocks that are 8 inches long. He lays 6 blocks end to end and puts a border that is 2 inches long along each end.

What is the total length of the garden bed?

Show your work.

Answer ____________ inches

Solving Measurement Problems – Practice Set 2

1 Leon fills his horse trough with 3 gallons of water every day. How much water would he use in 7 days?

Ⓐ 10 gallons

Ⓑ 14 gallons

Ⓒ 21 gallons

Ⓓ 24 gallons

2 At a recycling center, 425 pounds of cardboard is divided into bags of 25 pounds each. How many bags would be filled?

Ⓐ 11

Ⓑ 17

Ⓒ 41

Ⓓ 85

3 The diagram shows a balanced scale with a soccer ball and tennis balls.

If the soccer ball weighs 15 ounces, what does each tennis ball weigh?

Ⓐ 3 ounces

Ⓑ 5 ounces

Ⓒ 10 ounces

Ⓓ 45 ounces

4 The recipe for a cake states that it should be baked at 375°F. June decides to set the oven 15°F higher. What does June set the oven to?

Ⓐ 350°F

Ⓑ 360°F

Ⓒ 380°F

Ⓓ 390°F

5 A market sells spices for $8 per 50 grams. Danica bought spices with the weight below.

What would the total cost of the spices be? Write your answer below.

Answer $__________

6 A balanced scale is represented below.

The pumpkin weighs 12 pounds. How many 4-pound weights should be placed on the right to balance the scale? Write your answer below.

Answer __________

7 Jared wants to divide the oil in a container into 2-liter bottles. Which container below could he divide into 2-liter bottles and have no oil left over? Circle the letter of the correct answer.

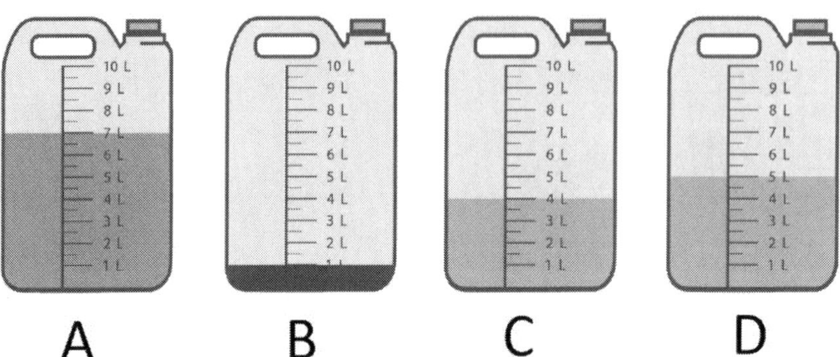

8 The length of a fork and a knife is shown below, in centimeters.

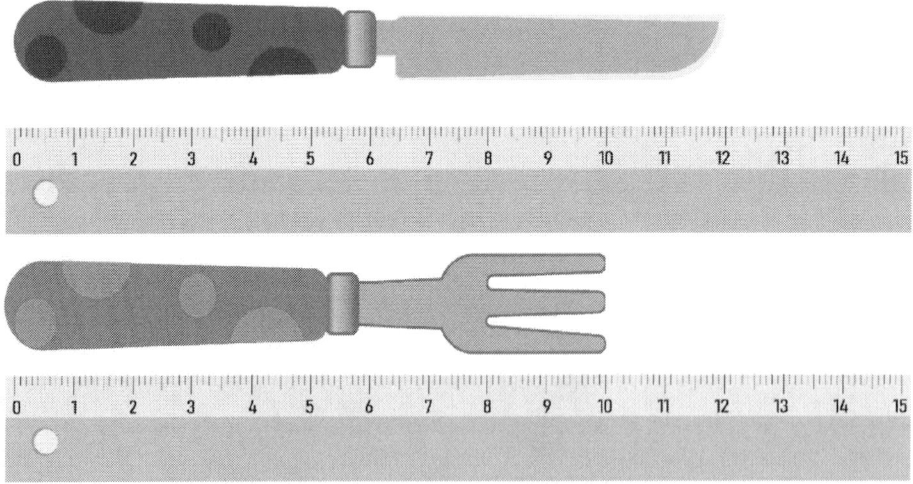

How much longer is the knife than the fork? Write your answer below.

Answer __________ cm

9 The thermometers show the high temperature on the first day of spring and the first day of summer.

Spring Summer

How much hotter was the first day of summer than the first day of spring? Write your answer on the line below.

Answer __________ °C

10 Erika has 20 yards of felt. She cuts 3 pieces of 4 yards each. How much felt would she have left over?

Show your work.

Answer ____________ yards

Solving Measurement Problems – Practice Set 3

1 Charlotte walks 650 meters of a hike. Then she walks another 850 meters to finish the hike. What is the total distance of the hike?

Ⓐ 1,300 meters

Ⓑ 1,400 meters

Ⓒ 1,500 meters

Ⓓ 1,600 meters

2 A scale has a 20-pound weight on one side. How many 5-pound weights should be placed on the other side to balance the scale?

Ⓐ 2

Ⓑ 4

Ⓒ 25

Ⓓ 100

3 Marcus placed a lemon and an orange on the scales, as shown below.

If the orange weighs 180 grams, what does the lemon weigh?

Ⓐ 95 grams

Ⓑ 100 grams

Ⓒ 105 grams

Ⓓ 110 grams

4 It takes 10,000 gallons of water to fill a swimming pool. A water truck can fill the pool at a rate of 100 gallons every minute. How long would it take to fill the swimming pool?

Ⓐ 10 minutes

Ⓑ 100 minutes

Ⓒ 1,000 minutes

Ⓓ 100,000 minutes

5 The diagram represents a balanced scale with weights in ounces.

If all the tomatoes have the same weight, what is the weight of each tomato?

Ⓐ 1 ounce

Ⓑ 2 ounces

Ⓒ 4 ounces

Ⓓ 8 ounces

6 Abigail bought 8 ounces of walnuts for $4 per ounce. How much change should she receive from $40? Write your answer on the line below.

Answer $______________

7 Katy divides the laundry liquid in the container below into bottles of 3 liters each.

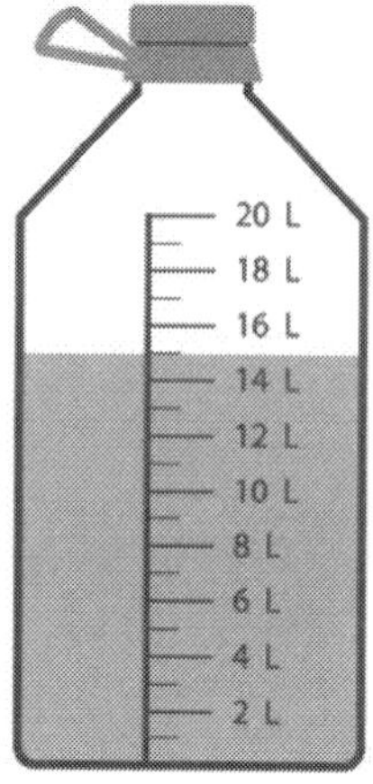

How many bottles would she fill? Write your answer on the line below.

Answer ____________

8 A scientist has a liquid at 40°C. He heats it by 15°C every 5 minutes. Complete the table with the temperature of the liquid at each time.

Minutes	Temperature (°C)
0	40
5	
10	
15	

9 The reading on a meat thermometer is shown below in degrees Celsius.

Jackson wants to keep cooking until the thermometer reads 90°C. How much does the temperature need to increase by? Write your answer on the line below.

Answer ______________ °C

10 Each storage box below has a height of 4 inches. Which stack of storage boxes has a total height of 20 inches? Circle the letter of the correct stack.

Solving Measurement Problems – Practice Set 4

1 A baby weighed 7 pounds 8 ounces when it was born. After 4 weeks, the baby was 1 pound 2 ounces heavier. What was the weight of the baby after 4 weeks?

Ⓐ 8 pounds 6 ounces

Ⓑ 8 pounds 10 ounces

Ⓒ 9 pounds 9 ounces

Ⓓ 10 pounds 8 ounces

2 The temperature outside is 51°F and the temperature inside is 73°F. What is the difference in temperature?

Ⓐ 22°F

Ⓑ 24°F

Ⓒ 122°F

Ⓓ 124°F

3 The diagram shows a balanced scale with lemons and a grapefruit.

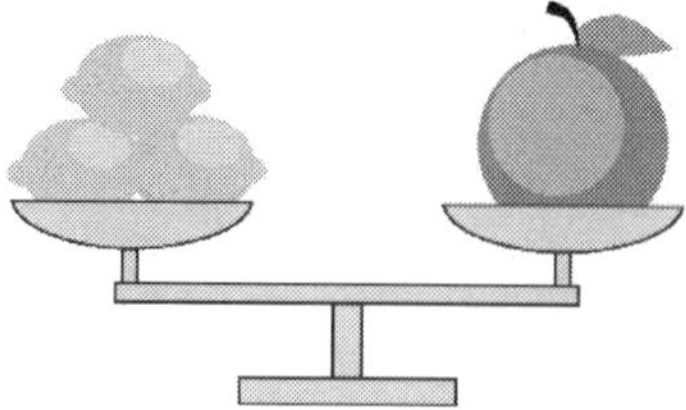

Based on the diagram, which statement is true?

Ⓐ Each lemon has the same weight as the grapefruit.

Ⓑ Each lemon is 3 times heavier than the grapefruit.

Ⓒ The grapefruit has a greater weight than each lemon.

Ⓓ The grapefruit is not as heavy as 3 lemons.

4 A box has a length of 6 inches. What is the greatest number of boxes that could be placed on a shelf with a length of 30 inches?

Ⓐ 4

Ⓑ 5

Ⓒ 8

Ⓓ 15

5 The diagram shows a balanced scale with 6 oranges and 3 apples.

If each orange weighs 4 ounces, what does each apple weigh?

Ⓐ 2 ounces

Ⓑ 8 ounces

Ⓒ 12 ounces

Ⓓ 24 ounces

6 India needs to give her cat the dose of medicine shown below every day for 5 days.

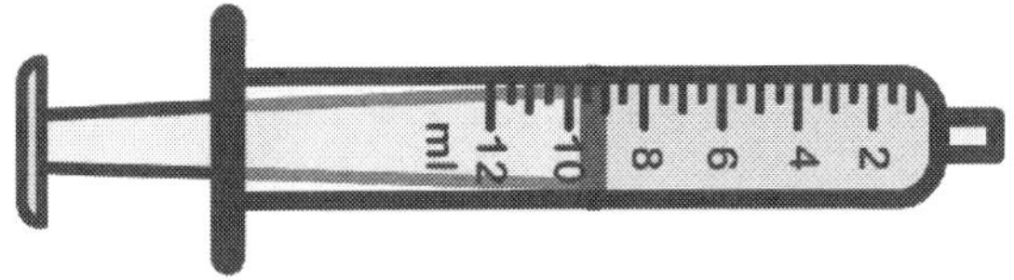

How much medicine would she use in 5 days? Write your answer below.

Answer __________ mL

7 The picture shows the high temperature each day in degrees Celsius.

Which day will have a high temperature greater than Monday?

Answer ________________

Which day will have a high temperature 5 degrees less than Monday?

Answer ________________

What is the difference between the greatest and least high temperature?

Answer ________°C

8 Audrey uses the plant food shown below on her apple trees. She uses 5 liters of plant food for each apple tree.

How many apple trees could she feed? Write your answer below.

Answer __________

9 The length of a sharpener and a pair of scissors is shown below, in centimeters.

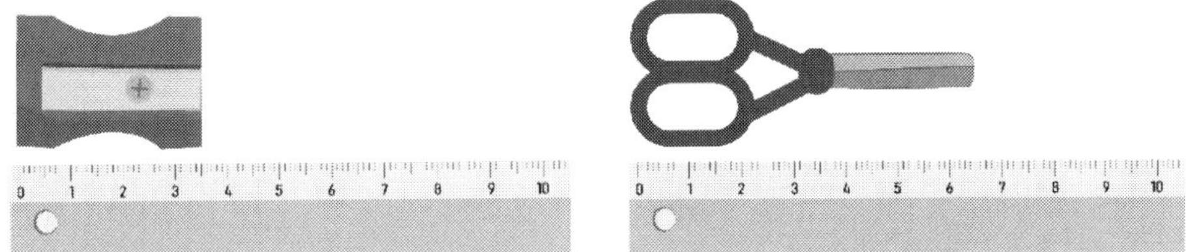

How much longer is the pair of scissors than the sharpener? Write your answer below.

Answer __________ cm

10 The mass of flour on a scale is shown below.

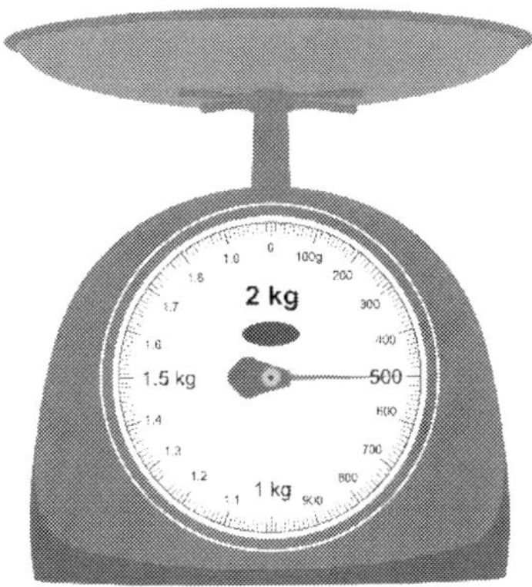

Sarah is making loaves of bread. She needs 200 grams of flour to make each loaf. How much more flour will she need to make 4 loaves of bread?

Show your work.

Answer ____________ grams

Solving Measurement Problems – Practice Set 5

1 A male lion weighs 490 pounds. A female lion weighs 320 pounds. What is the difference in mass between the male and female lion?

Ⓐ 130 pounds

Ⓑ 150 pounds

Ⓒ 170 pounds

Ⓓ 190 pounds

2 A running track has a length of 400 meters. Kai runs 6 laps of the track. What is the total distance he has run?

Ⓐ 2,400 meters

Ⓑ 3,000 meters

Ⓒ 3,200 meters

Ⓓ 4,600 meters

3 A balanced scale is represented below.

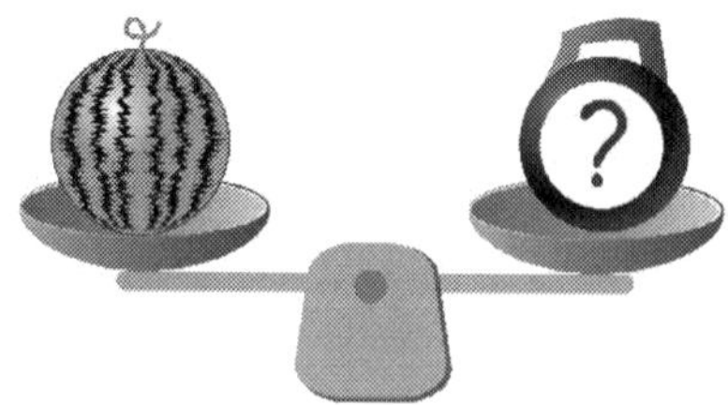

If the watermelon weighs 20 pounds, how many 4-pound weights should be placed on the right side to balance the scale? Write your answer on the line below.

Answer __________

4 Oliver makes 30 quarts of orange juice. He sells it for $3 per quart and makes $60 in sales. How much orange juice would he have left over?

Ⓐ 5 quarts

Ⓑ 10 quarts

Ⓒ 20 quarts

Ⓓ 25 quarts

5 A farmer collects apples with the total weight shown below.

He sorts the apples into boxes of 5 kilograms each. How many boxes would he fill?

Ⓐ 16

Ⓑ 20

Ⓒ 85

Ⓓ 400

6 The thermometer shows the temperature of a beaker of water.

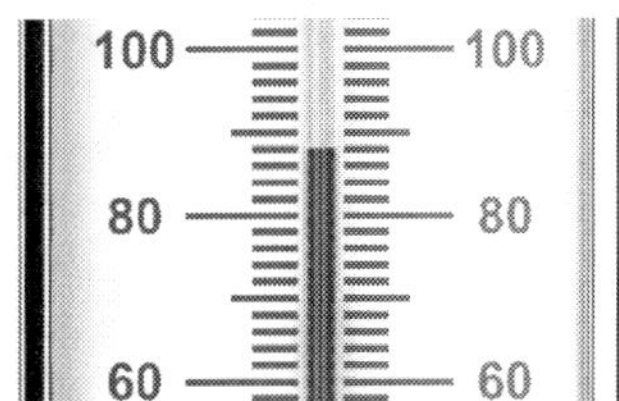

Water boils at 100°C. How much would the temperature need to increase by for the water to boil? Write your answer on the line below.

Answer __________ °C

7 Jordan has the five weights shown below. Tick the boxes of the weights he could add to the left side to balance the scale.

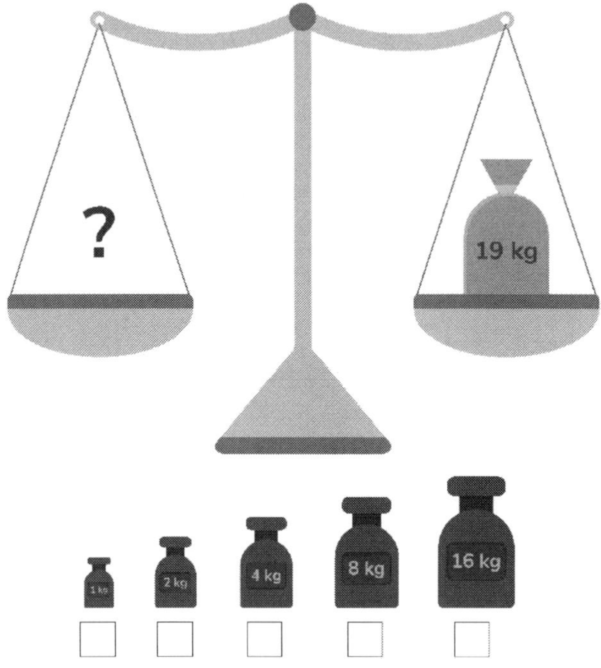

8 Kieran adds 6 liters of oil to his car from the container below.

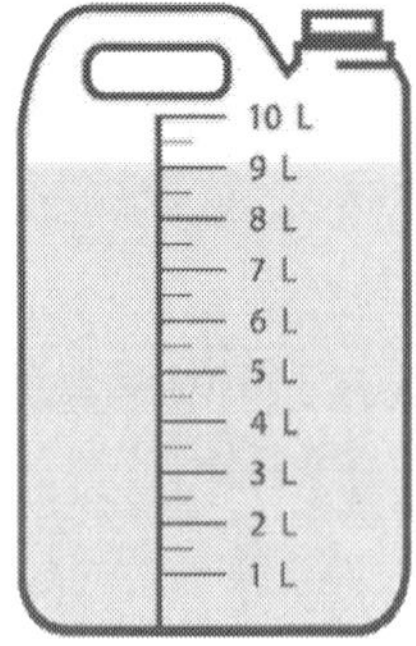

How much oil would be left over? Write your answer on the line below.

Answer __________ L

9 Which thermometer below shows a temperature closest to 45°F? Circle the letter of the correct thermometer.

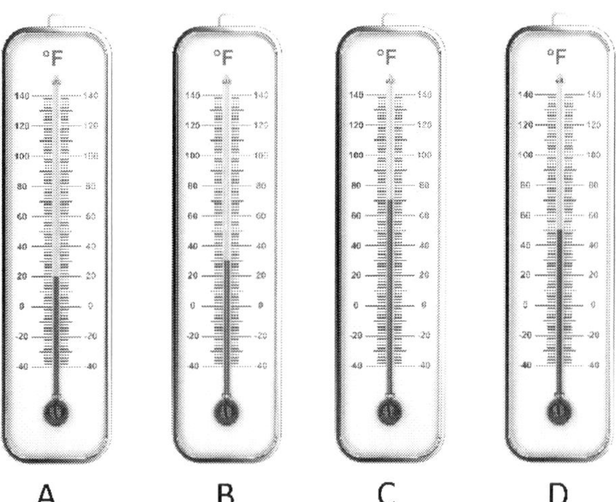

10 Darren is fencing 4 paddocks on his farm. He needs 80 meters of wire fencing to fence each paddock. The wire fencing costs $3 for each meter. How much would he pay for all the wire fencing he needs?

Show your work.

Answer $____________

Measurement

Telling Time and Solving Time Problems

B.E.S.T. Standards

MA.3.M.2 Tell and write time and solve problems involving time.

MA.3.M.2.1
Using analog and digital clocks tell and write time to the nearest minute using a.m. and p.m. appropriately.

MA.3.M.2.2
Solve one- and two-step real-world problems involving elapsed time.

Telling Time and Solving Time Problems – Practice Set 1

1 What time is the same as quarter past three in the afternoon?

Ⓐ 3:15 a.m.

Ⓑ 3:15 p.m.

Ⓒ 3:45 a.m.

Ⓓ 3:45 p.m.

2 Joe started a walk at 8:45 a.m. He walked for 45 minutes. What time did he finish the walk?

Ⓐ 9:15 a.m.

Ⓑ 9:30 a.m.

Ⓒ 10:15 a.m.

Ⓓ 10:30 a.m.

3 What time is shown on the clock below?

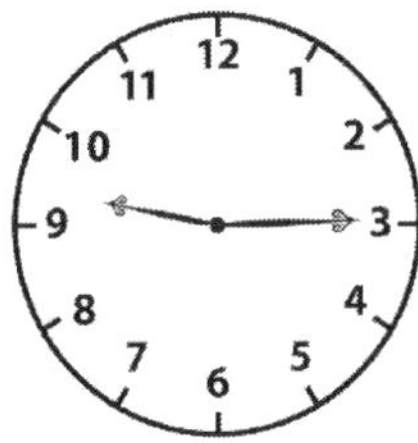

Ⓐ 9:03

Ⓑ 9:15

Ⓒ 9:30

Ⓓ 9:45

4 A flight took off at 8:15 in the morning and landed at 11:58 in the morning. How long was the flight?

Ⓐ 3 hours, 43 minutes

Ⓑ 3 hours, 53 minutes

Ⓒ 4 hours, 43 minutes

Ⓓ 4 hours, 53 minutes

5 Meredith caught a train at the time shown below.

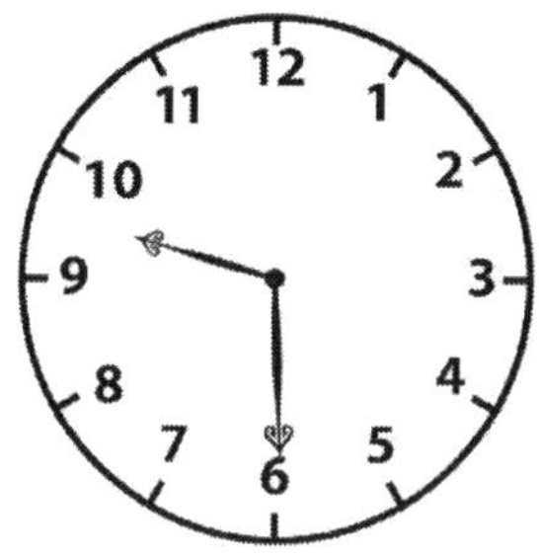

What time did she catch the train?

Ⓐ 6:30

Ⓑ 6:45

Ⓒ 9:30

Ⓓ 9:45

6 Stephanie starts a coding class at quarter to four in the afternoon. What is this time written as digital time? Write your answer on the line below.

Answer ________:________ p.m.

7 Write the correct number in the empty box to show the time shown on each clock.

8 Write the time shown on each clock on the line below it.

9 The clocks show a time one morning and a time the same afternoon. Write the time shown on each clock in the empty space.

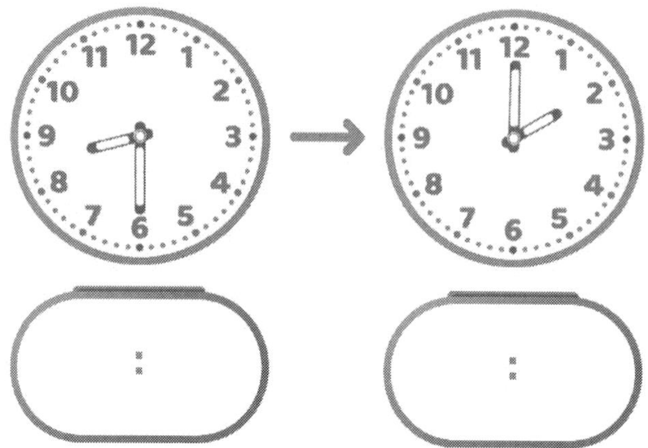

How much time has passed between the two times? Write your answer on the lines below.

Answer ________ hours and ________ minutes

10 Kim hires a bike. The bike is charged at a rate of \$6 for each half hour. She hires the bike from 10:30 a.m. until noon. How much would she be charged for the bike hire?

Show your work.

Answer \$____________

Telling Time and Solving Time Problems – Practice Set 2

1 Which time is closest to midnight?

Ⓐ 11:55 a.m.

Ⓑ 12:06 a.m.

Ⓒ 11:50 p.m.

Ⓓ 12:03 p.m.

2 A fishing charter left at 6:20 in the morning and returned at 10:35 in the morning. How long was the fishing charter?

Ⓐ 3 hours, 15 minutes

Ⓑ 3 hours, 25 minutes

Ⓒ 4 hours, 15 minutes

Ⓓ 4 hours, 25 minutes

3 The clock shows a time that a movie starts.

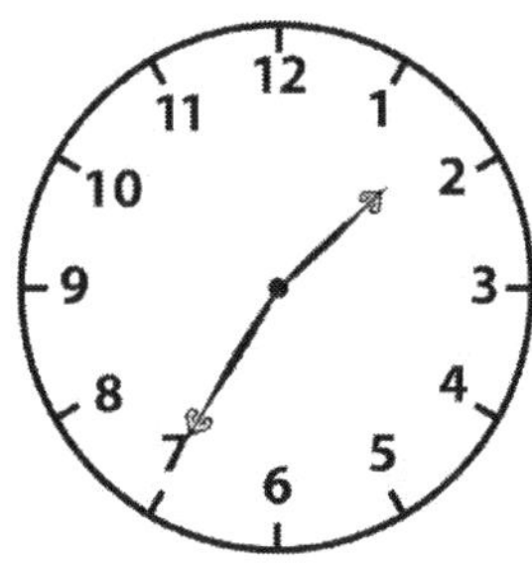

What time does the movie start?

Ⓐ 1:07

Ⓑ 1:10

Ⓒ 1:25

Ⓓ 1:35

4 A history exam started at 2:20 and went for 80 minutes. What time did the exam finish?

Ⓐ 2:40

Ⓑ 3:00

Ⓒ 3:40

Ⓓ 3:50

5 A tour bus runs at 1 p.m. in the afternoon and then every 2 hours all day. Select **all** the times that the tour bus would run. Tick the boxes under the clocks to select all the correct answers.

6 What time is shown on the clock? Write your answer on the line below.

Answer ______:______

7 Write the time shown on each clock on the line below it.

8 The clocks below show the time that Phil started work and the time he finished work.

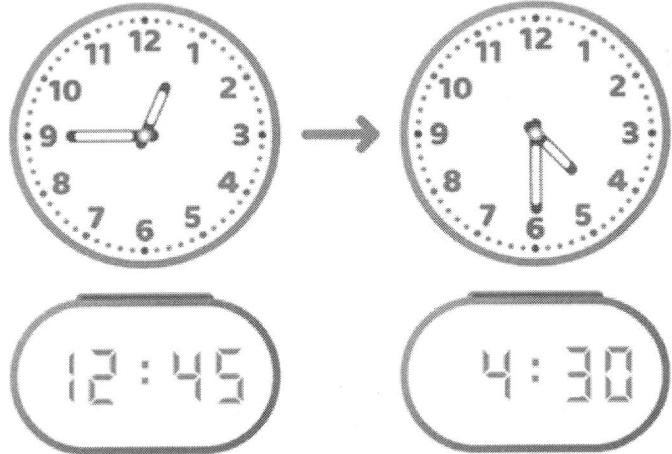

How long did Phil work for? Write your answer on the lines below.

Answer ________ h ________ min

9 Draw a first and second hand on each clock to show the time given under the clock.

10 Moira charges $12 per hour to do ironing. She starts ironing at 7:30 a.m. and finishes at 11:30 a.m. How much would she charge?

Show your work.

Answer $____________

Telling Time and Solving Time Problems – Practice Set 3

1 Stella put a cake in the oven at 10:25 in the morning. She needs to bake it for 55 minutes. What time should she take it out of the oven?

Ⓐ 11:10

Ⓑ 11:20

Ⓒ 11:30

Ⓓ 11:40

2 What time is the same as quarter to five in the afternoon?

Ⓐ 4:15 p.m.

Ⓑ 4:45 p.m.

Ⓒ 5:15 p.m.

Ⓓ 5:45 p.m.

3 The clock shows the time that Toby had lunch.

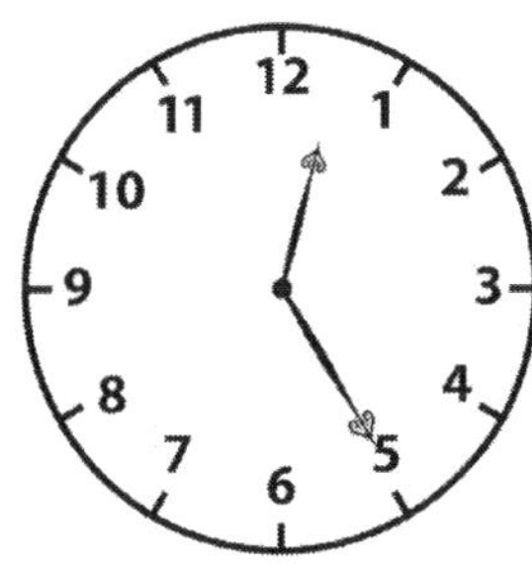

What time did Toby have lunch?

Ⓐ 12:05

Ⓑ 12:15

Ⓒ 12:25

Ⓓ 12:50

4 A marathon runner started a race at 5:35 in the morning and finished it at 9:52 in the morning. How long did it take the runner to finish the race?

Ⓐ 4 hours, 17 minutes

Ⓑ 4 hours, 27 minutes

Ⓒ 5 hours, 17 minutes

Ⓓ 5 hours, 27 minutes

5 What time is shown on the clock below?

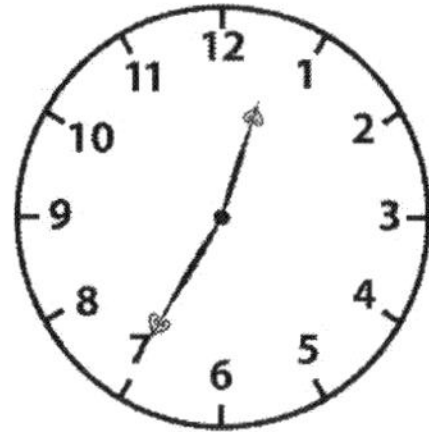

Ⓐ 12:07

Ⓑ 12:25

Ⓒ 12:35

Ⓓ 12:37

6 The clocks below show the time in London and New York one day. What time would it be in New York when it is 2 o'clock in London? Write your answer on the line below.

Answer ________ o'clock

7 The clocks show a time one afternoon and a time the same evening. Write the time shown on each clock in the empty space.

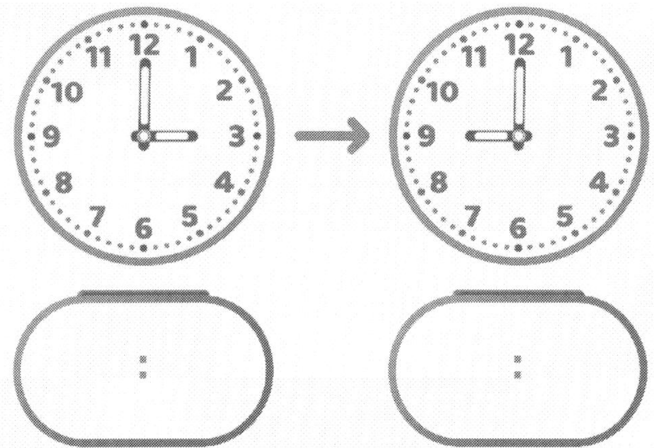

How much time has passed between the two times? Write your answer on the line below.

Answer ________ hours

8 Write the time shown on each clock on the line below it.

9 Draw a first and second hand on each clock to show the time given under the clock.

10 The instructions for a roast state to cook it for 45 minutes per 500 grams. Alex has a roast weighing 2,000 grams. If he puts it in the oven at 3 p.m., what time would it be ready?

Show your work.

Answer ________:________ p.m.

Telling Time and Solving Time Problems – Practice Set 4

1 Which time is closest to noon?

Ⓐ 11:35 a.m.

Ⓑ 12:10 p.m.

Ⓒ 11:55 p.m.

Ⓓ 12:05 a.m.

2 A motorcycle race started at 2:55 in the afternoon and finished at 3:29 in the afternoon. How long was the race?

Ⓐ 24 minutes

Ⓑ 26 minutes

Ⓒ 34 minutes

Ⓓ 39 minutes

3 The clock shows the time that the town library opens each day.

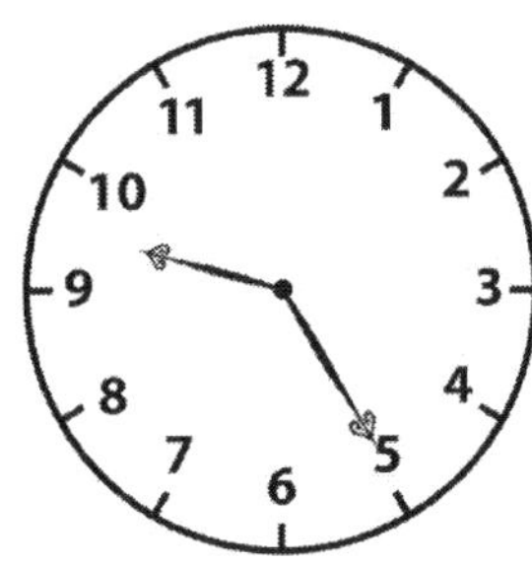

What time does the town library open?

Ⓐ 9:05

Ⓑ 9:25

Ⓒ 9:35

Ⓓ 9:50

4 Morgan called her grandmother at 7:55. She spoke to her for 35 minutes. What time did the phone call end?

Ⓐ 8:10

Ⓑ 8:20

Ⓒ 8:30

Ⓓ 8:40

5 Kris starts babysitting at noon and babysits for 3 hours. Select the clock that shows the time that Kris finishes babysitting.

6 What time is shown on the clock? Write your answer on the line below.

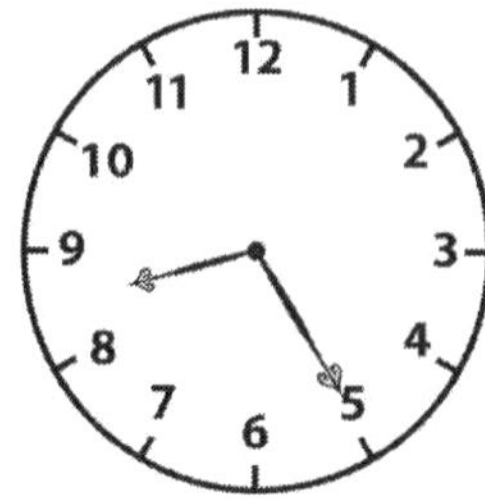

Answer ______:______

7 Write the time shown on each clock on the line below it.

8 Draw lines to match the times shown on the clocks.

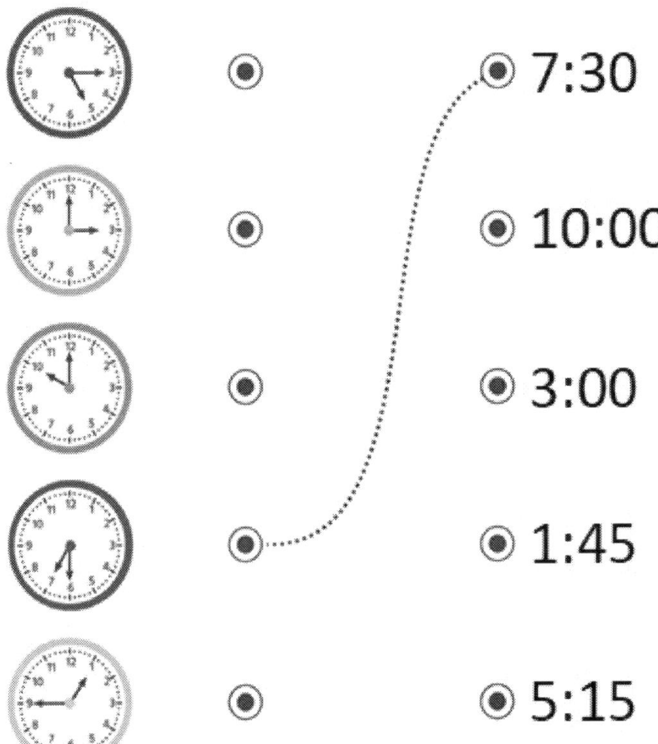

9 The clocks below show the time that a play started and the time that a play ended one morning.

How long did the play go for? Write your answer on the lines below.

Answer ________ h ________ min

10 A restaurant promises to deliver all local orders within 45 minutes. Andy orders some meals at 5:28 p.m. The meals are delivered at 6:19 p.m. How late is the order delivered?

Show your work.

Answer ____________ minutes

Telling Time and Solving Time Problems – Practice Set 5

1 What time is the same as ten to eight in the morning?

Ⓐ 7:50 a.m.

Ⓑ 8:50 a.m.

Ⓒ 7:50 p.m.

Ⓓ 8:50 p.m.

2 The clocks below show the time in the afternoon a train left Stafford and the time that evening the train arrived in Everton.

How long was the train trip?

Ⓐ 7 hours, 31 minutes

Ⓑ 7 hours, 41 minutes

Ⓒ 8 hours, 31 minutes

Ⓓ 8 hours, 41 minutes

3 What time is shown on the clock below?

Ⓐ 8:40

Ⓑ 8:45

Ⓒ 9:40

Ⓓ 9:45

4 Samantha was meant to arrive for a meeting at 8:10. Samantha arrived 25 minutes early. What time did Samantha arrive?

Ⓐ 7:35

Ⓑ 7:40

Ⓒ 7:45

Ⓓ 7:50

5 The clock shows the time that a parcel was delivered.

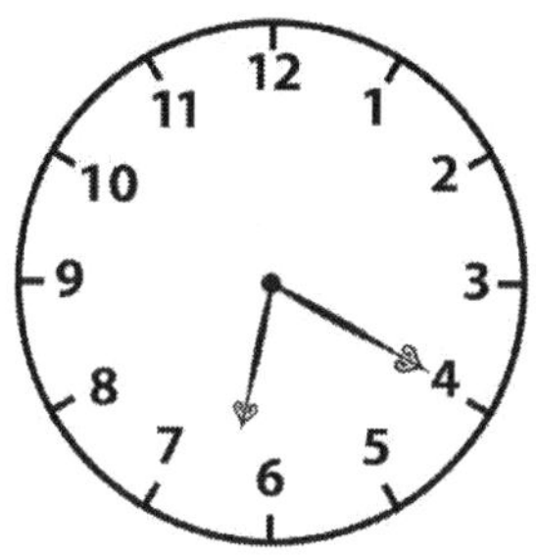

What time was the parcel delivered?

Ⓐ 6:04

Ⓑ 6:20

Ⓒ 6:35

Ⓓ 6:40

6 Brayden starts basketball practice at quarter past four in the afternoon. What is this time written as digital time? Write your answer on the line below.

Answer ________:________ p.m.

7 Draw a first and second hand on each clock to show the time given under the clock.

8 The clocks show two times one afternoon. Write the time shown on each clock in the blank space.

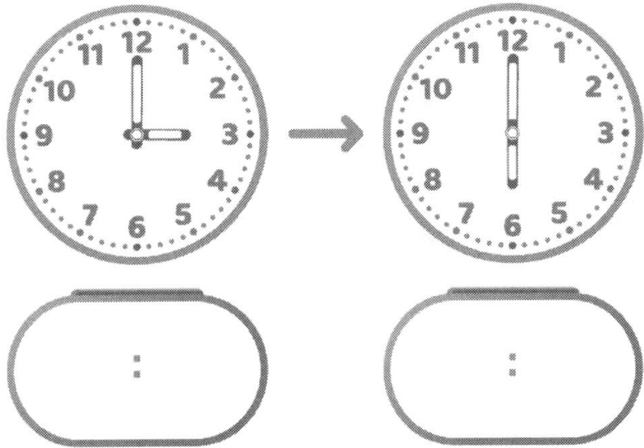

How much time has passed between the two times? Write your answer on the line below.

Answer ________ hours

9 Write the time shown on each clock on the line below it.

10 Mandy earns extra money looking after people's dogs. She charges $8 per hour. The clocks below show when she started and finished looking after a dog one Saturday afternoon.

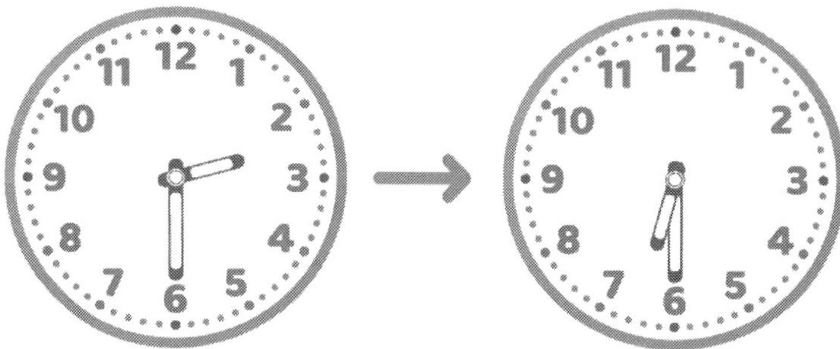

How much would she charge for looking after the dog?

Show your work.

Answer $____________

Geometric Reasoning

Lines, Quadrilaterals, and Symmetry

B.E.S.T. Standards

MA.3.GR.1 Describe and identify relationships between lines and classify quadrilaterals.

MA.3.GR.1.1
Describe and draw points, lines, line segments, rays, intersecting lines, perpendicular lines and parallel lines. Identify these in two-dimensional figures.

MA.3.GR.1.2
Identify and draw quadrilaterals based on their defining attributes. Quadrilaterals include parallelograms, rhombi, rectangles, squares and trapezoids.

MA.3.GR.1.3
Draw line(s) of symmetry in a two-dimensional figure and identify line-symmetric two-dimensional figures.

Lines, Quadrilaterals, and Symmetry – Practice Set 1

1 Based on the diagram below, how many lines of symmetry does a square have?

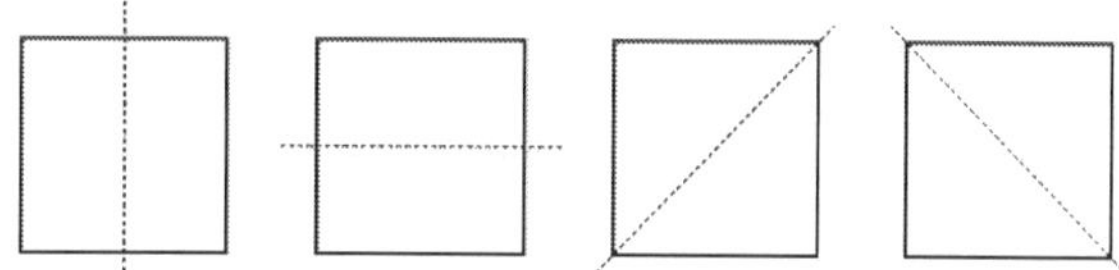

Ⓐ 2

Ⓑ 4

Ⓒ 8

Ⓓ 16

2 How many endpoints does a line segment have?

Ⓐ 0

Ⓑ 1

Ⓒ 2

Ⓓ 4

3 Which letter on the sign below has exactly one line of symmetry?

Ⓐ O

Ⓑ P

Ⓒ E

Ⓓ N

4 Which term describes the lines below?

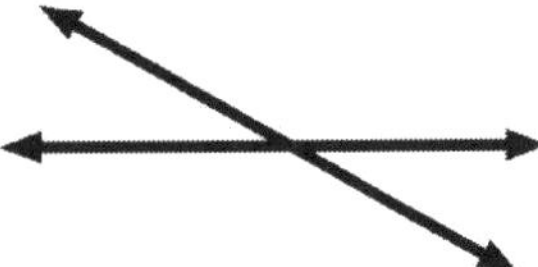

Ⓐ curved

Ⓑ intersecting

Ⓒ parallel

Ⓓ perpendicular

5 A symbol is shown below.

How many lines of symmetry does the symbol have?

Ⓐ 0

Ⓑ 1

Ⓒ 2

Ⓓ 3

6 How many pairs of parallel sides does a parallelogram have? Write your answer on the line below.

Answer __________

7 Which letters have a pair of parallel lines? Select the **two** correct answers.

☐ F

☐ G

☐ H

☐ K

☐ L

☐ S

8 Draw a line of symmetry on the figure below.

9 Shade the **two** shapes with 4 equal sides.

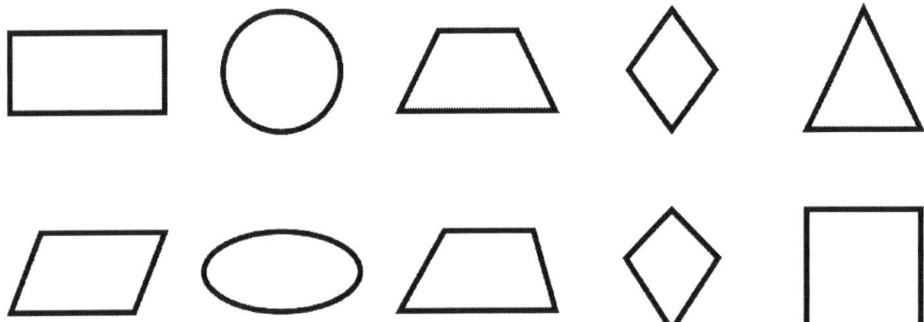

What two types of shapes did you shade? Write the names of the two shapes on the lines below.

Answer _______________ and _______________

10 Draw a rectangle with side lengths of 2 units and 3 units on the grid below.

Lines, Quadrilaterals, and Symmetry – Practice Set 2

1 Circle the term that describes the two upright posts shown below.

intersecting parallel perpendicular

2 Which of the following has two endpoints?

Ⓐ line

Ⓑ line segment

Ⓒ point

Ⓓ ray

3 A set of letters is shown below.

L M N O

Which letter has exactly one line of symmetry?

Ⓐ L

Ⓑ M

Ⓒ N

Ⓓ O

4 Which quadrilateral has 4 equal sides, but no right angles?

Ⓐ rectangle

Ⓑ rhombus

Ⓒ square

Ⓓ trapezoid

5 The shape of a roof is shown below.

Which term best describes the shape of the roof?

Ⓐ parallelogram

Ⓑ rectangle

Ⓒ trapezoid

Ⓓ triangle

6 Which diagrams below show a line of symmetry? Tick the box under each diagram that shows a correct line of symmetry.

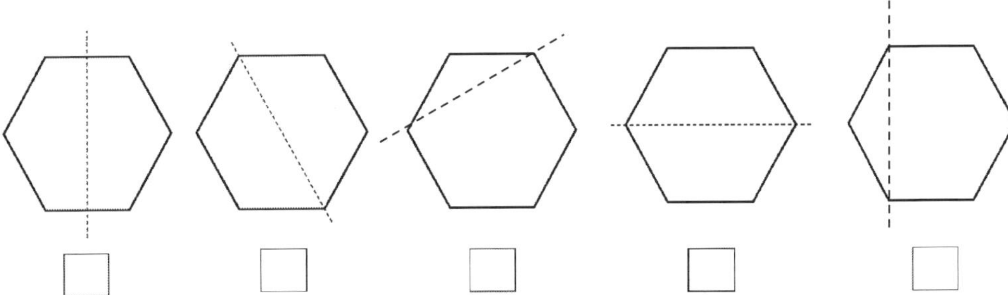

7 Dion has a collection of felt shapes. He wants to sort the shapes into those that have at least one line of symmetry and those that do not have a line of symmetry. Shade **all** the shapes below that Dion should sort into the category of shapes that do not have a line of symmetry.

8 Draw lines to match each shape shown with its correct name.

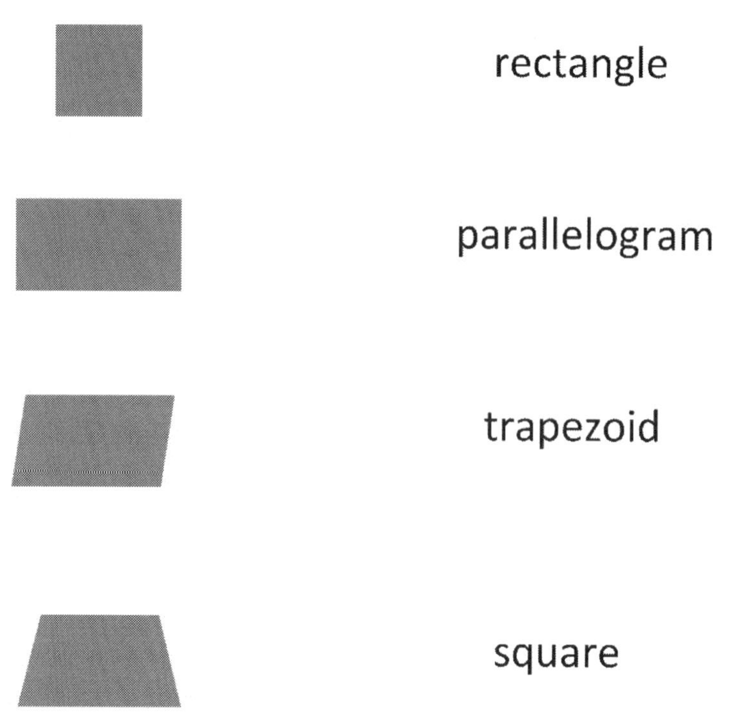

9 Half a heart and its line of symmetry is shown below. Shade squares to show the second half of the heart.

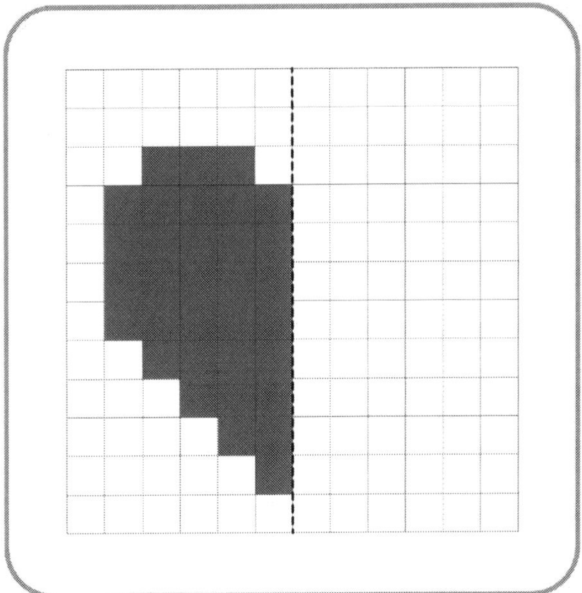

10 Circle the **two** clocks where the hands are perpendicular to each other.

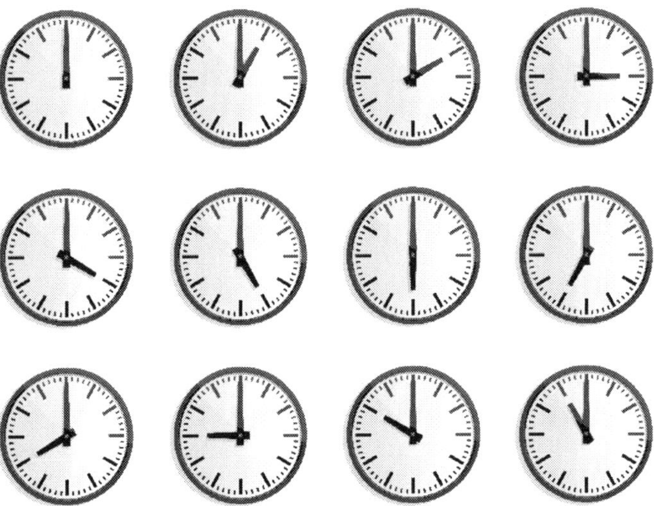

Lines, Quadrilaterals, and Symmetry – Practice Set 3

1 Based on the diagram below, how many lines of symmetry does a regular pentagon have?

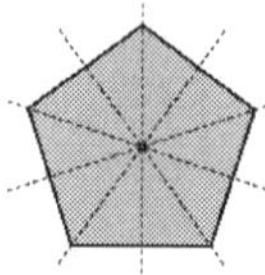

Ⓐ 1

Ⓑ 5

Ⓒ 6

Ⓓ 10

2 How many pairs of parallel sides does a rectangle have?

Ⓐ 1

Ⓑ 2

Ⓒ 4

Ⓓ 8

3 Caitlyn draws a line through the shape below.

Which of these would be a line of symmetry?

Ⓐ a line from the left corner to the right corner

Ⓑ a line from the top center to the right corner

Ⓒ a line from the left to the right through the center

Ⓓ a line from the top to the bottom through the center

4 Gemma drew a quadrilateral with 4 right angles, 2 sides of 3 inches, and 2 sides of 5 inches. What type of quadrilateral did Gemma draw?

Ⓐ rectangle

Ⓑ rhombus

Ⓒ square

Ⓓ trapezoid

5 A set of letters is shown below.

H M P S

Which letter has two lines of symmetry?

Ⓐ H

Ⓑ M

Ⓒ P

Ⓓ S

6 Which terms describe the lines below? Select **all** the correct answers.

☐ curved

☐ intersecting

☐ parallel

☐ perpendicular

☐ straight

7 Draw a line of symmetry on the shape on the grid.

8 Draw lines to match the term below with the number of endpoints.

Term	Number of Endpoints
ray	0
line segment	1
line	2

9 The picture below represents the blades of a windmill.

What shape are the blades? Write your answer on the line below.

Answer ____________________

10 Draw a square with side lengths of 4 units on the grid below.

Lines, Quadrilaterals, and Symmetry – Practice Set 4

1 Which of the following is shown below?

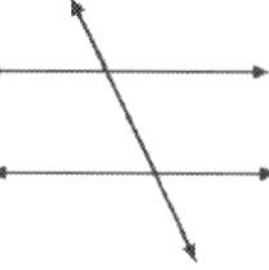

Ⓐ 2 parallel lines and an intersecting line

Ⓑ 2 parallel lines and a perpendicular line

Ⓒ 2 perpendicular lines and an intersecting line

Ⓓ 2 perpendicular lines and a parallel line

2 Which statement describes how a square and a parallelogram are similar?

Ⓐ They both have 4 equal angles.

Ⓑ They both have 4 equal sides.

Ⓒ They both have 2 pairs of parallel sides.

Ⓓ They both have 2 pairs of perpendicular sides.

3 How many lines of symmetry does the symbol below have?

Ⓐ 0

Ⓑ 2

Ⓒ 4

Ⓓ 8

4 A shape has 4 sides of 3 inches. Which of these could the shape be?

Ⓐ rectangle

Ⓑ rhombus

Ⓒ trapezoid

Ⓓ triangle

5 Jessica shaded squares on a grid to show the shape of a flowerpot.

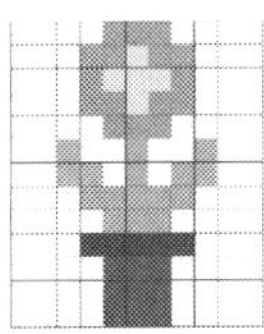

Which statement describes the symmetry of the flowerpot?

Ⓐ It has symmetry because the top and bottom are the same.

Ⓑ It has symmetry because the left and right sides are the same.

Ⓒ It does not have symmetry because it is taller than it is wide.

Ⓓ It does not have symmetry because it has an uneven number of squares.

6 Marshall has a puzzle game where wooden puzzle pieces of different shapes are fitted onto a base. The six pieces are shown below.

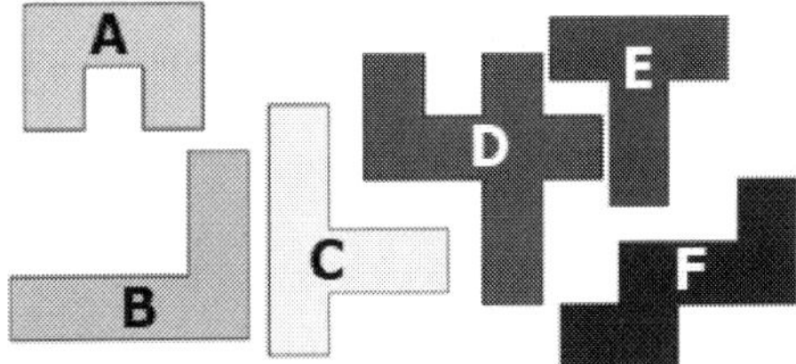

Which two pieces have a line of symmetry? Write the letters of the two pieces on the lines below.

Answer _______ and _______

7 Which letters have a pair of perpendicular lines? Select the **two** correct answers.

☐ A

☐ L

☐ N

☐ T

☐ V

☐ Z

8 Circle the angle shown below that is formed by two perpendicular rays.

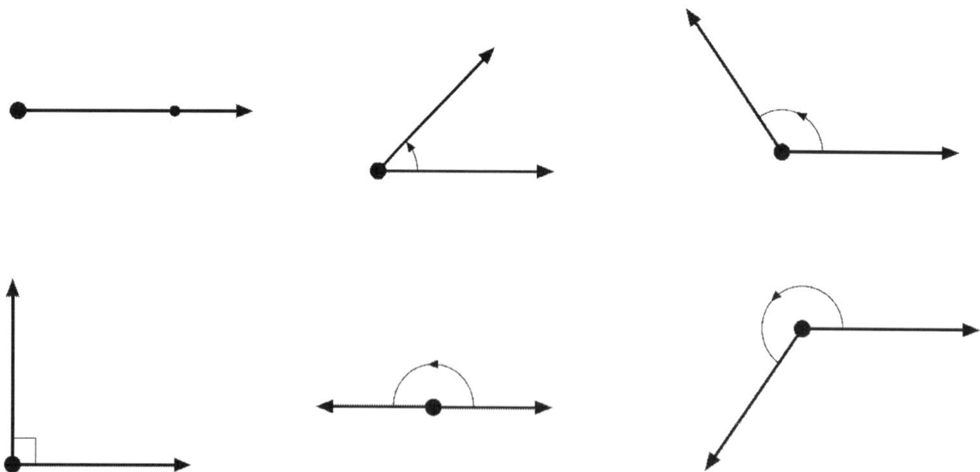

9 On the grid below, draw the other half of the triangle to show a triangle with the line of symmetry shown.

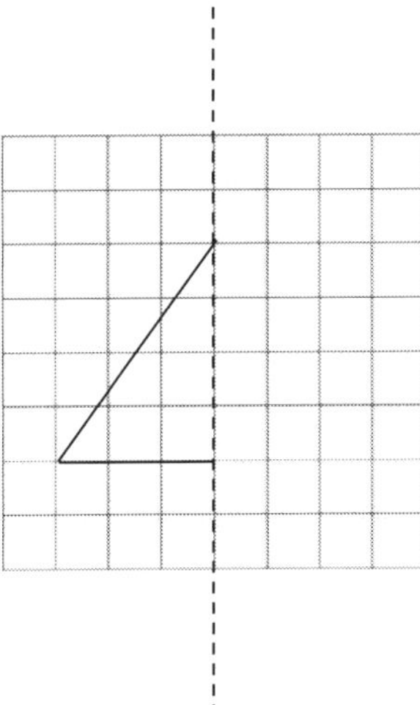

10 Shade **all** the shapes below that have 4 equal angles.

What two types of shapes did you shade? Write the names of the two shapes on the lines below.

Answer ________________ and ________________

Lines, Quadrilaterals, and Symmetry – Practice Set 5

1 How many lines of symmetry does the window below have?

Ⓐ 0

Ⓑ 1

Ⓒ 2

Ⓓ 4

2 Circle the letters of the **two** lines that are parallel.

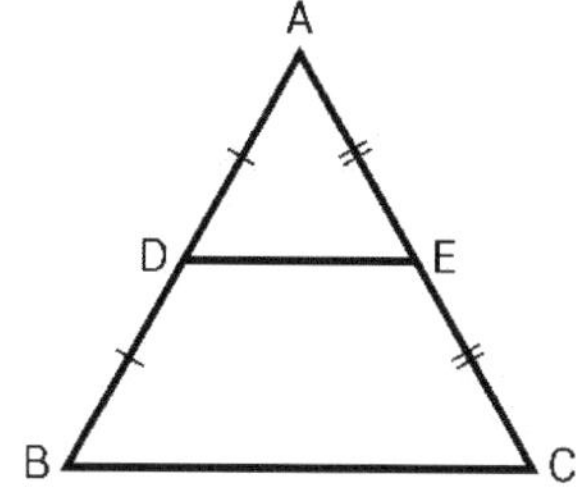

AD AE DE DB EC BC

3 Which letter shown below does not have a line of symmetry?

A L T C

Ⓐ A

Ⓑ L

Ⓒ T

Ⓓ C

4 Which of these does the diagram below show?

Ⓐ line

Ⓑ point

Ⓒ line segment

Ⓓ ray

5 Jacob shaded squares on a grid to show the shape of an ice block.

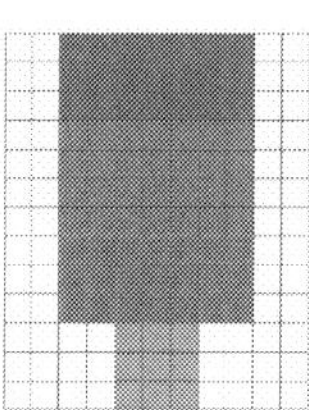

Which statement describes the symmetry of the ice block?

Ⓐ It has symmetry because the top and bottom are the same.

Ⓑ It has symmetry because the left and right sides are the same.

Ⓒ It does not have symmetry because it is taller than it is wide.

Ⓓ It does not have symmetry because it has an odd number of squares.

6 What type of shape is drawn on the grid? Write your answer on the line.

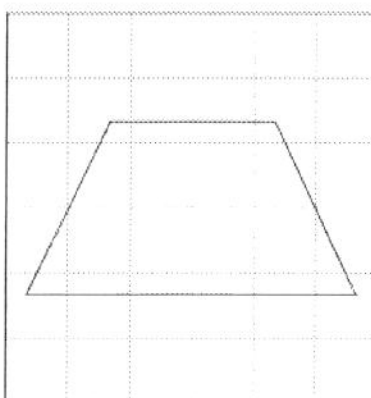

Answer ______________________

7 Which terms describe the lines below? Select **all** the correct answers.

☐ curved

☐ intersecting

☐ parallel

☐ perpendicular

☐ straight

8 The first side of a parallelogram is shown on the grid. Complete a drawing of a parallelogram by drawing three more lines.

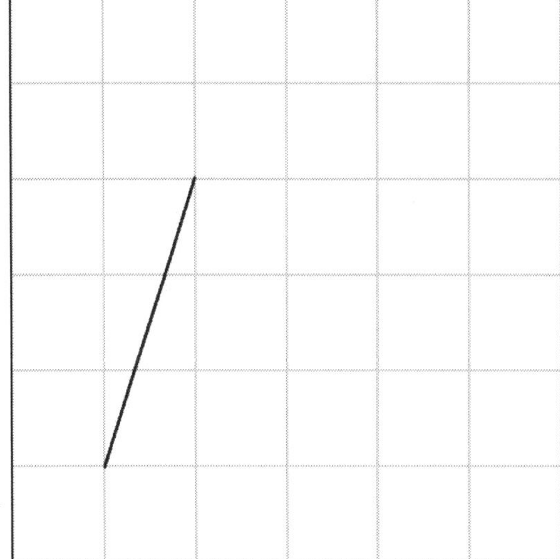

9 Draw a line of symmetry on the bottle shown on the grid.

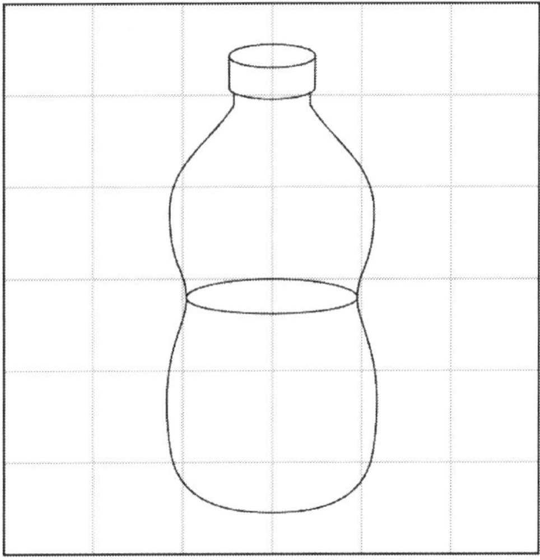

10 Shade the shape below that has the same number of equal side lengths as a square.

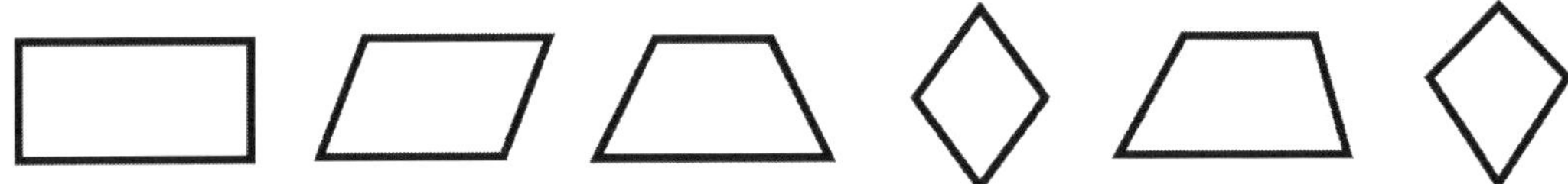

Shade the shape below that has the same number of right angles as a square.

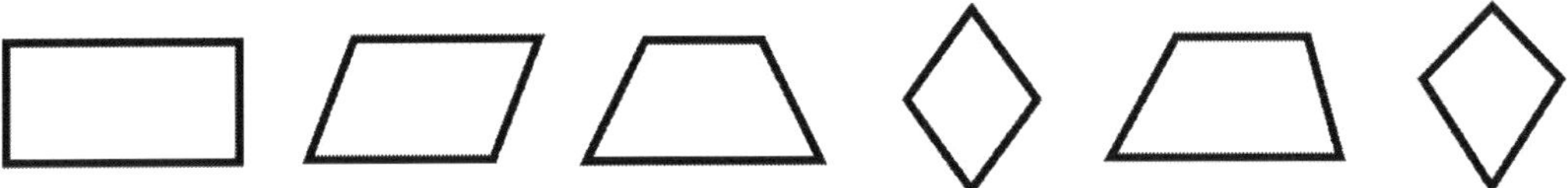

Geometric Reasoning

Area and Perimeter

B.E.S.T. Standards

MA.3.GR.2 Solve problems involving the perimeter and area of rectangles.

MA.3.GR.2.1
Explore area as an attribute of a two-dimensional figure by covering the figure with unit squares without gaps or overlaps. Find areas of rectangles by counting unit squares.

MA.3.GR.2.2
Find the area of a rectangle with whole-number side lengths using a visual model and a multiplication formula.

MA.3.GR.2.3
Solve mathematical and real-world problems involving the perimeter and area of rectangles with whole-number side lengths using a visual model and a formula.

MA.3.GR.2.4
Solve mathematical and real-world problems involving the perimeter and area of composite figures composed of non-overlapping rectangles with whole-number side lengths.

Area and Perimeter – Practice Set 1

1 Which of these shows how to calculate the area of a square with side lengths of 6 inches, in square inches?

Ⓐ 6×2

Ⓑ 6×6

Ⓒ $6 + 6 + 6 + 6$

Ⓓ $(6 + 6) \times 2$

2 Which of these describes the area of a classroom?

Ⓐ The distance along the four walls is 36 meters.

Ⓑ It covers a total of 80 square meters.

Ⓒ It is 10 meters long.

Ⓓ It is 8 meters wide.

3 Sonja wants to find the area of the heart shaded on the grid. Which of these would give Sonja the area?

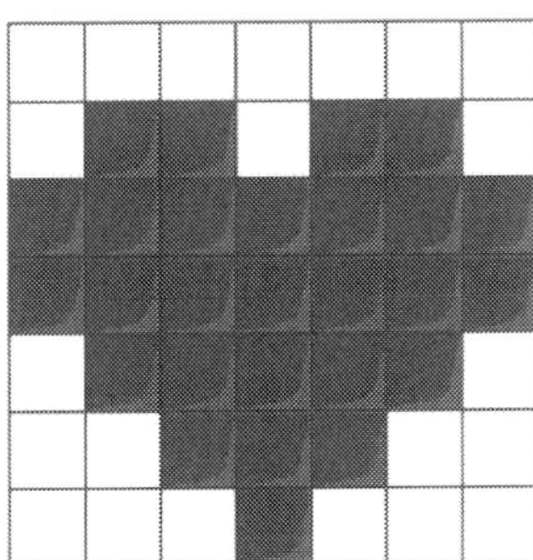

Ⓐ count the number of shaded squares

Ⓑ multiply the height by the width

Ⓒ subtract the number of empty squares from the shaded squares

Ⓓ find the total number of edges on all four sides

4 Oscar is mowing a rectangular lawn that is 10 meters by 12 meters. How many square meters of lawn is Oscar mowing?

Ⓐ 22 square meters

Ⓑ 44 square meters

Ⓒ 60 square meters

Ⓓ 120 square meters

5 Each square below has side lengths of 1 inch.

What is the area of the rectangle?

Ⓐ 9 square inches

Ⓑ 12 square inches

Ⓒ 18 square inches

Ⓓ 24 square inches

6 What is the area of the shape shaded below, in square units? Write your answer on the line below.

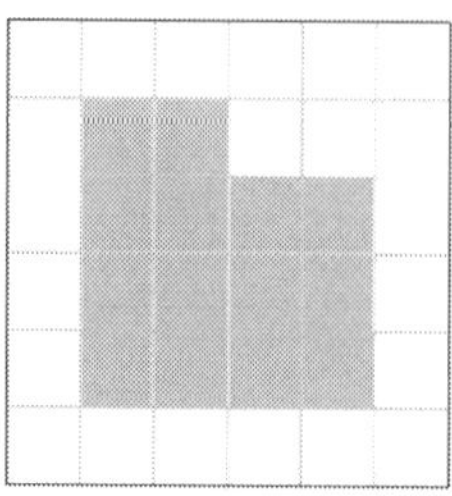

Answer __________ square units

7 What is the perimeter and area of the letter shaded on the grid below?

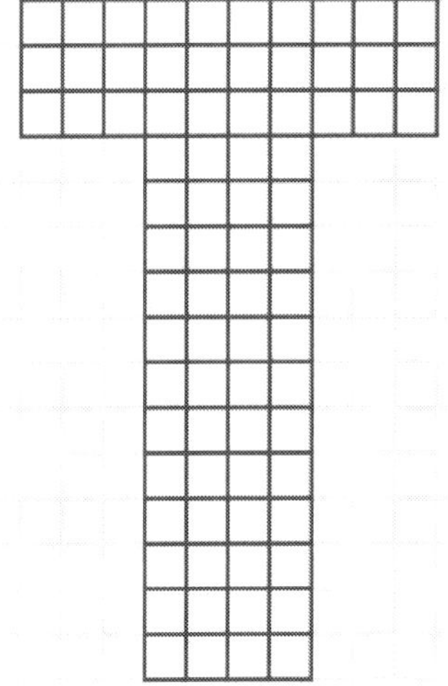

Perimeter __________ units **Area** __________ square units

8 Hayden is making rectangular photo frames. The table below shows the height and length of three different photo frames. Complete the table by adding the perimeter of each photo frame.

Photo Frame Sizes

Height (inches)	Length (inches)	Perimeter (inches)
7	5	
12	9	
10	8	

9 The diagram shows the size of a tile in millimeters. Complete the equation to show how to find the perimeter of the tile.

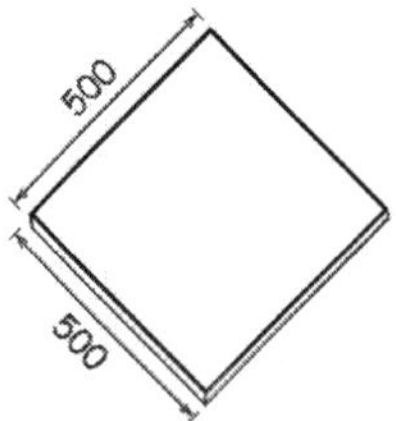

2 × (______ + ______) = ______

What is the perimeter of the tile? Write your answer below.

Answer __________ millimeters

10 Emilia is choosing a canvas to paint on. One canvas is 12 inches by 12 inches. The other canvas is 16 inches by 20 inches.

What is the difference between the area of the large and small canvas?

Show your work.

Answer ____________ square inches

Area and Perimeter – Practice Set 2

1 Which of these would find the perimeter of a rectangular sports field?

Ⓐ walk all the edges with a measuring wheel and record the distance

Ⓑ walk from one end to the other and time how long it takes

Ⓒ multiply the length of the field by the width of the field

Ⓓ lay 1-meter square flags on the field and count how many cover it

2 Which of these gives a measure of area? Select the **two** correct answers.

☐ 20 inches

☐ 20 square feet

☐ 20 centimeters

☐ 20 yards

☐ 20 square meters

3 Jay counts the number of squares shaded to form the picture of the ice block. Which of these is Jay finding a measure of?

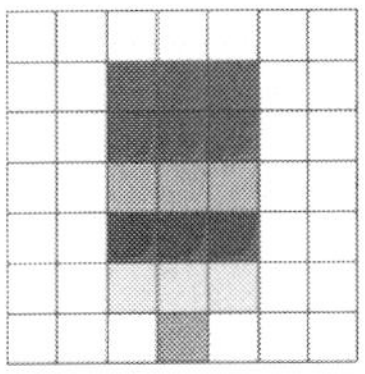

Ⓐ area

Ⓑ length

Ⓒ perimeter

Ⓓ volume

4 What is the perimeter of the rectangle shown below?

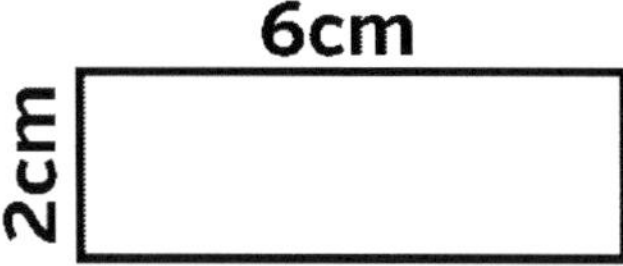

Ⓐ 12 cm

Ⓑ 16 cm

Ⓒ 20 cm

Ⓓ 24 cm

5 What is the area of the letter shaded below?

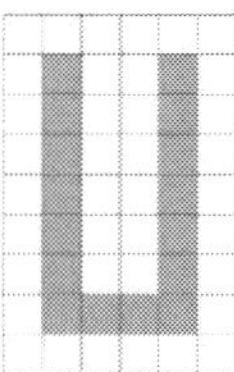

Ⓐ 14 square units

Ⓑ 16 square units

Ⓒ 24 square units

Ⓓ 28 square units

6 What is the area of the billboard below? Write your answer on the line.

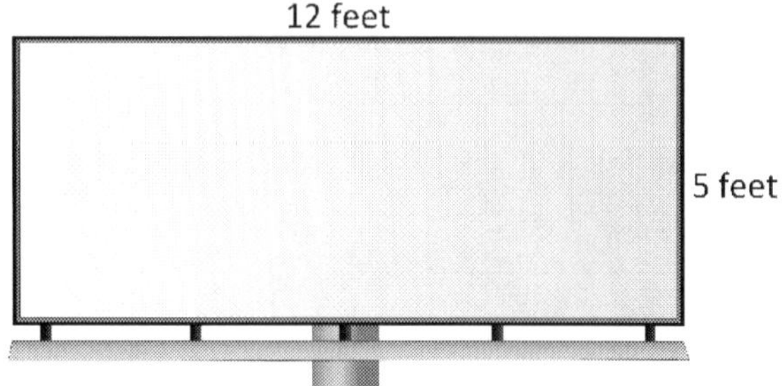

Answer ____________ square feet

7 The diagram below shows the dimensions of a shape in inches. Complete the calculation to find the total area of the shape.

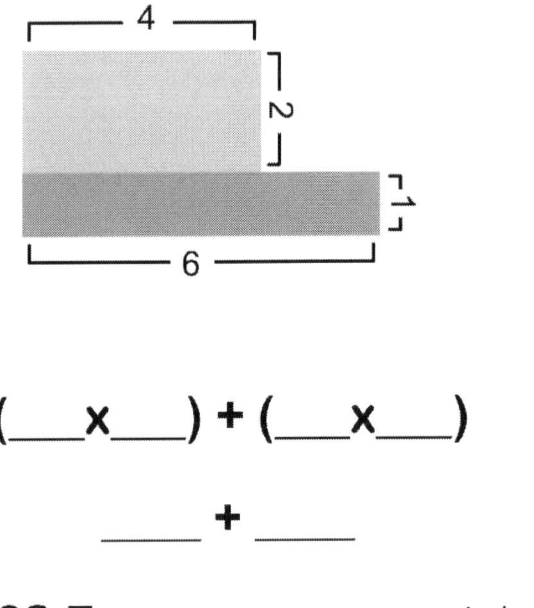

(___x___) + (___x___)

____ + ____

Area = __________ square inches

8 Complete the table below by finding the area of each rectangle with the dimensions given.

Area of Rectangles

Length (centimeters)	Height (centimeters)	Area (square centimeters)
2	6	
5	7	
3	9	

9 Complete the calculation to find the area of the rectangle shown below.

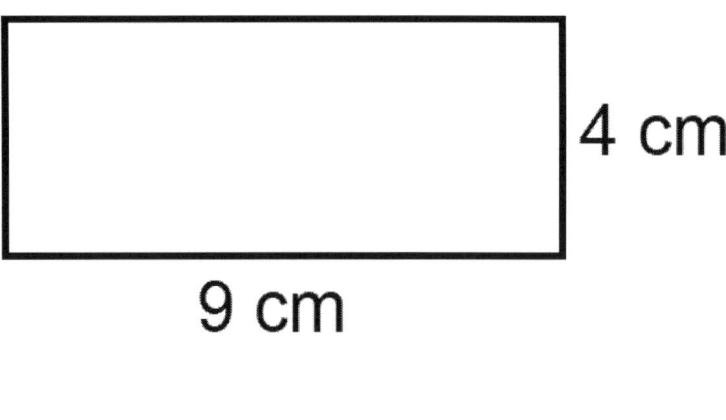

_______ × _______ = _______

What is the area of the rectangle? Write your answer on the line below.

Answer __________ square centimeters

10 Holly cut out the cardboard bookmark shown below. What is the perimeter of the bookmark? Write your answer on the line below.

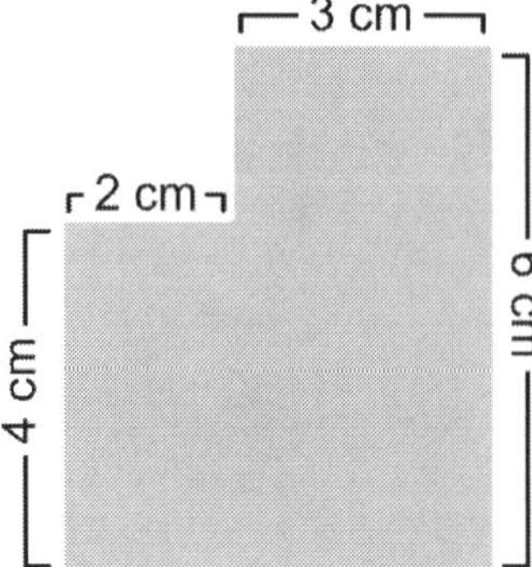

Answer ____________ cm

Area and Perimeter – Practice Set 3

1 Which of these describes the perimeter of a blanket?

Ⓐ The distance around the 4 edges is 30 feet.

Ⓑ It covers a total of 50 square feet.

Ⓒ It is 10 feet long.

Ⓓ It is 5 feet wide.

2 What is the area of the base of the box shown below?

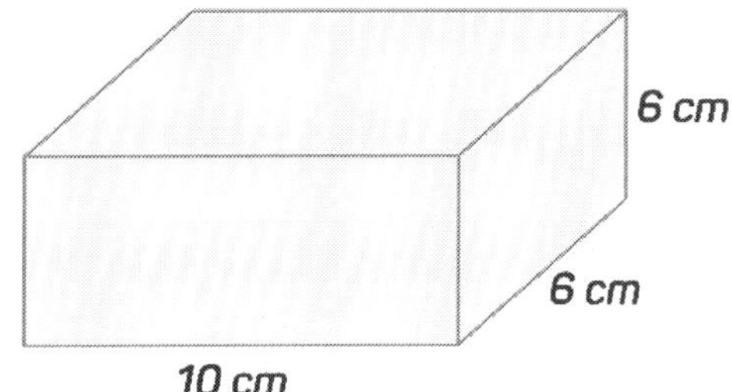

Ⓐ 16 square centimeters

Ⓑ 32 square centimeters

Ⓒ 48 square centimeters

Ⓓ 60 square centimeters

3 What is the perimeter of the rectangle shown below?

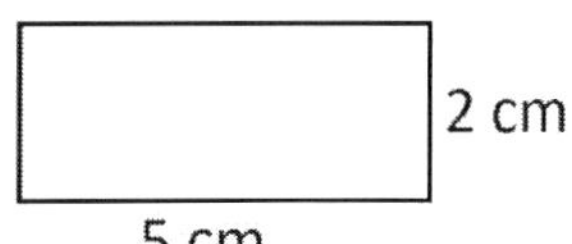

Ⓐ 10 cm

Ⓑ 12 cm

Ⓒ 14 cm

Ⓓ 20 cm

4 What is the area of a square sandpit with side lengths of 3 yards?

Ⓐ 6 square yards

Ⓑ 9 square yards

Ⓒ 12 square yards

Ⓓ 18 square yards

5 Which shapes shown below have equal areas?

Ⓐ 1 and 2

Ⓑ 1 and 3

Ⓒ 2 and 3

Ⓓ 1, 2, and 3

6 What is the area of the tree shaded below, in square units? Write your answer on the line below.

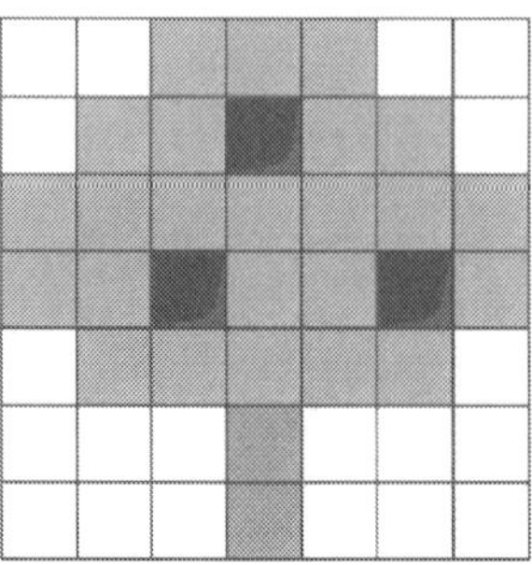

Answer __________ square units

7 What is the perimeter and area of the letter shaded on the grid below?

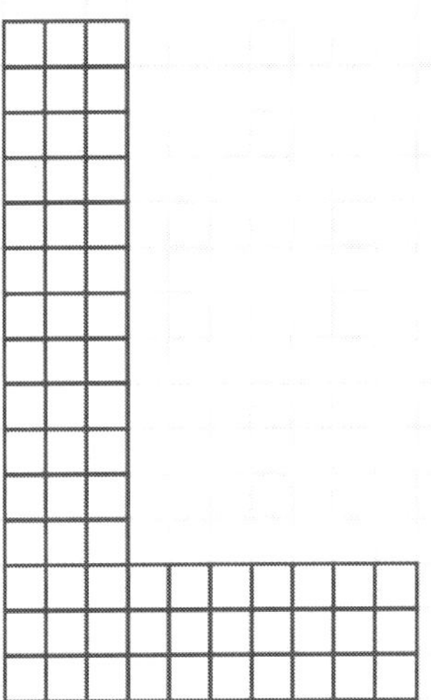

Perimeter ___________ units **Area** ___________ square units

8 Complete the table below by finding the area of each rectangle with the dimensions given.

Area of Rectangles

Length (inches)	Height (inches)	Area (square inches)
9	8	
4	6	
5	7	

9 Each square of the rectangle below has side lengths of 1 inch. Complete the calculation to find the area of the rectangle.

What is the area of the rectangle? Write your answer on the line below.

Answer __________ square inches

10 Ryan drew the diagram below to show a wall he is painting. He is painting the whole wall except for the window.

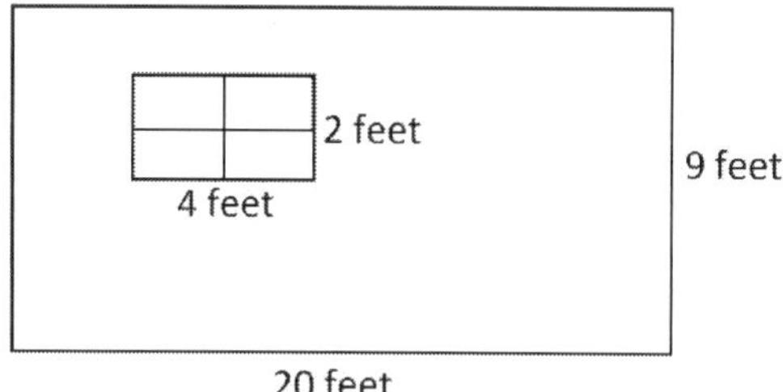

What is the area of wall that is being painted?

Show your work.

Answer ____________ square feet

Area and Perimeter – Practice Set 4

1 Which of these shows how to calculate the area of a rectangle with side lengths of 3 inches and 8 inches, in square inches?

Ⓐ 3 × 8

Ⓑ 3 + 8

Ⓒ (3 × 8) × 2

Ⓓ (3 + 8) × 2

2 What is the area of the rectangle below?

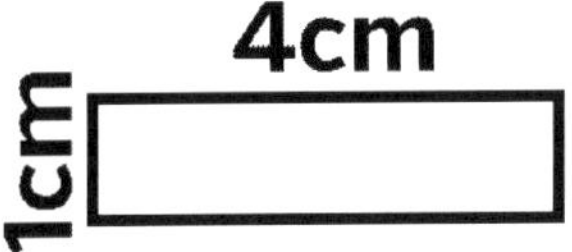

Ⓐ 4 square centimeters

Ⓑ 5 square centimeters

Ⓒ 8 square centimeters

Ⓓ 10 square centimeters

3 What is the area of the shape shaded on the grid below?

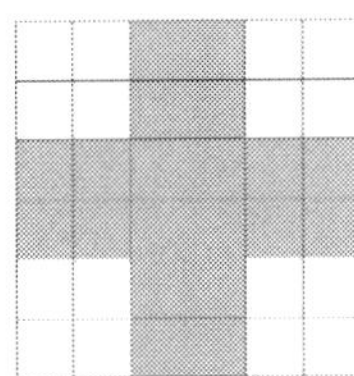

Ⓐ 16 square units

Ⓑ 20 square units

Ⓒ 24 square units

Ⓓ 36 square units

4 Which of these describes the area of a rectangular flag?

Ⓐ The total length of the 4 edges is 18 feet.

Ⓑ It is made of 20 square feet of material.

Ⓒ It is 5 feet long.

Ⓓ It is 4 feet wide.

5 AJ wants to estimate the area of the pencil shaded on the grid. Which of these would give AJ the estimated area?

Ⓐ count the number of shaded squares

Ⓑ multiply the length by the width

Ⓒ subtract the number of empty squares from the shaded squares

Ⓓ measure and add the lengths of the five edges

6 Each square below has side lengths of 1 inch.

What is the area of the rectangle? Write your answer on the line below.

Answer __________ square inches

7 The diagram below shows the dimensions of a shape in inches. Complete the calculation to find the total area of the shape.

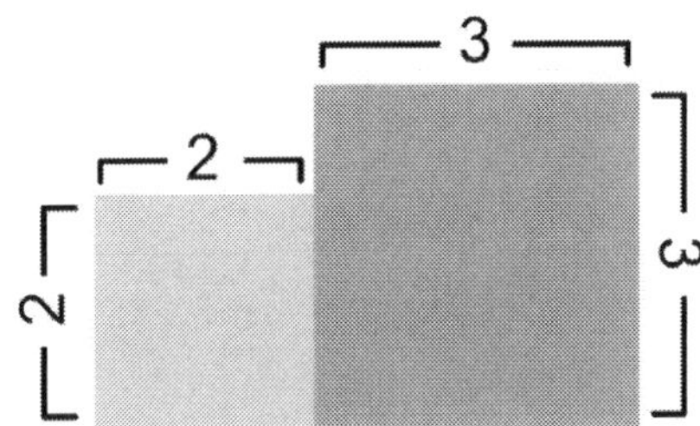

(___x___) + (___x___)

_____ + _____

Area = ____________ square inches

8 Camilla is making a rectangular vegetable garden. The table below shows the width and length of three different gardens she is planning. Complete the table by adding the perimeter of each garden.

Vegetable Garden Sizes

Width (feet)	Length (feet)	Perimeter (feet)
5	12	
8	15	
3	7	

9 The diagram shows the size of a doormat in millimeters. Complete the equation to show how to find the perimeter of the doormat.

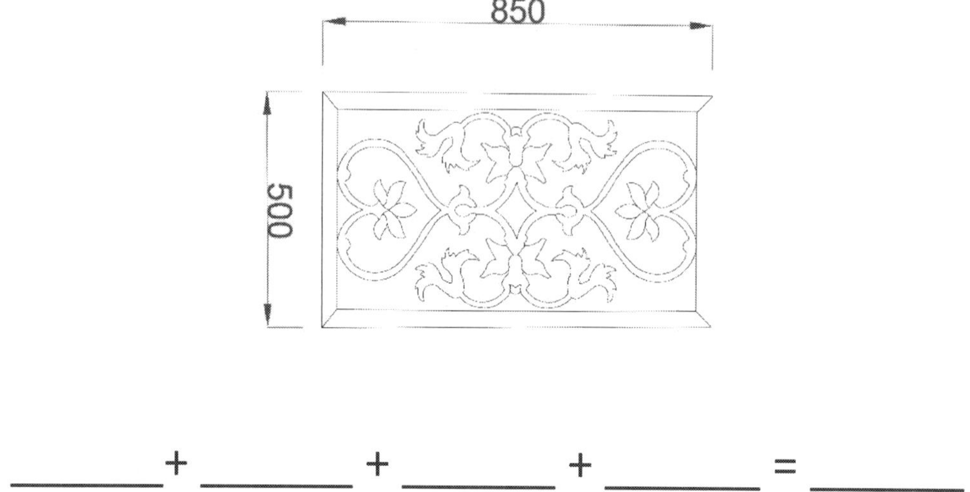

_______ + _______ + _______ + _______ = _______

What is the perimeter of the doormat? Write your answer below.

Answer __________ millimeters

10 The shape of a sticker is shown below. What is the perimeter of the sticker? Write your answer on the line below.

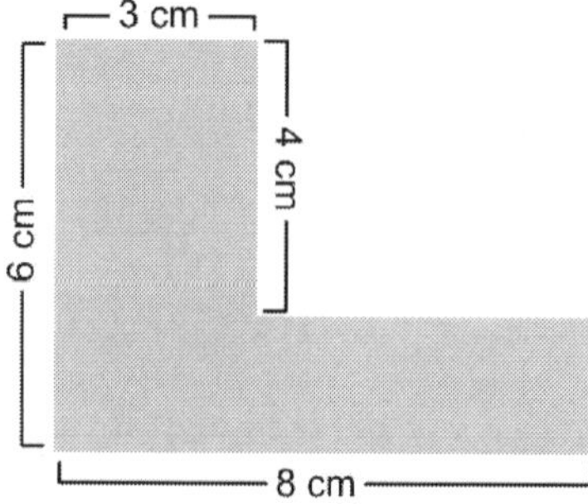

Answer ____________ cm

Area and Perimeter – Practice Set 5

1 Which of these would find the perimeter of a rectangular paddock?

Ⓐ walk all the edges with a measuring wheel and record the distance

Ⓑ walk from one end to the other and time how long it takes

Ⓒ multiply the length of the paddock by the width of the paddock

Ⓓ count how many 1-meter squares the paddock could be divided into

2 Which of these gives a measure of area?

Ⓐ 8 feet

Ⓑ 8 yards

Ⓒ 8 square inches

Ⓓ 8 meters per hour

3 The diagram below shows the size of a chalkboard.

36 inches

24 inches

What is the perimeter of the chalkboard? Write your answer on the line below.

Answer __________ inches

4 What is the area of a rectangular serving platter that is 20 centimeters long and 10 centimeters wide?

Ⓐ 30 square centimeters

Ⓑ 60 square centimeters

Ⓒ 100 square centimeters

Ⓓ 200 square centimeters

5 Tamara counts the number of squares shaded to form the picture of the present. Which of these is Tamara finding a measure of?

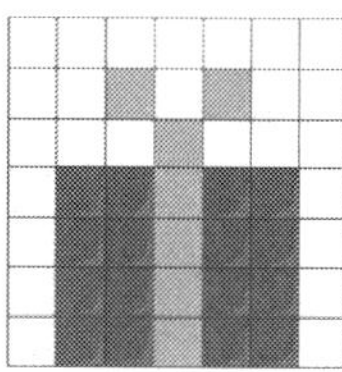

Ⓐ area

Ⓑ length

Ⓒ perimeter

Ⓓ volume

6 What is the area of the shape shaded below, in square units? Write your answer on the line below.

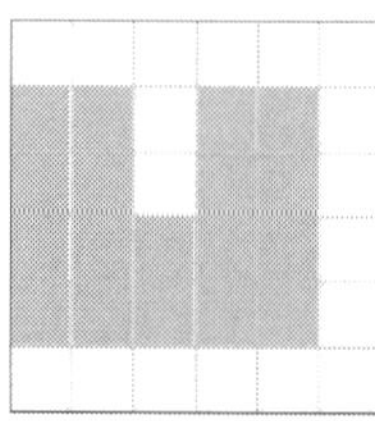

Answer __________ square units

7 The diagram below shows the dimensions of a shape in inches. Complete the calculation to find the total area of the shape.

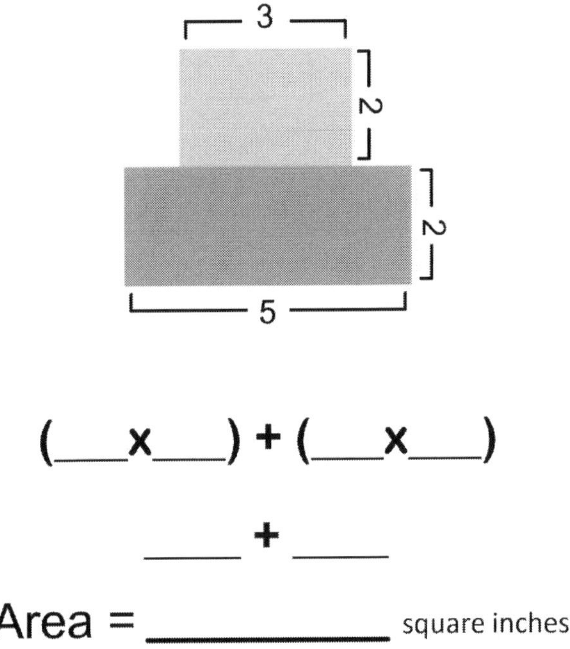

(___x___) + (___x___)

____ + ____

Area = __________ square inches

8 Complete the table below by finding the area of each rectangle with the dimensions given.

Area of Rectangles

Length (centimeters)	Height (centimeters)	Area (square centimeters)
3	6	
8	4	
10	9	

9 Complete the calculation to find the area of the rectangle shown below.

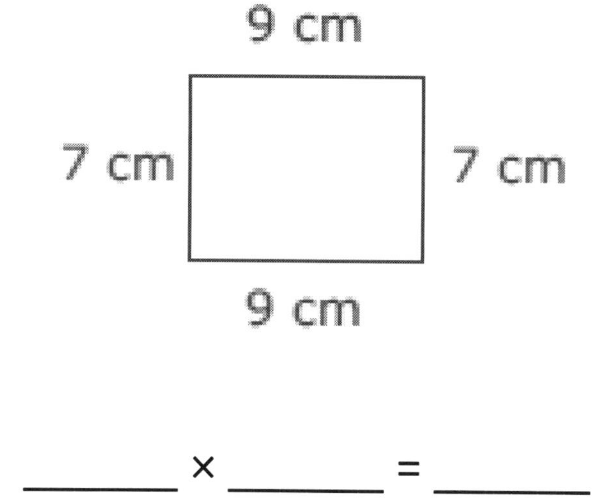

_______ × _______ = _______

What is the area of the rectangle? Write your answer on the line below.

Answer __________ square centimeters

10 Reynold made a garden with the shape shown below. What is the perimeter of the garden? Write your answer on the line below.

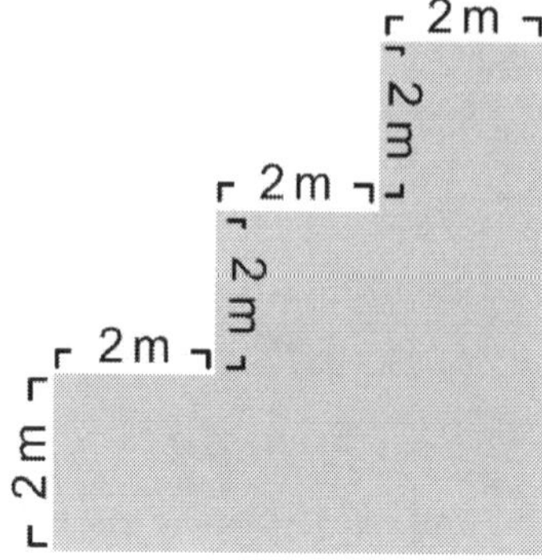

Answer ___________ m

Data Analysis and Probability

Collect and Represent Data

B.E.S.T. Standards

MA.3.DP.1 Collect, represent and interpret numerical and categorical data.

MA.3.DP.1.1
Collect and represent numerical and categorical data with whole-number values using tables, scaled pictographs, scaled bar graphs or line plots. Use appropriate titles, labels and units.

Collect and Represent Data – Practice Set 1

1 Kim wants to determine whether the students in her class prefer apples or oranges. Which question would Kim be best to ask all the students?

Ⓐ What do you like most about oranges?

Ⓑ Do you like apples or oranges more?

Ⓒ How many apples do you eat each week?

Ⓓ Do you think apples and oranges are good for you?

2 Odin is creating a pictograph where each symbol Δ will represent 5 houses. Which of these would he add to the graph to show 30 houses?

Ⓐ Δ Δ Δ

Ⓑ Δ Δ Δ Δ Δ Δ

Ⓒ Δ Δ Δ Δ Δ Δ Δ Δ Δ Δ

Ⓓ Δ Δ Δ Δ Δ Δ Δ Δ Δ Δ Δ Δ Δ Δ Δ

3 Mr. Daniels recorded how many sales his 6 salespeople made one week. The number of sales made by each salesperson is listed below.

18, 24, 16, 24, 30, 13

Mr. Daniels decides to make a bar graph showing the data. Which of these would be the title of the horizontal axis?

Ⓐ Amount ($)

Ⓑ Number of Sales

Ⓒ Best Salespeople

Ⓓ Weekly Sales by Salesperson

4 Hayden recorded how many sales he made each day of the week. The data is shown below.

Day	M	T	W	T	F	S	S
Sales	45	41	47	57	55	43	42

Hayden wants to make a bar graph of the data. Which of these would be the best scale for the bar graph?

Ⓐ 0 to 40 in units of 5

Ⓑ 40 to 50 in units of 1

Ⓒ 40 to 60 in units of 2

Ⓓ 0 to 100 in units of 10

5 Tyson asked students how long they read for one day. He collected the data in the table below.

Minutes of Reading Completed

Minutes of Reading	Number of Students
15 minutes or less	7
30 minutes	9
45 minutes	12
60 minutes or more	5

Tyson creates a display where he uses a symbol of a book to represent the number of students for each time. What type of display has Tyson created?

Ⓐ circle graph

Ⓑ pictograph

Ⓒ bar graph

Ⓓ line plot

6 Which of these are labels on the graph? Select the **two** correct answers.

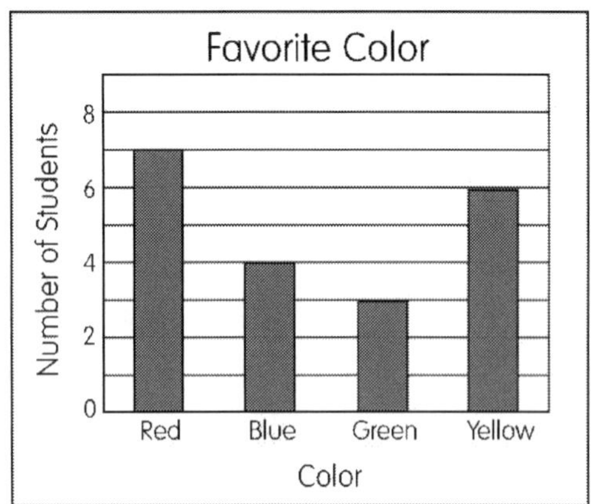

☐ Favorite Color

☐ Number of Students

☐ 0, 2, 4, 6, 8

☐ Red, Blue, Green, Yellow

☐ Color

7 Charlotte recorded data on how many points she scored on ten different science quizzes. The data is listed below. Complete the line plot below with the data.

5, 8, 6, 7, 6, 5, 8, 8, 7, 7

Charlotte's Science Quiz Scores

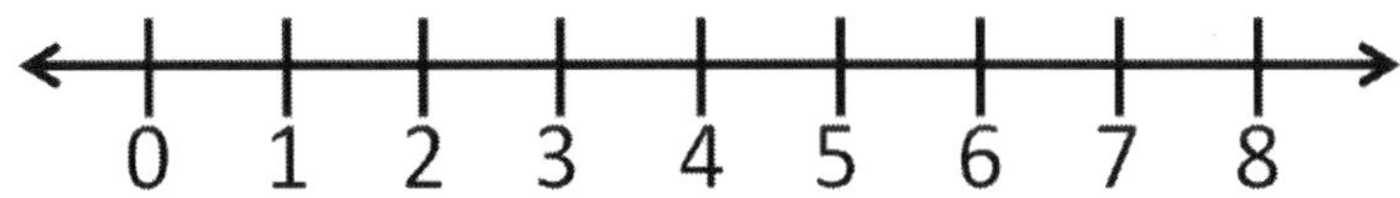

8 Andre used the data in a frequency table to complete the graph below.

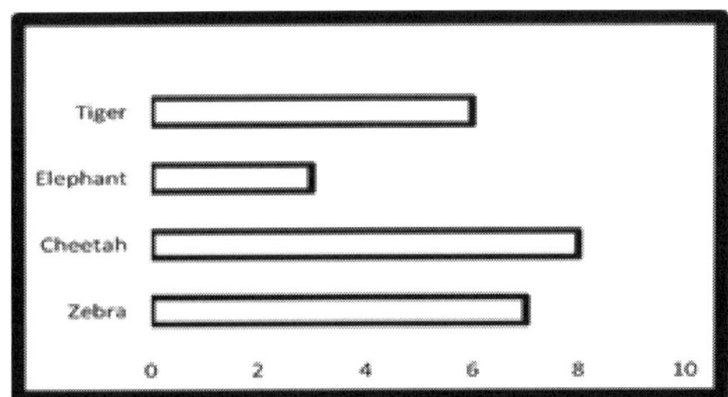

Which of these would have been the frequency in the table for cheetah?

Ⓐ 𝍸

Ⓑ 𝍸 |||

Ⓒ 𝍸 ||||

Ⓓ 𝍸 𝍸

9 Jamal counted the number of free point shots he made out of 20 at each training session one week. The data he collected is shown below.

- Monday - 16
- Tuesday – 18
- Wednesday – 12
- Thursday – 14
- Friday – 14

Complete the pictograph below with the data.

Jamal's Basketball Shots Made

Monday	O O O O O O O O
Tuesday	
Wednesday	
Thursday	
Friday	

Each O represents 2 shots.

10 The table below shows how much money Levi saved each month.

Levi's Savings

Month	Savings
March	$60
April	$70
May	$110
June	$120

Complete the column graph below to represent Levi's savings.

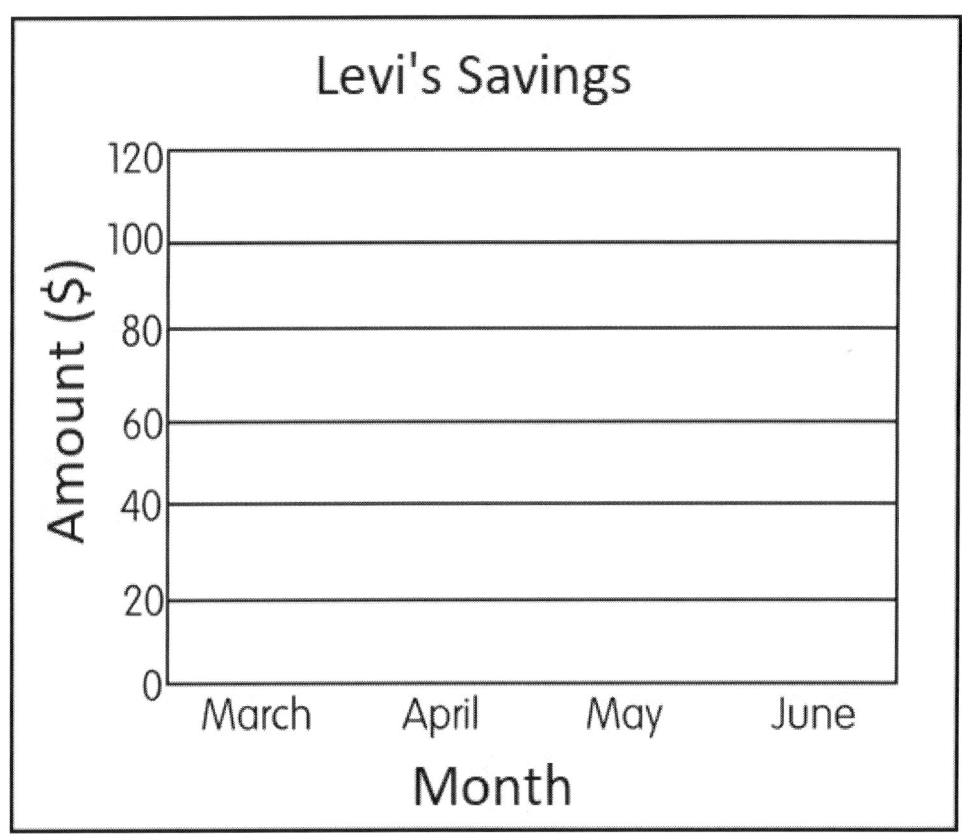

Collect and Represent Data – Practice Set 2

1 Isla wants to find out how much television students watch. Which survey question would she be best to ask to collect the data?

Ⓐ What is your favorite television show?

Ⓑ How many hours do you watch television for each day?

Ⓒ Do you watch television in the evening?

Ⓓ Would you prefer watching television or using a computer?

2 Emily is creating a pictograph where each symbol $ will represent $4. Which of these would she add to the graph to show $12?

Ⓐ $ $ $

Ⓑ $ $ $ $

Ⓒ $ $ $ $ $ $ $ $

Ⓓ $ $ $ $ $ $ $ $ $ $ $ $

3 What type of data display is represented below?

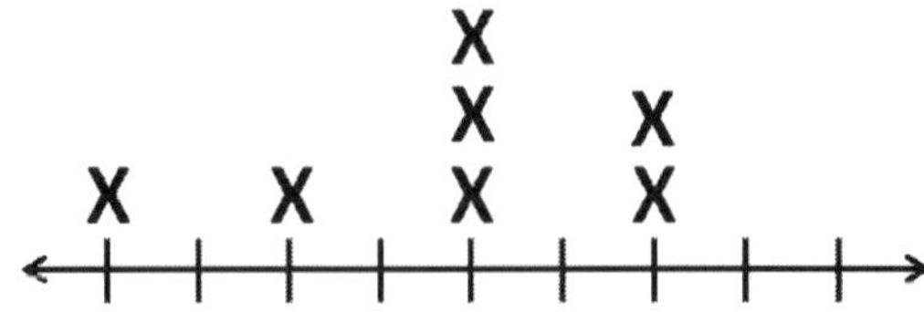

Ⓐ bar graph

Ⓑ pie chart

Ⓒ line plot

Ⓓ tally chart

4 A farmer collected eggs and observed them. Which of these would be recorded with a measurement?

Ⓐ shape

Ⓑ color

Ⓒ texture

Ⓓ weight

5 Which of these is the categories on the graph below?

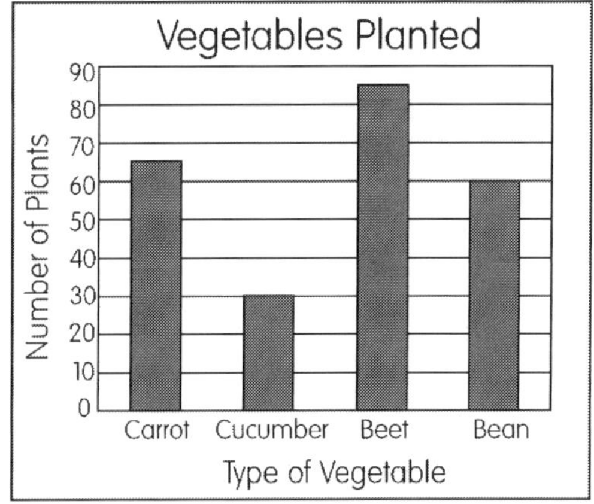

Ⓐ Number of Plants

Ⓑ 0 to 90

Ⓒ Carrot, Cucumber, Beef, Bean

Ⓓ Vegetables Planted

6 On a pictograph, each ☼ symbol represents 4 sunny days. How many ☼ symbols would represent 20 sunny days? Write your answer below.

Answer ____________

7 Elijah recorded the ages of the 12 students in his karate class. The ages are listed below.

11, 12, 12, 13, 13, 13, 13, 14, 14, 14, 15, 15

Complete the line plot below with the data.

Ages of Students in a Karate Class

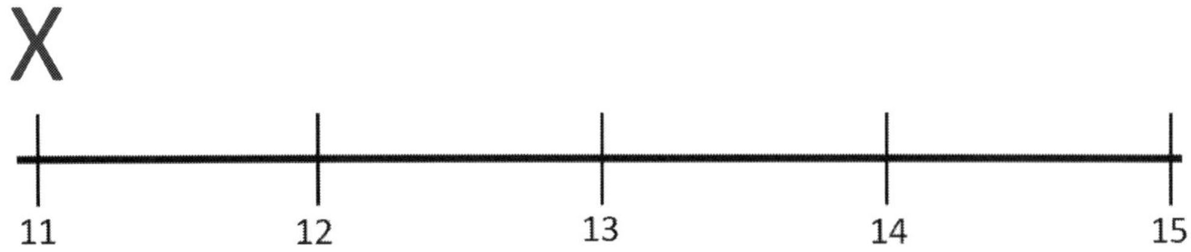

8 Complete the table below by adding the number represented by each set of tally marks.

Tally marks	Number
||||	
𝍸 |||	
𝍸 |	
||	
𝍸	

9 Emilia started a business selling T-shirts. The table below shows her orders in the first four months.

T-Shirt Orders

Month	Number Ordered
January	300
February	500
March	800
April	1,100

Use the data to complete the column graph below.

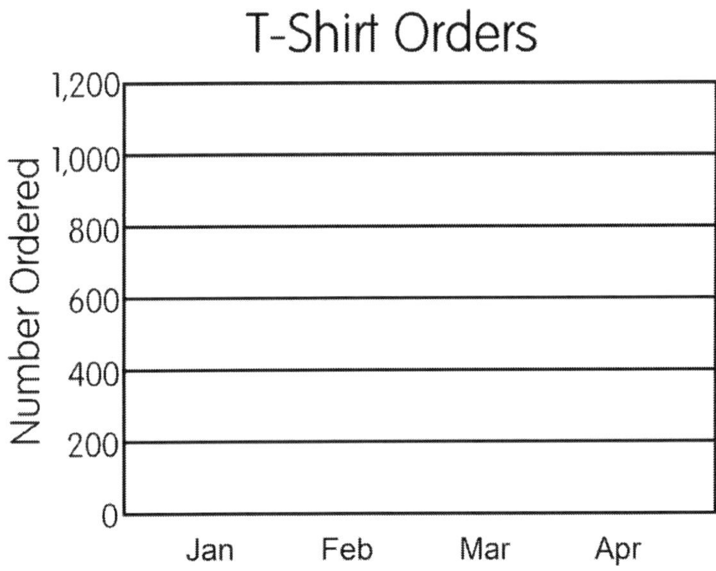

10 The grade 3 classes at Walker's school raised money to start a school garden. The list below shows how much the four classes raised.

- Mr. Jackson – \$110
- Miss Drake – \$70
- Mrs. Elliott – \$60
- Mr. Rossi – \$80

Complete the pictograph below with the data.

Money Raised by Each Class

Mr. Jackson	**\$ \$ \$ \$ \$ \$ \$ \$ \$ \$ \$**
Miss Drake	
Mrs. Elliott	
Mr. Rossi	

Each \$ represents \$10.

Collect and Represent Data – Practice Set 3

1 Which of these are labels on the graph below? Select the **two** correct answers.

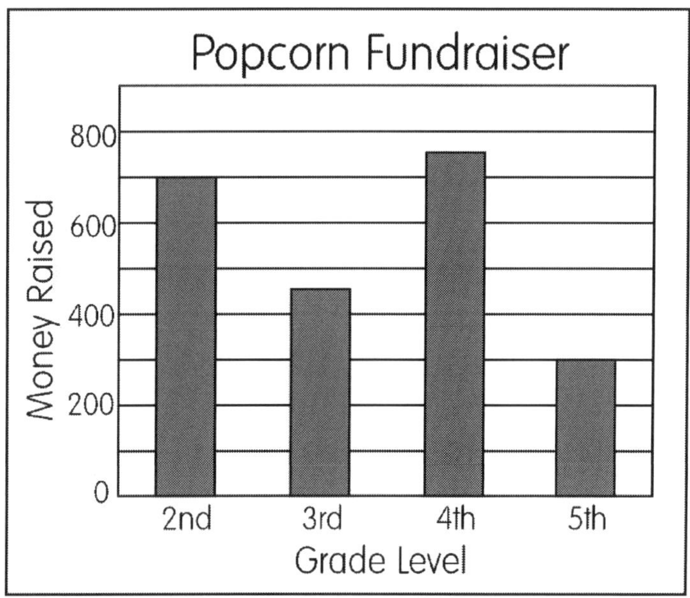

☐ Popcorn Fundraiser

☐ Money Raised

☐ 0, 200, 400, 600, 800

☐ 2nd, 3rd, 4th, 5th

☐ Grade Level

2 Erik wants to find out which genre of fiction book is most popular with the students in his class. Which question would Erik be best to ask?

Ⓐ What type of fiction book is your favorite?

Ⓑ How many fiction books have you read this month?

Ⓒ Do you enjoy reading science fiction books?

Ⓓ On a scale of 1 to 10, how much do you enjoy reading?

3 A teacher did a survey asking whether students were for or against having a class pet. The results are shown below.

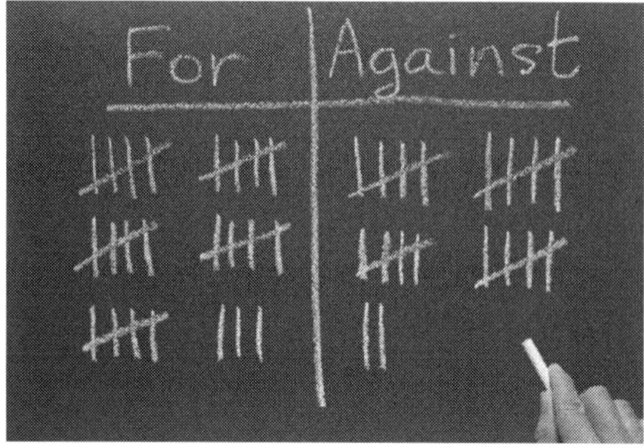

How many students were for having a class pet? Write your answer below.

Answer ____________________

4 The table below shows the number of sandwiches of each type on a platter.

Type of Sandwich	Number of Sandwiches
Ham	10
Chicken	6
Egg	3
Salad	8

Adam wants to create a pictograph where each ☐ symbol represents 2 sandwiches. Which sandwich would be represented by ☐ ☐ ☐?

Ⓐ Ham

Ⓑ Chicken

Ⓒ Egg

Ⓓ Salad

5 Samantha counted the number of customers that entered a store one morning. The tally she kept is shown below.

How many customers did she count?

Ⓐ 4

Ⓑ 16

Ⓒ 19

Ⓓ 23

6 Luna recorded the temperature at noon every day for 7 days, in Fahrenheit. The data is listed below.

72, 73, 73, 74, 76, 78, 80

Complete the line plot below with the data.

Temperature at Noon (°F)

7 Trudy used the data in a frequency table to complete the graph below.

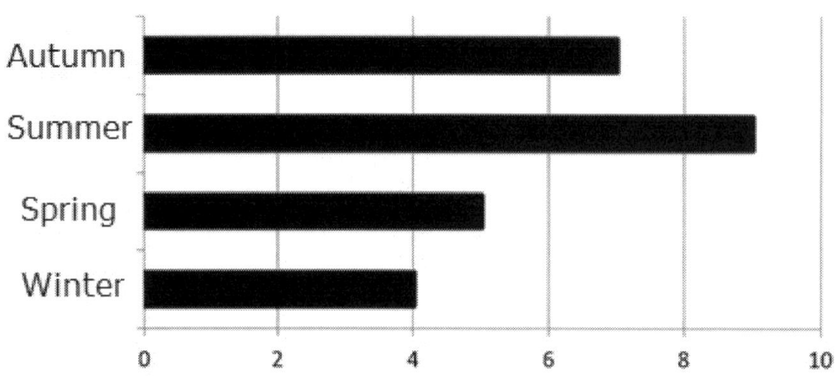

Complete the table below with the frequency for spring and winter.

Favorite Season of the Year

Season	Frequency
Autumn	7
Summer	9
Spring	
Winter	

8 Robert asked 20 students to choose their favorite pet. The results of the survey are shown below.

Favorite Pets

Pet	**Number of Students**
Cat	~~IIII~~ II
Dog	~~IIII~~ III
Fish	IIII
Bird	I

Represent the data in the table on the column graph below.

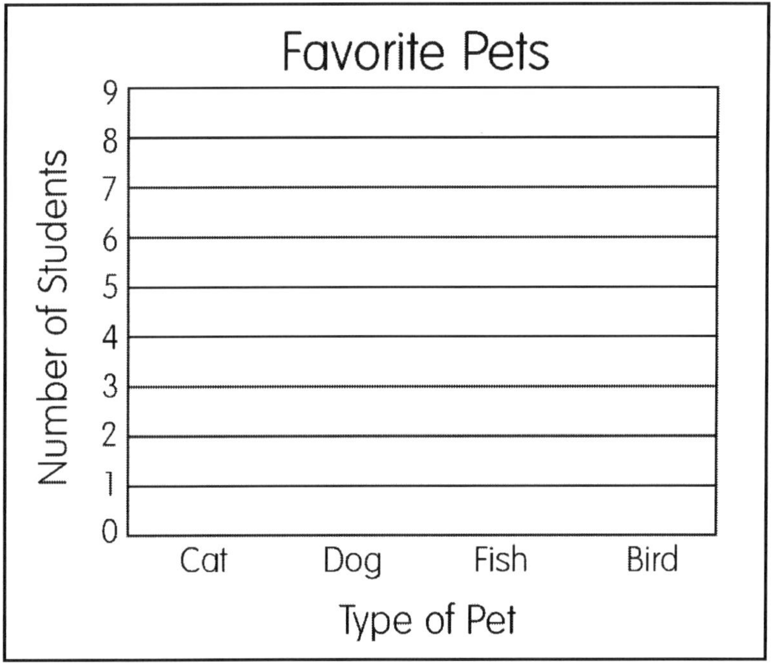

9 Oscar counted the number of students on his school bus each morning one week. The data he collected is shown below.

- Monday – 25
- Tuesday – 30
- Wednesday – 35
- Thursday – 40
- Friday – 25

Complete the pictograph below with the data.

Students on Oscar's School Bus

Monday	**X X X X X**
Tuesday	
Wednesday	
Thursday	
Friday	

Each X represents 5 people.

10 Zachary is part of a cycling club that rides every weekend. He collected data on how far he biked each month. The data he collected is shown below.

Distance Biked Each Month

Month	**Kilometers**
March	80
April	100
May	90
June	60

Use the data to complete the column graph below.

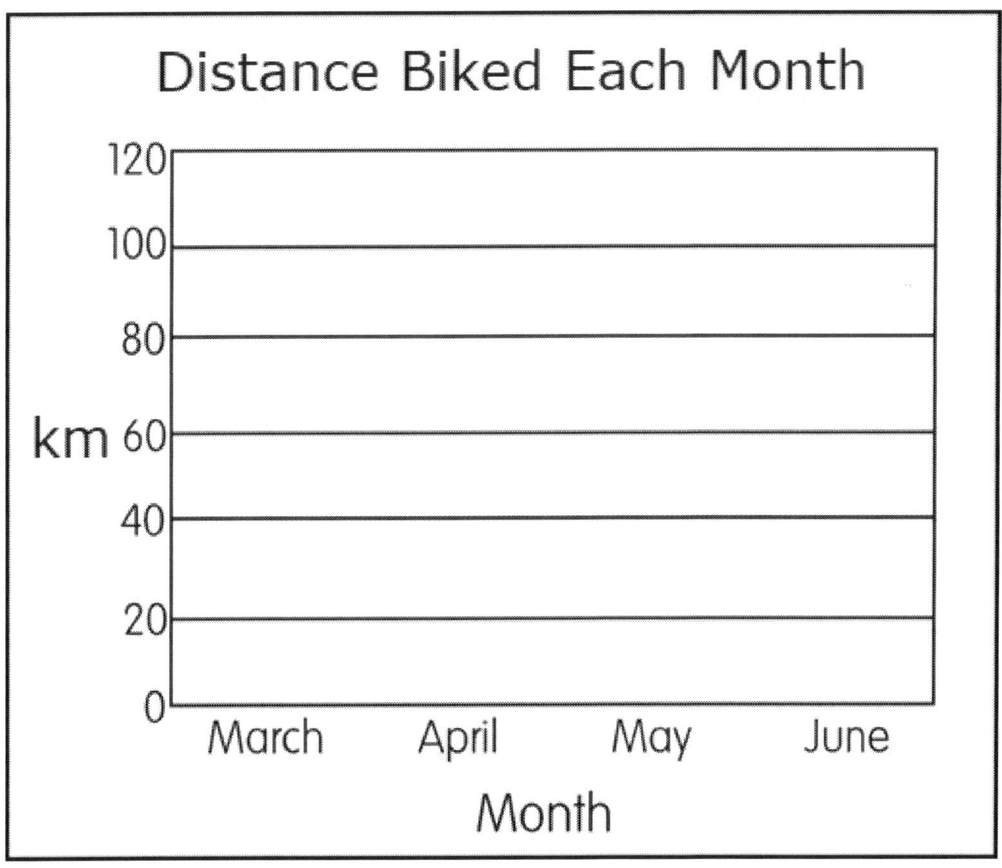

Collect and Represent Data – Practice Set 4

1 Abby measured the weight of a kitten every day and recorded the weight in grams. Which of these would Abby be best to use to show how the kitten's weight changed over time?

Ⓐ circle graph

Ⓑ line plot

Ⓒ bar graph

Ⓓ tally chart

2 Lennox is creating a pictograph where each symbol ¢ will represent 10 cents. Which of these would be represented by ¢ ¢ ¢ ¢?

Ⓐ 4 cents

Ⓑ 14 cents

Ⓒ 40 cents

Ⓓ 44 cents

3 What type of data display is represented below?

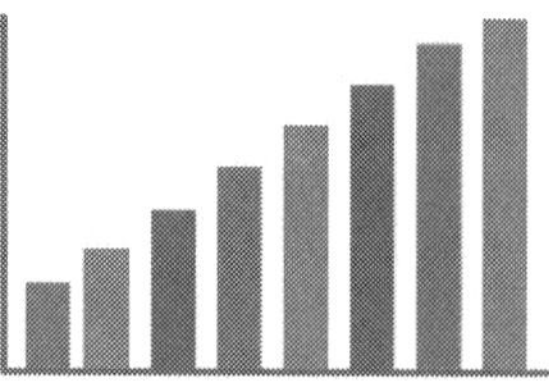

Ⓐ column graph

Ⓑ pie chart

Ⓒ line plot

Ⓓ tally chart

4 Trent collected shells from a beach and observed them. Which of these would be recorded with a measurement?

Ⓐ shape

Ⓑ color

Ⓒ texture

Ⓓ length

5 Lawson asked some students to vote on their favorite game. The table below shows his results.

Favorite Games

Game	Number of Students
Checkers	30
Chess	15
Cards	35
Dominoes	25

Lawson wants to make a bar graph of the results. Which of these would be the best scale for the bar graph?

Ⓐ 0 to 20 in units of 2

Ⓑ 0 to 25 in units of 5

Ⓒ 0 to 50 in units of 5

Ⓓ 0 to 100 in units of 10

6 On a pictograph, each ✉ symbol represents 10 emails. How many ✉ symbols would represent 60 emails? Write your answer below.

Answer ____________

7 Amelia recorded data on how many points she scored in ten netball games she played. The data is listed below.

11, 14, 15, 12, 12, 15, 13, 13, 12, 12

Complete the line plot below with the data.

Points Scored by Amelia in Netball Games

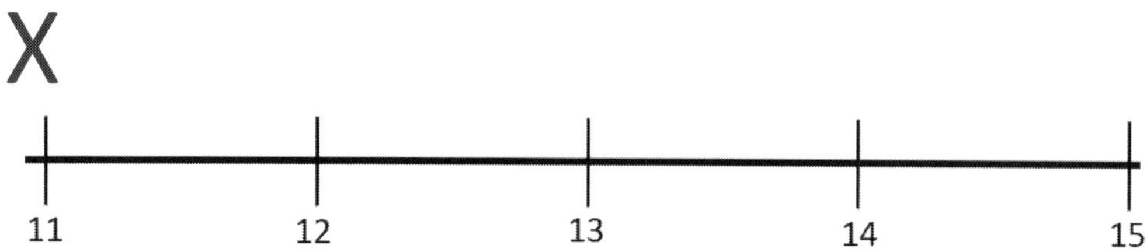

8 Complete the table below by adding the number represented by each set of tally marks.

Tally marks	Number
𝍸 II	
𝍸	
III	
𝍸 𝍸	
𝍸 IIII	

9 Mandy is the goalkeeper of her soccer team. She kept a record of how many goals she saved in five games. The data is listed below.

- Game 1 – 7
- Game 2 – 6
- Game 3 – 9
- Game 4 – 6
- Game 5 – 8

Complete the pictograph below with the data.

Goals Saved by Mandy

Game 1	O O O ◖
Game 2	
Game 3	
Game 4	
Game 5	

Each O represents 2 goals.

10 Sarah recorded how many tomatoes were on each of her tomato plants. The table below shows her data.

Plant	Number of Tomatoes
1	6
2	7
3	9
4	8
5	5

Complete the column graph below to represent the data.

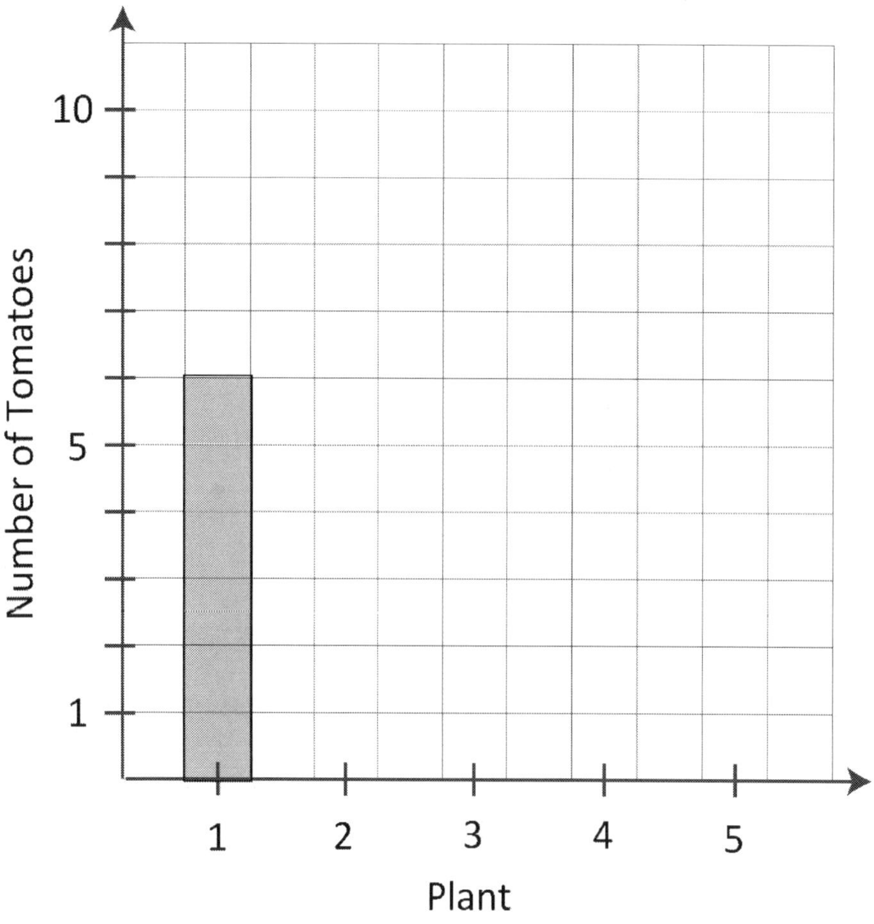

Collect and Represent Data – Practice Set 5

1 Anna wants to find out how common it is for students to have breakfast. Which survey question would Anna be best to ask in a survey?

Ⓐ What do you like most about breakfast?

Ⓑ What time did you have breakfast today?

Ⓒ How many days a week do you usually have breakfast?

Ⓓ Are you more likely to have a hot or a cold breakfast?

2 Alison counted the number of students on the playground at different times. The table below shows her results.

Students on the Playground

Time	Number of Students
11:00	15
11:30	25
12:00	55
12:30	50

Alison is completing a pictograph where each ☺ symbol will represent 5 students. For which time should Alison put five ☺ symbols?

Ⓐ 11:00

Ⓑ 11:30

Ⓒ 12:00

Ⓓ 12:30

3 Marley is creating a pictograph where each symbol ☺ will represent 6 people. How many people would be represented by ☺ ☺ ☺ ☺? Write your answer on the line below.

Answer __________

4 Jake did a survey asking people about their favorite fruit. The results are shown below.

How many people chose banana as their favorite fruit? Write your answer on the line below.

Answer __________

5 Kieran counted the number of snails in his yard one morning. The tally he kept is shown below.

How many snails did he see?

Ⓐ 9

Ⓑ 12

Ⓒ 14

Ⓓ 17

6 Ellie recorded how many people in her class were away sick each day for 5 days. Her data is listed below.

1, 3, 3, 3, 5

Complete the line plot below with the data.

Number of People Away Sick

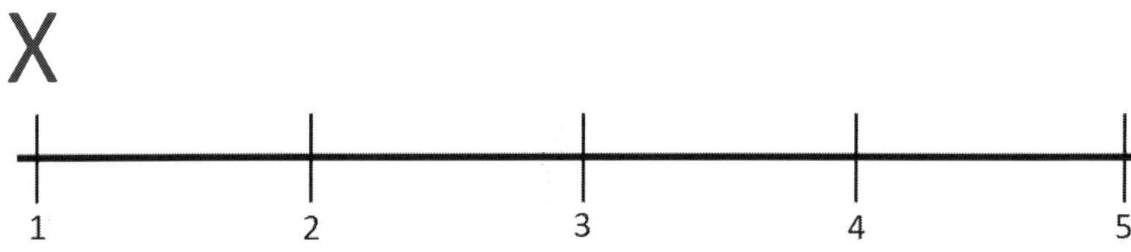

7 The table below shows how many employees Katie's business had since she started it in 2015.

Katie's Nail Salon

Year	Number of Employees
2015	5
2016	15
2017	25
2018	40

Use the data to complete the column graph below.

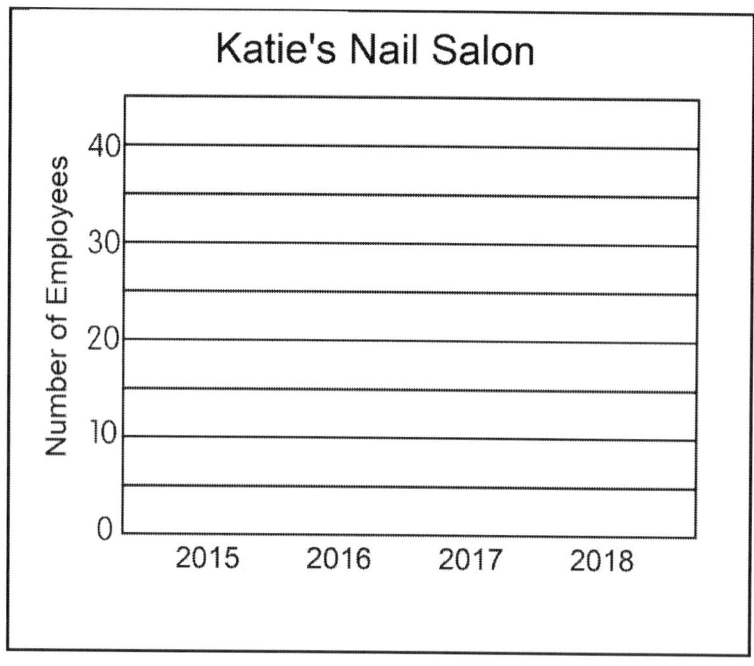

8 Which graph below represents a column graph? Tick the circle under the correct graph.

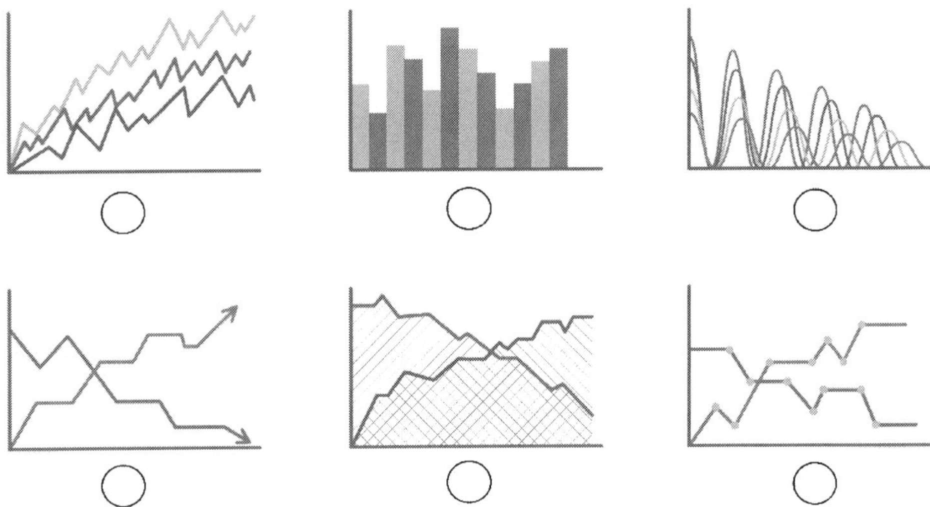

9 At a local fair, a food truck had ready to sell 200 fresh sandwiches, 200 grilled sandwiches, 300 burgers, and 400 cartons of fries. Complete the pictograph below with the missing data.

Each star symbol represents 100 items.

10 Lola asked the students in her class to choose their favorite pet. The results of the survey are shown below.

Favorite Pets

Pet	Number of Students
Cat	卌 II
Dog	卌 III
Fish	卌
Bird	IIII

Represent the data in the table on the column graph below.

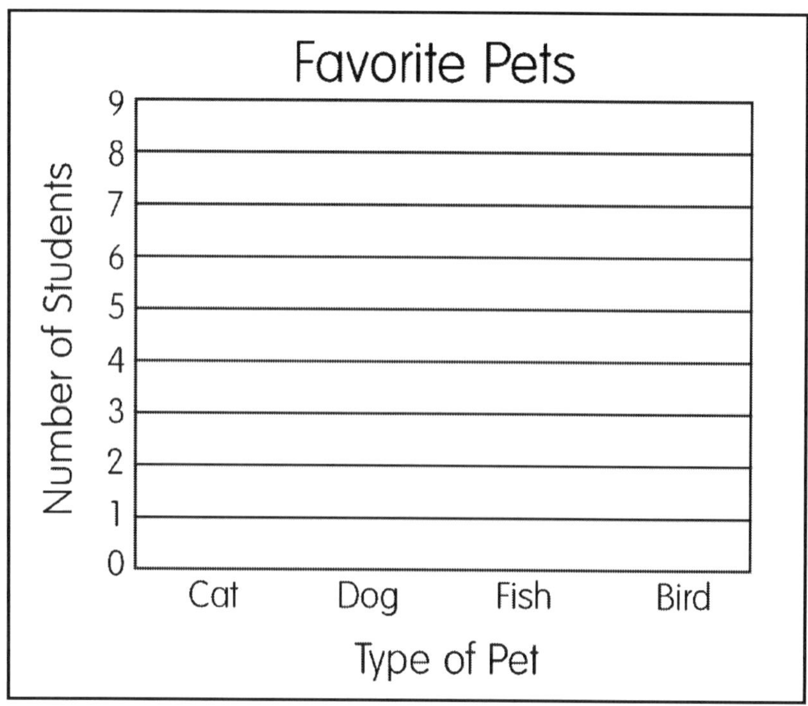

Data Analysis and Probability

Interpret Data

B.E.S.T. Standards

MA.3.DP.1 Collect, represent and interpret numerical and categorical data.

MA.3.DP.1.2
Interpret data with whole-number values represented with tables, scaled pictographs, circle graphs, scaled bar graphs or line plots by solving one- and two-step problems.

Interpret Data – Practice Set 1

1 Rachel found the weight of 14 pumpkins. The line plot shows her data.

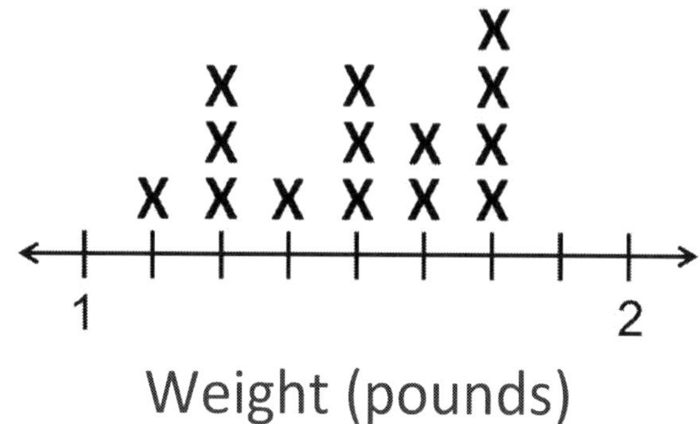

How many pumpkins had a weight of $1\frac{1}{2}$ pounds? Write your answer below.

Answer ________

2 The graph below represents the votes four students received for captain of the school hockey team. Which student received a quarter of the vote?

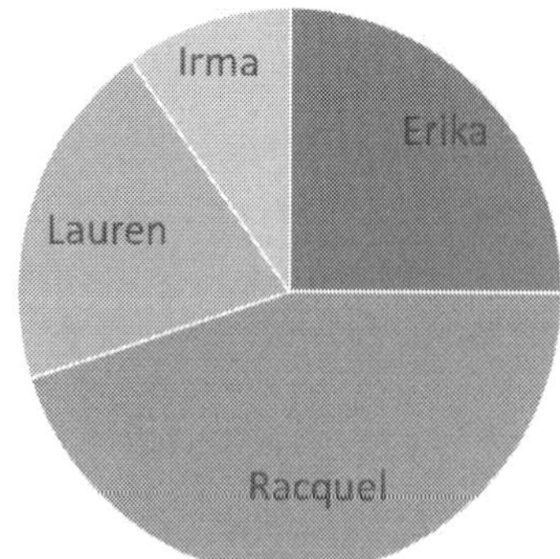

Ⓐ Erika

Ⓑ Irma

Ⓒ Lauren

Ⓓ Racquel

3 The graph below represents how many emails Angela sent each day.

Angela's Emails Sent

What is the greatest number of emails sent in one day? Write your answer on the line below.

Answer ____________

4 The line plot shows how many siblings a group of students have.

Number of Siblings

```
X
X   X
X   X   X
X   X   X
X   X   X
X   X   X   X       X
1   2   3   4   5   6   7
```

How many students have 1 or 2 siblings? Write your answer below.

Answer ____________

5 An art contest had a prize for the people's choice where students voted for their favorite artwork. The table shows the number of votes that the four students who entered got.

Artist	Number of Votes
Bethany	79
Leanne	85
Perry	81
Anthony	77

Which student got the most votes? Write your answer on the line below.

Answer ____________________

6 The graph below shows the results of a survey on which fruit students would most prefer to eat on a hot day.

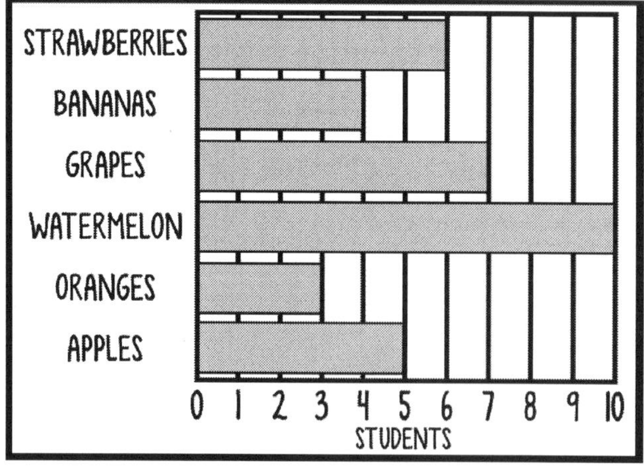

How many more students would prefer watermelon than bananas? Write your answer on the line below.

Answer ______________________

7 Dina asked students if they had visited the tourist attractions below. She collected the data in the table below.

Attractions Visited by Students

Attraction	**Number of Students**
Empire State Building	𝍸 𝍸 𝍸 III
Grand Canyon	𝍸 𝍸 𝍸 𝍸 I
Golden Gate Bridge	𝍸 I
Mount Rushmore	IIII

How many students had visited the Empire State Building?

Ⓐ 6

Ⓑ 13

Ⓒ 15

Ⓓ 18

8 The line plot shows how a class scored on a science test.

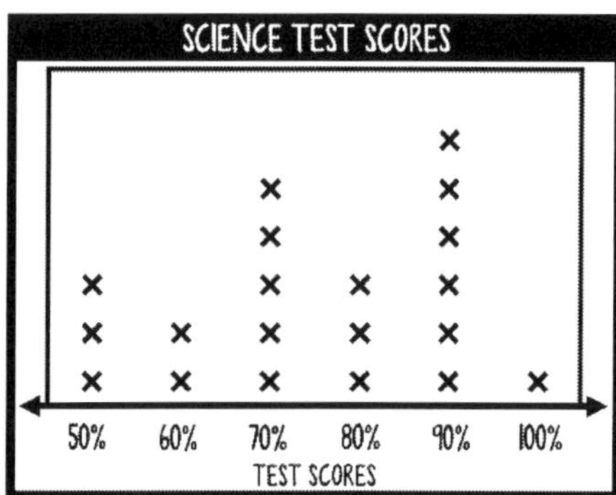

Which score was most common? Circle the correct answer.

50% 60% 70% 80% 90% 100%

9 The pictograph represents the type of vegetable students chose to plant in the school garden.

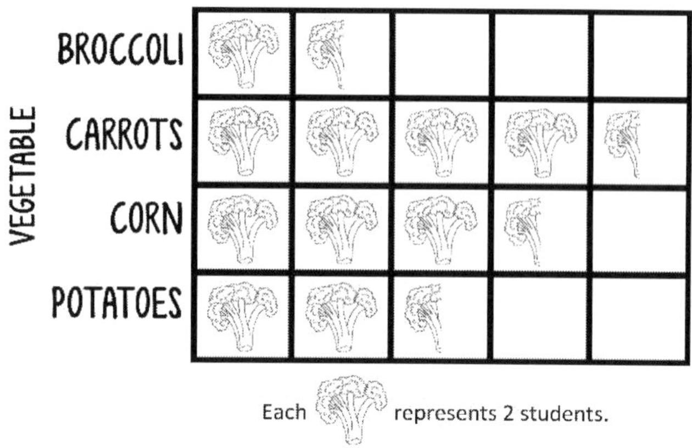

How many more students chose to plant carrots than corn? Write your answer on the line below.

Answer _______________

10 The graph shows how many items were collected for a school supply drive.

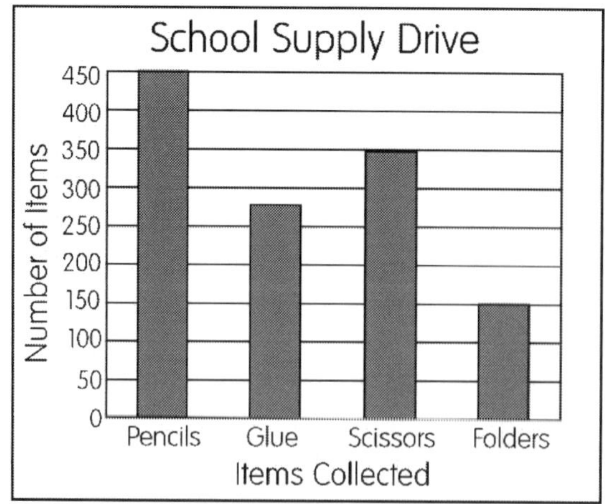

How many pencils and folders were collected in all? Write your answer on the line below.

Answer ____________________

Interpret Data – Practice Set 2

1 The students in a geography class voted on which country they would most like to study. The circle graph shows the results.

Vote for Country to Study

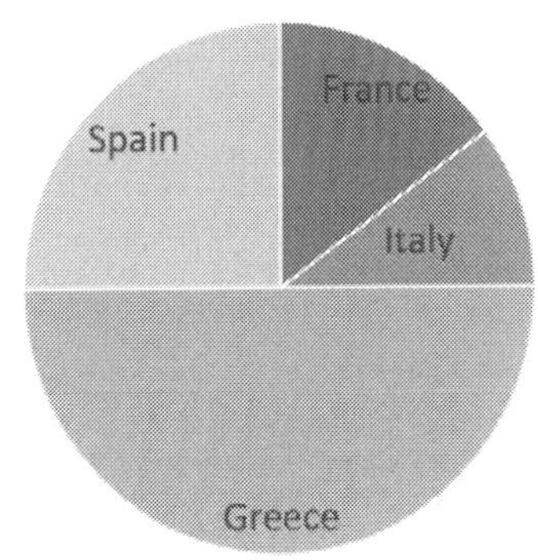

If 10 students voted for Spain, how many voted for Greece?

Ⓐ 5

Ⓑ 12

Ⓒ 20

Ⓓ 25

2 The pictograph shows how many fish a pet store sold one week.

Number of Fish Sold at the Pet Store

Monday

Tuesday

Wednesday

Thursday

Key

= 2 fish

How many fish were sold on Tuesday? Write your answer below.

Answer ________________

3 The line plot shows the time it took 10 students to solve a slide puzzle.

Time to Complete Slide Puzzle

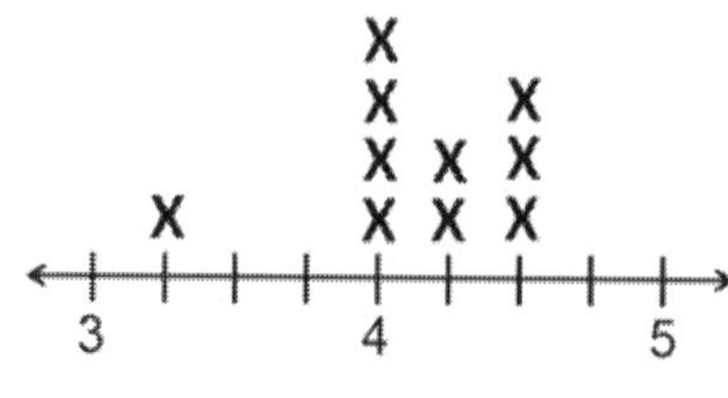

Time (minutes)

How many students took 4 minutes or more to solve the puzzle?

Ⓐ 4

Ⓑ 5

Ⓒ 9

Ⓓ 10

4 The table below shows how many cupcakes of each flavor Marcia sold. If Marcia sold each cupcake for $3, how much did she make from the sale of chocolate and strawberry cupcakes? Write your answer on the line below.

CHOCOLATE	9
VANILLA	4
STRAWBERRY	6
BIRTHDAY CAKE	8
COOKIES & CREAM	5

Answer $____________

5 The table shows the time that four students took to run a race of 5 kilometers.

Student	Time (minutes)
Renee	39
Abby	55
Tina	68
Venus	71

Which student completed the race in the fastest time?

Ⓐ Renee

Ⓑ Abby

Ⓒ Tina

Ⓓ Venus

6 The graph below shows the results of a survey on which animal students would prefer for a school mascot.

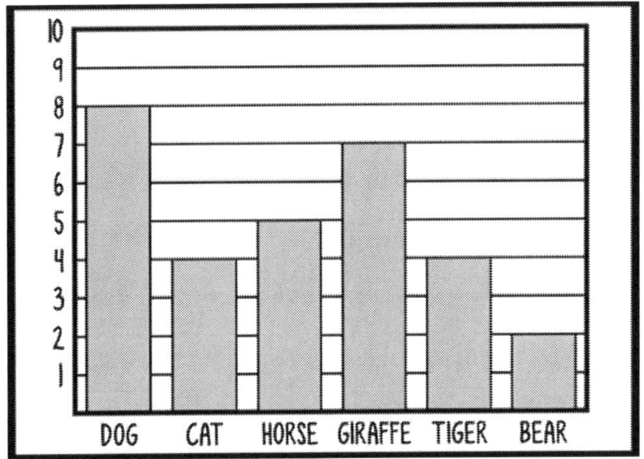

Which animal was chosen by twice as many people as tiger? Write your answer on the line below.

Answer ____________________

7 The graph below shows the items of clothing collected by a clothing drive.

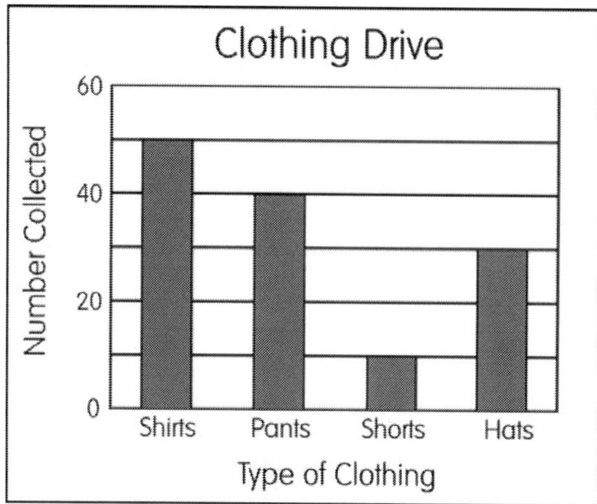

How many items of clothing were collected in all? Write your answer on the line below.

Answer __________

8 Emilio played a game where he tried to grab as many pennies as he could with one hand. The line plot below shows his results in 22 attempts.

Pennies Grabbed with One Hand

30	31	32	33	34	35	36
X	X X	X X X X	X X X X X X	X X X X X	X	X X X

How many times did he grab 34 or more pennies? Write your answer below.

Answer ___________

9 The pictograph shows the raffle tickets sold by four grades.

How many raffle tickets were sold by the second and third grade in all? Write your answer on the line below.

Answer _______________

10 Students at Hunter Elementary School had to choose one sport from four choices. The graph below shows how many students chose each sport.

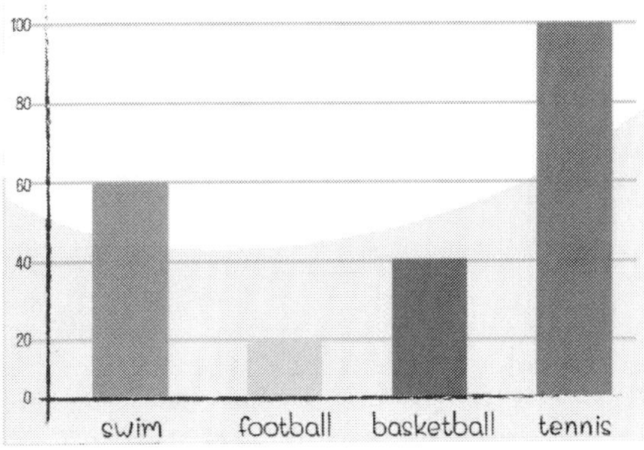

How many more students chose tennis than basketball? Write your answer on the line below.

Answer _______________

Interpret Data – Practice Set 3

1 Arlo recorded how many points his basketball team scored in 23 matches. The line plot below shows the results.

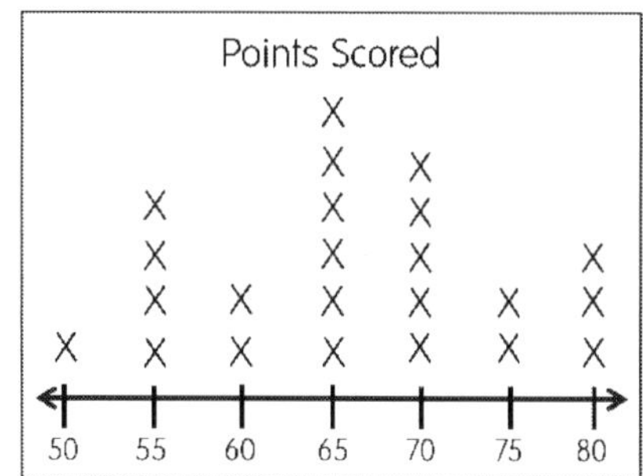

How many times did the team score 70 or more points?

Ⓐ 5

Ⓑ 7

Ⓒ 8

Ⓓ 10

2 The graph below shows the results of a survey on which fruit students would most prefer to eat with cereal.

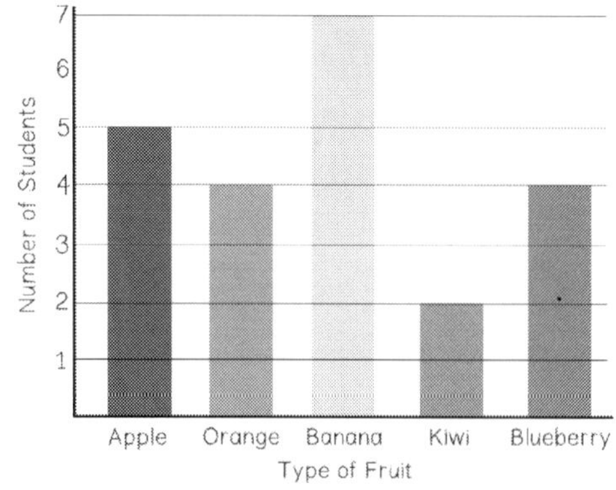

How many more students chose banana than blueberry? Write your answer on the line below.

Answer ______________

3 The pictograph shows the number of pie sales at a school fair.

How many apple and pumpkin pies were sold in all?

Ⓐ 50

Ⓑ 100

Ⓒ 150

Ⓓ 175

4 The members of a marching band voted on which color they would prefer for their uniform. The circle graph shows the results.

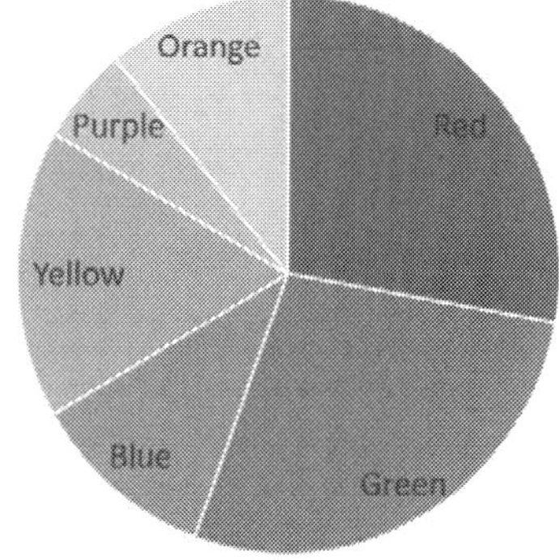

Which two colors had the most votes? Write your answer on the lines below.

Answer ____________ and ____________

5 The table below shows data Evelyn collected one week.

Number of Passengers on Public Transportation	
Monday	48
Tuesday	63
Wednesday	26
Thursday	49

What is the difference between the greatest and the lowest number of passengers? Write your answer on the line below.

Answer ____________

6 The graph below shows the results of a survey on favorite school subject.

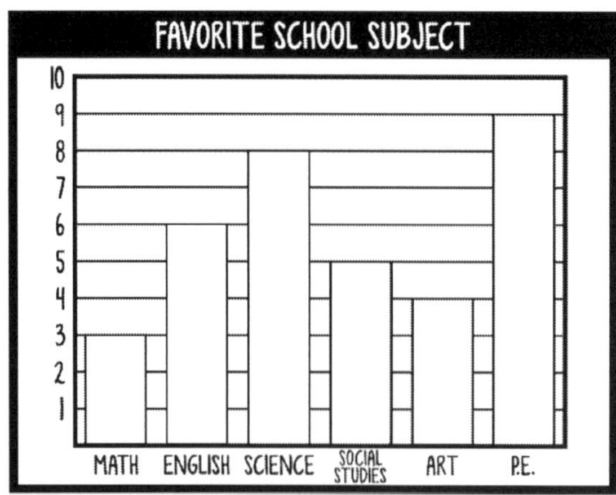

Which subject was chosen by twice as many students as math? Write your answer on the line below.

Answer ______________________

7 Lori asked students to choose one of four activities they would most like to do for an end-of-year party.

End-of-Year Party Activities

Activity	Number of Students
Bowling	𝍸 II
Minigolf	𝍸 IIII
Ice skating	𝍸 𝍸 II
Movies	𝍸

How many students chose ice skating? Write your answer on the line below.

Answer ____________

8 Tina counted the vehicles of each color in a parking lot. The line plot below shows the results.

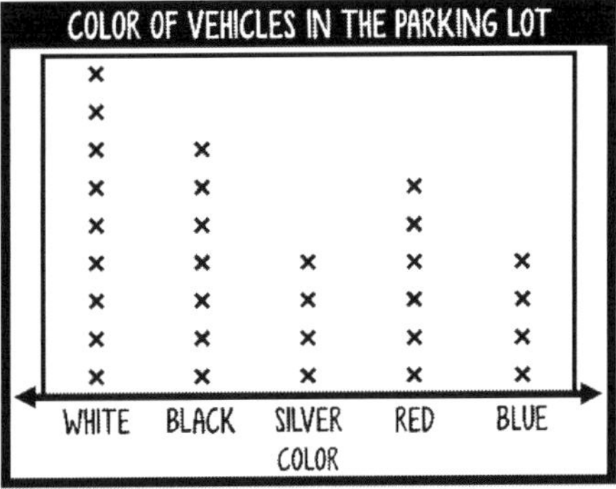

How many more vehicles were white than silver? Write your answer on the line below.

Answer ____________

9 Ava sold boxes of cookies to raise money for a school camp. The graph below shows how many boxes of cookies of each type she sold.

If she sold each box of cookies for $6, how much more did she make from the sale of oatmeal cookies than from ginger snap cookies? Write your answer on the line below.

Answer $__________

10 The graph below shows the results of a survey on favorite pizza topping.

Which pizza topping was selected by a quarter of the people surveyed? Write your answer on the line below.

Answer __________________

Interpret Data – Practice Set 4

1 Jacinta recorded how long she spent reading each evening for 23 days. The line plot below shows the results.

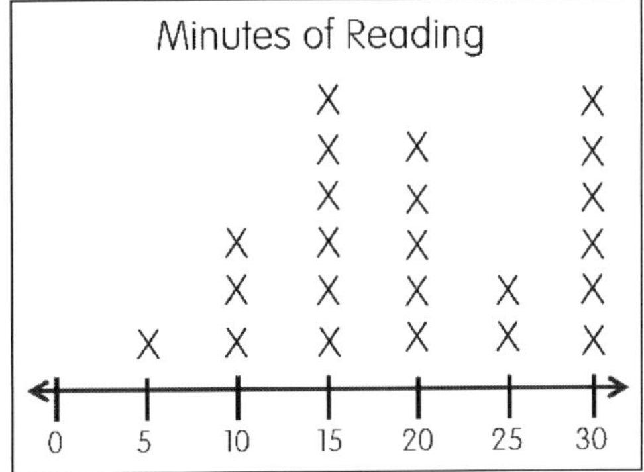

On how many days did she read for 20 minutes or more?

Ⓐ 3

Ⓑ 5

Ⓒ 8

Ⓓ 13

2 The pictograph shows the lunches that students chose one day.

How many students chose either a pizza or a burger? Write your answer below.

Answer ________________

3 The graph shows the number of people who visited a website for 5 days.

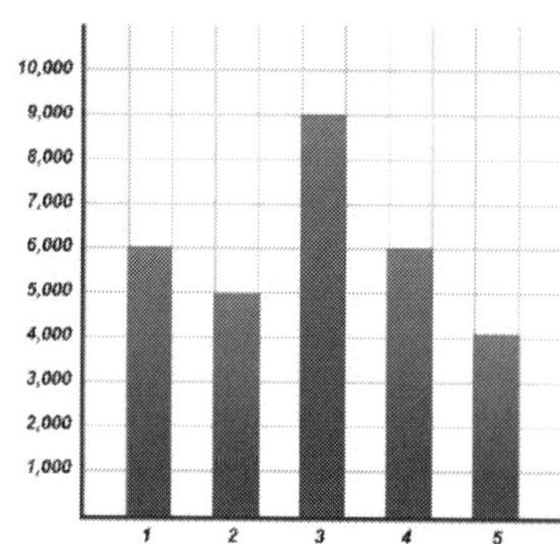

How many more people visited the website on Day 3 than on Day 2?

Ⓐ 3,000

Ⓑ 4,000

Ⓒ 9,000

Ⓓ 14,000

4 The circle graph shows the results of a survey Ken did.

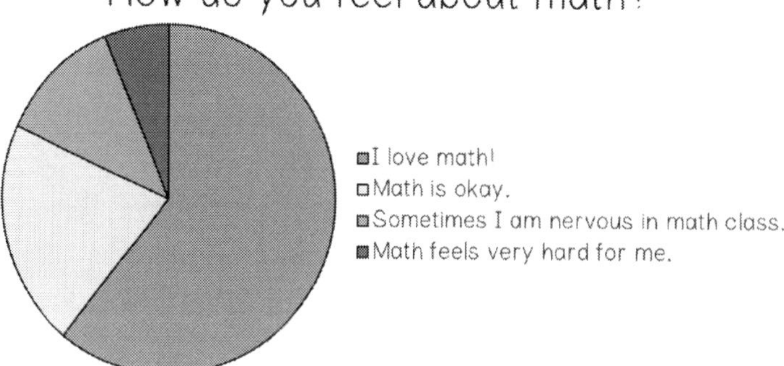

Which response to the survey question was least common?

Ⓐ I love math!

Ⓑ Math is okay.

Ⓒ Sometimes I am nervous in math class.

Ⓓ Math feels very hard for me.

5 Margo made the graph below to show the results of a survey she did on people's favorite season.

Based on the graph, how many people did Margo survey?

Ⓐ 100

Ⓑ 150

Ⓒ 200

Ⓓ 250

6 Maxine asked students about their favorite thing to bake. She made the pictograph below to show the results.

Which two items combined were chosen by the same number of students as cookies? Write your answer on the line below.

Answer ____________________ and ____________________

7 The students at Louise's school had to choose one sport to play. Louise made the graph below to show how many students chose each sport.

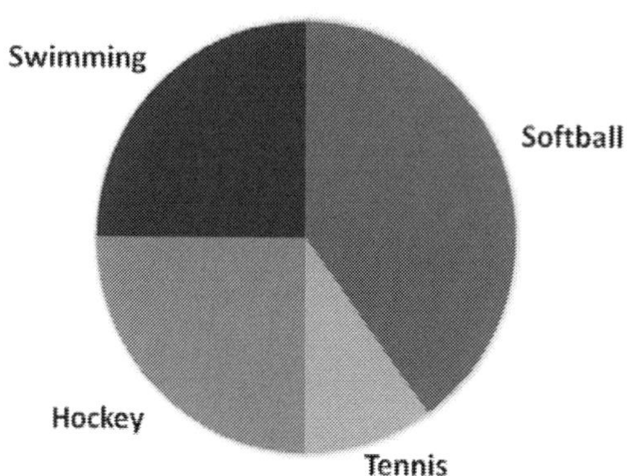

Which sport was the most popular?

Answer ____________________

Which two sports were chosen by the same number of students?

Answer ____________________ and ____________________

8 The table below shows how many email messages Ari received each day.

Day	Mon	Tue	Wed	Thu	Fri	Sat	Sun
Number of Emails	30	42	36	28	26	33	36

On how many days did Ari receive 30 or more emails? Write your answer below.

Answer ____________

9 The graph below shows the number of cars that Paul sold each day.

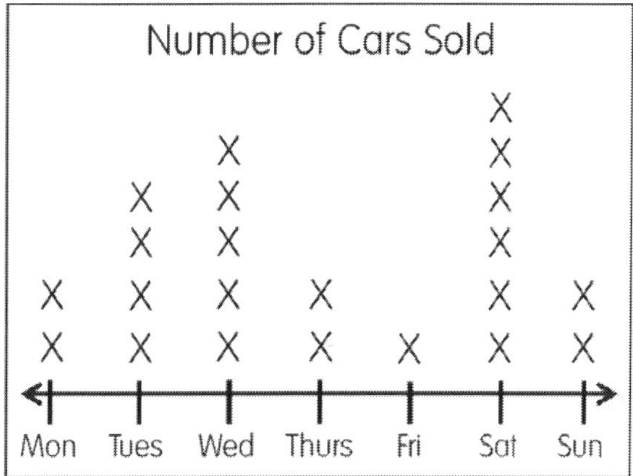

What is the difference between the greatest and least number of cars sold?

Ⓐ 2

Ⓑ 3

Ⓒ 5

Ⓓ 6

10 Based on the data in the table, which topping is twice as popular as only cheese? Write your answer on the line below.

FAVORITE PIZZA TOPPINGS	
Pepperoni	𝍸 |||
Sausage	𝍸
Pineapple	|||
Onions & Peppers		
Only Cheese	||||

Answer ______________________

Interpret Data – Practice Set 5

1 The pictograph shows the number of boxes of each fruit a farmer took to the markets one day. Each symbol of a fruit represents 10 boxes.

How many boxes of apples and oranges did the farmer take?

Ⓐ 4

Ⓑ 8

Ⓒ 40

Ⓓ 80

2 Kevin made the line plot to show the height of students in his class.

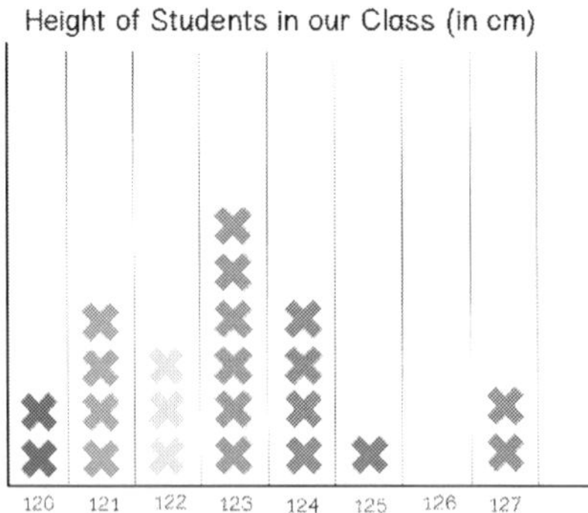

How many students were either 120 or 121 centimeters tall?

Ⓐ 2

Ⓑ 4

Ⓒ 6

Ⓓ 8

3 The graph below shows the results of a survey on which activity students would most like to do at a camp.

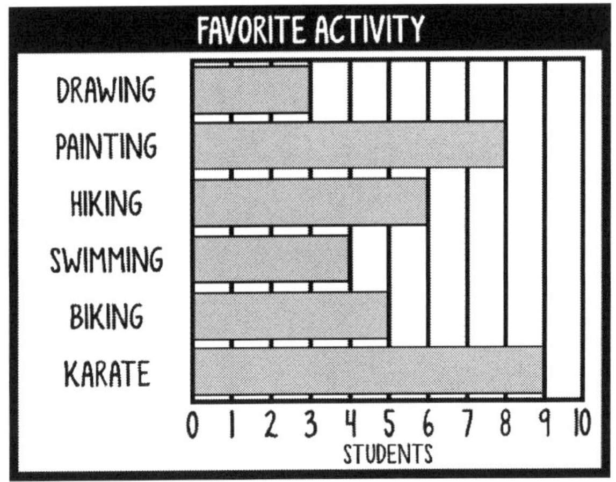

Which activity was twice as popular as swimming?

Ⓐ painting

Ⓑ hiking

Ⓒ biking

Ⓓ karate

4 Based on the data in the table, how many more students chose Harry Potter than Matilda? Write your answer on the line below.

FAVORITE CHAPTER BOOK

CHARLOTTE'S WEB	𝍸 II
HARRY POTTER	𝍸 𝍸
THE BFG	𝍸 I
MATILDA	III
PETER PAN	IIII

Answer ___________

5 The graph below shows the results of a survey on favorite food.

Which food was selected by the most people? Circle the **one** correct answer.

pizza **tacos** **hamburger**

hot dog **chicken nuggets**

6 The pictograph shows how much was raised from the sale of baked goods.

How much was raised from the sale of cookies? Write your answer on the line below.

Answer $___________

7 Gavin made the line plot below to show how long 12 staff members worked one Saturday.

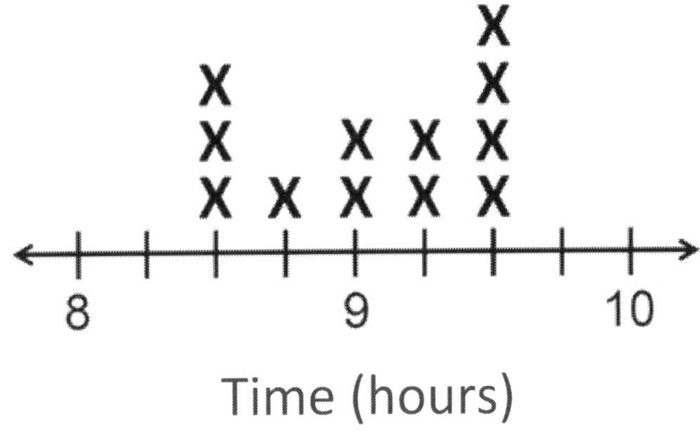

How many staff members worked 9 or more hours? Write your answer on the line below.

Answer ____________

8 Based on the data in the table, which animal is the least favorite? Write your answer on the line below.

FAVORITE ANIMALS	
Cat	5
Dog	10
Rabbit	1
Bird	2
Horse	4

Answer ____________________

9 Alexandra sold snow cones of different flavors at a weekend market. She made the pictograph below to show her sales.

If she sold each snow cone for $3, how much did she make from the sale of cherry snow cones? Write your answer on the line below.

Answer $____________

10 Students at a fun park were able to choose one superhero to have a photo taken with. The graph shows the superheroes chosen.

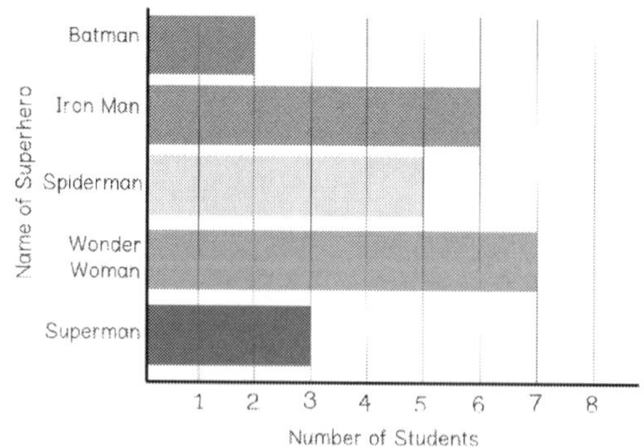

How many students chose either Batman or Superman? Write your answer on the line below.

Answer __________

ANSWER KEY

Introducing the B.E.S.T. Standards for Mathematics

In 2020, the state of Florida introduced the B.E.S.T. standards. The standards describe the skills and knowledge that students are expected to have and replace the previous MAFS standards. The new standards will begin to be introduced in 2020-2021 and will be fully introduced by 2022-2023. The state tests will assess these new standards beginning with the 2022-2023 school year.

About the B.E.S.T. Standards for Mathematics

The B.E.S.T. Standards are divided into six strands. These are listed below.

- Number Sense and Operations
- Fractions
- Algebraic Reasoning
- Measurement
- Geometric Reasoning
- Data Analysis and Probability

Within each strand, there are standards describing an overall skill and then benchmarks within that standard describing specific skills. The answer key that follows lists the specific benchmark covered by each question.

Number Sense and Operations – Place Value

Place Value – Practice Set 1

Question	Answer	B.E.S.T Standard
1	B	Compose and decompose four-digit numbers in multiple ways using thousands, hundreds, tens and ones. Demonstrate each composition or decomposition using objects, drawings and expressions or equations.
2	2,507	Read and write numbers from 0 to 10,000 using standard form, expanded form and word form.
3	C	Compose and decompose four-digit numbers in multiple ways using thousands, hundreds, tens and ones. Demonstrate each composition or decomposition using objects, drawings and expressions or equations.
4	3,000 + 80 + 5	Read and write numbers from 0 to 10,000 using standard form, expanded form and word form.
5	C	Plot, order and compare whole numbers up to 10,000.
6	600	Round whole numbers from 0 to 1,000 to the nearest 10 or 100.
7	2nd, 6th	Compose and decompose four-digit numbers in multiple ways using thousands, hundreds, tens and ones. Demonstrate each composition or decomposition using objects, drawings and expressions or equations.
8	<, <, >	Plot, order and compare whole numbers up to 10,000.
9	35 plotted	Plot, order and compare whole numbers up to 10,000.
10	350, 330, 320, 320	Round whole numbers from 0 to 1,000 to the nearest 10 or 100.

Place Value – Practice Set 2

Question	Answer	B.E.S.T Standard
1	D	Read and write numbers from 0 to 10,000 using standard form, expanded form and word form.
2	C	Round whole numbers from 0 to 1,000 to the nearest 10 or 100.
3	B	Compose and decompose four-digit numbers in multiple ways using thousands, hundreds, tens and ones. Demonstrate each composition or decomposition using objects, drawings and expressions or equations.
4	169 < 178 < 187 < 196	Plot, order and compare whole numbers up to 10,000.
5	C	Plot, order and compare whole numbers up to 10,000.
6	9,530	Read and write numbers from 0 to 10,000 using standard form, expanded form and word form.
7	3rd, 5th	Plot, order and compare whole numbers up to 10,000.
8	6, 8 68 680	Compose and decompose four-digit numbers in multiple ways using thousands, hundreds, tens and ones. Demonstrate each composition or decomposition using objects, drawings and expressions or equations.
9	7, 8 78	Compose and decompose four-digit numbers in multiple ways using thousands, hundreds, tens and ones. Demonstrate each composition or decomposition using objects, drawings and expressions or equations.
10	400, 400, 500	Round whole numbers from 0 to 1,000 to the nearest 10 or 100.

Place Value – Practice Set 3

Question	Answer	B.E.S.T Standard
1	C	Read and write numbers from 0 to 10,000 using standard form, expanded form and word form.
2	D	Compose and decompose four-digit numbers in multiple ways using thousands, hundreds, tens and ones. Demonstrate each composition or decomposition using objects, drawings and expressions or equations.
3	B	Plot, order and compare whole numbers up to 10,000.
4	7,000 + 600 + 3	Read and write numbers from 0 to 10,000 using standard form, expanded form and word form.
5	B	Round whole numbers from 0 to 1,000 to the nearest 10 or 100.
6	121	Compose and decompose four-digit numbers in multiple ways using thousands, hundreds, tens and ones. Demonstrate each composition or decomposition using objects, drawings and expressions or equations.
7	2nd, 3rd, 4th	Round whole numbers from 0 to 1,000 to the nearest 10 or 100.
8	>, >, >	Plot, order and compare whole numbers up to 10,000.
9	2,708 < 2,754 < 2,812	Plot, order and compare whole numbers up to 10,000.
10	63 squares shaded 63	Compose and decompose four-digit numbers in multiple ways using thousands, hundreds, tens and ones. Demonstrate each composition or decomposition using objects, drawings and expressions or equations.

Place Value – Practice Set 4

Question	Answer	B.E.S.T Standard
1	A	Compose and decompose four-digit numbers in multiple ways using thousands, hundreds, tens and ones. Demonstrate each composition or decomposition using objects, drawings and expressions or equations.
2	C	Plot, order and compare whole numbers up to 10,000.
3	C	Plot, order and compare whole numbers up to 10,000.
4	C	Round whole numbers from 0 to 1,000 to the nearest 10 or 100.
5	B	Compose and decompose four-digit numbers in multiple ways using thousands, hundreds, tens and ones. Demonstrate each composition or decomposition using objects, drawings and expressions or equations.
6	8,207	Read and write numbers from 0 to 10,000 using standard form, expanded form and word form.
7	1st, 6th	Plot, order and compare whole numbers up to 10,000.
8	300, 4 8,304	Read and write numbers from 0 to 10,000 using standard form, expanded form and word form.
9	4, 7 47 470	Compose and decompose four-digit numbers in multiple ways using thousands, hundreds, tens and ones. Demonstrate each composition or decomposition using objects, drawings and expressions or equations.
10	130, 120, 140, 130	Round whole numbers from 0 to 1,000 to the nearest 10 or 100.

Place Value – Practice Set 5

Question	Answer	B.E.S.T Standard
1	D	Compose and decompose four-digit numbers in multiple ways using thousands, hundreds, tens and ones. Demonstrate each composition or decomposition using objects, drawings and expressions or equations.
2	3,017	Read and write numbers from 0 to 10,000 using standard form, expanded form and word form.
3	309 < 318 < 326 < 370	Plot, order and compare whole numbers up to 10,000.
4	6, 5, 7	Read and write numbers from 0 to 10,000 using standard form, expanded form and word form.
5	238	Compose and decompose four-digit numbers in multiple ways using thousands, hundreds, tens and ones. Demonstrate each composition or decomposition using objects, drawings and expressions or equations.
6	670	Plot, order and compare whole numbers up to 10,000.
7	3rd, 4th	Round whole numbers from 0 to 1,000 to the nearest 10 or 100.
8	23 squares shaded	Compose and decompose four-digit numbers in multiple ways using thousands, hundreds, tens and ones. Demonstrate each composition or decomposition using objects, drawings and expressions or equations.
9	180, 30, 70, 760, 850, 620, 730, 210	Round whole numbers from 0 to 1,000 to the nearest 10 or 100.
10	>, >, <	Plot, order and compare whole numbers up to 10,000.

Number Sense and Operations – Addition, Subtraction, Multiplication, and Division

Addition, Subtraction, Multiplication, and Division – Practice Set 1

Question	Answer	B.E.S.T Standard
1	C	Explore multiplication of two whole numbers with products from 0 to 144, and related division facts.
2	A	Multiply two whole numbers from 0 to 12 and divide using related facts with procedural reliability.
3	D	Add and subtract multi-digit whole numbers including using a standard algorithm with procedural fluency.
4	B	Multiply a one-digit whole number by a multiple of 10, up to 90, or a multiple of 100, up to 900, with procedural reliability.
5	C	Explore multiplication of two whole numbers with products from 0 to 144, and related division facts.
6	727	Add and subtract multi-digit whole numbers including using a standard algorithm with procedural fluency.
7	1st, 5th	Multiply a one-digit whole number by a multiple of 10, up to 90, or a multiple of 100, up to 900, with procedural reliability.
8	8 × 8 = 64	Explore multiplication of two whole numbers with products from 0 to 144, and related division facts.
9	96, 67, 99, 57	Add and subtract multi-digit whole numbers including using a standard algorithm with procedural fluency.
10	12 × 6 = 72 72	Multiply two whole numbers from 0 to 12 and divide using related facts with procedural reliability.

Addition, Subtraction, Multiplication, and Division – Practice Set 2

Question	Answer	B.E.S.T Standard
1	B	Multiply a one-digit whole number by a multiple of 10, up to 90, or a multiple of 100, up to 900, with procedural reliability.
2	D	Multiply two whole numbers from 0 to 12 and divide using related facts with procedural reliability.
3	C	Explore multiplication of two whole numbers with products from 0 to 144, and related division facts.
4	11	Multiply two whole numbers from 0 to 12 and divide using related facts with procedural reliability.
5	A	Add and subtract multi-digit whole numbers including using a standard algorithm with procedural fluency.
6	5 + 5 + 5 + 5 4 + 4 + 4 + 4 + 4	Explore multiplication of two whole numbers with products from 0 to 144, and related division facts.
7	2nd, 4th	Add and subtract multi-digit whole numbers including using a standard algorithm with procedural fluency.
8	+, +, +, -	Add and subtract multi-digit whole numbers including using a standard algorithm with procedural fluency.
9	3 × 4 = 12	Explore multiplication of two whole numbers with products from 0 to 144, and related division facts.
10	40	Multiply a one-digit whole number by a multiple of 10, up to 90, or a multiple of 100, up to 900, with procedural reliability.

Addition, Subtraction, Multiplication, and Division – Practice Set 3

Question	Answer	B.E.S.T Standard
1	C	Add and subtract multi-digit whole numbers including using a standard algorithm with procedural fluency.
2	A	Multiply a one-digit whole number by a multiple of 10, up to 90, or a multiple of 100, up to 900, with procedural reliability.
3	B	Explore multiplication of two whole numbers with products from 0 to 144, and related division facts.
4	C	Multiply two whole numbers from 0 to 12 and divide using related facts with procedural reliability.
5	B	Multiply a one-digit whole number by a multiple of 10, up to 90, or a multiple of 100, up to 900, with procedural reliability.
6	6,251	Add and subtract multi-digit whole numbers including using a standard algorithm with procedural fluency.
7	1st, 6th	Explore multiplication of two whole numbers with products from 0 to 144, and related division facts.
8	78, 15, 87, 21	Add and subtract multi-digit whole numbers including using a standard algorithm with procedural fluency.
9	6 × 5 30	Explore multiplication of two whole numbers with products from 0 to 144, and related division facts.
10	6 × 9 or 9 × 6	Multiply two whole numbers from 0 to 12 and divide using related facts with procedural reliability.

Addition, Subtraction, Multiplication, and Division – Practice Set 4

Question	Answer	B.E.S.T Standard
1	C	Add and subtract multi-digit whole numbers including using a standard algorithm with procedural fluency.
2	B	Multiply a one-digit whole number by a multiple of 10, up to 90, or a multiple of 100, up to 900, with procedural reliability.
3	C	Explore multiplication of two whole numbers with products from 0 to 144, and related division facts.
4	C	Multiply two whole numbers from 0 to 12 and divide using related facts with procedural reliability.
5	C	Explore multiplication of two whole numbers with products from 0 to 144, and related division facts.
6	6 + 6 + 6 3 + 3 + 3 + 3 + 3 + 3	Explore multiplication of two whole numbers with products from 0 to 144, and related division facts.
7	4 + 6 8 + 2 1 + 9 5 + 5	Add and subtract multi-digit whole numbers including using a standard algorithm with procedural fluency.
8	7, 9, 11, 7	Multiply two whole numbers from 0 to 12 and divide using related facts with procedural reliability.
9	69, 8, 40, 49	Add and subtract multi-digit whole numbers including using a standard algorithm with procedural fluency.
10	3 × 10 = 30	Multiply a one-digit whole number by a multiple of 10, up to 90, or a multiple of 100, up to 900, with procedural reliability.

Addition, Subtraction, Multiplication, and Division – Practice Set 5

Question	Answer	B.E.S.T Standard
1	C	Explore multiplication of two whole numbers with products from 0 to 144, and related division facts.
2	D	Add and subtract multi-digit whole numbers including using a standard algorithm with procedural fluency.
3	A	Explore multiplication of two whole numbers with products from 0 to 144, and related division facts.
4	D	Multiply two whole numbers from 0 to 12 and divide using related facts with procedural reliability.
5	C	Explore multiplication of two whole numbers with products from 0 to 144, and related division facts.
6	4,850	Add and subtract multi-digit whole numbers including using a standard algorithm with procedural fluency.
7	4th, 6th	Multiply a one-digit whole number by a multiple of 10, up to 90, or a multiple of 100, up to 900, with procedural reliability.
8	24, 36, 48	Multiply two whole numbers from 0 to 12 and divide using related facts with procedural reliability.
9	100, 9, 7	Multiply a one-digit whole number by a multiple of 10, up to 90, or a multiple of 100, up to 900, with procedural reliability.
10	20, 10, 17	Add and subtract multi-digit whole numbers including using a standard algorithm with procedural fluency.

Fractions – Understanding Fractions

Understanding Fractions – Practice Set 1

Question	Answer	B.E.S.T Standard
1	C	Represent and interpret fractions, including fractions greater than one, in the form of m/n as the result of adding the unit fraction $1/n$ to itself m times.
2	B	Read and write fractions, including fractions greater than one, using standard form, numeral-word form and word form.
3	B	Represent and interpret unit fractions in the form $1/n$ as the quantity formed by one part when a whole is partitioned into n equal parts.
4	B	Read and write fractions, including fractions greater than one, using standard form, numeral-word form and word form.
5	C	Represent and interpret unit fractions in the form $1/n$ as the quantity formed by one part when a whole is partitioned into n equal parts.
6	$\frac{2}{3}$	Represent and interpret fractions, including fractions greater than one, in the form of m/n as the result of adding the unit fraction $1/n$ to itself m times.
7	1st	Represent and interpret unit fractions in the form $1/n$ as the quantity formed by one part when a whole is partitioned into n equal parts.
8	5 parts shaded $\frac{5}{4}$ or $1\frac{1}{4}$	Represent and interpret fractions, including fractions greater than one, in the form of m/n as the result of adding the unit fraction $1/n$ to itself m times.
9	$\frac{1}{10}$	Represent and interpret unit fractions in the form $1/n$ as the quantity formed by one part when a whole is partitioned into n equal parts.
10	point at $\frac{1}{4}$	Represent and interpret unit fractions in the form $1/n$ as the quantity formed by one part when a whole is partitioned into n equal parts.

Understanding Fractions – Practice Set 2

Question	Answer	B.E.S.T Standard
1	A	Represent and interpret fractions, including fractions greater than one, in the form of m/n as the result of adding the unit fraction $1/n$ to itself m times.
2	C	Read and write fractions, including fractions greater than one, using standard form, numeral-word form and word form.
3	$\frac{1}{5}$	Represent and interpret unit fractions in the form $1/n$ as the quantity formed by one part when a whole is partitioned into n equal parts.
4	B	Read and write fractions, including fractions greater than one, using standard form, numeral-word form and word form.
5	B	Represent and interpret unit fractions in the form $1/n$ as the quantity formed by one part when a whole is partitioned into n equal parts.
6	$\frac{1}{5}$	Represent and interpret unit fractions in the form $1/n$ as the quantity formed by one part when a whole is partitioned into n equal parts.
7	4 parts shaded $\frac{4}{3}$ or $1\frac{1}{3}$	Represent and interpret fractions, including fractions greater than one, in the form of m/n as the result of adding the unit fraction $1/n$ to itself m times.
8	1 part shaded	Represent and interpret unit fractions in the form $1/n$ as the quantity formed by one part when a whole is partitioned into n equal parts.
9	1, 1	Represent and interpret fractions, including fractions greater than one, in the form of m/n as the result of adding the unit fraction $1/n$ to itself m times.
10	$\frac{6}{8}, \frac{9}{3}, \frac{5}{6}, \frac{3}{10}$	Read and write fractions, including fractions greater than one, using standard form, numeral-word form and word form.

Understanding Fractions – Practice Set 3

Question	Answer	B.E.S.T Standard
1	B	Represent and interpret fractions, including fractions greater than one, in the form of m/n as the result of adding the unit fraction $1/n$ to itself m times.
2	B	Read and write fractions, including fractions greater than one, using standard form, numeral-word form and word form.
3	A	Represent and interpret unit fractions in the form $1/n$ as the quantity formed by one part when a whole is partitioned into n equal parts.
4	D	Read and write fractions, including fractions greater than one, using standard form, numeral-word form and word form.
5	C	Represent and interpret unit fractions in the form $1/n$ as the quantity formed by one part when a whole is partitioned into n equal parts.
6	$\frac{7}{8}$	Read and write fractions, including fractions greater than one, using standard form, numeral-word form and word form.
7	$\frac{7}{10}$	Represent and interpret fractions, including fractions greater than one, in the form of m/n as the result of adding the unit fraction $1/n$ to itself m times.
8	top right	Represent and interpret unit fractions in the form $1/n$ as the quantity formed by one part when a whole is partitioned into n equal parts.
9	1, 1, 1 2	Represent and interpret fractions, including fractions greater than one, in the form of m/n as the result of adding the unit fraction $1/n$ to itself m times.
10	point at $\frac{1}{6}$	Represent and interpret unit fractions in the form $1/n$ as the quantity formed by one part when a whole is partitioned into n equal parts.

Understanding Fractions – Practice Set 4

Question	Answer	B.E.S.T Standard
1	B	Represent and interpret fractions, including fractions greater than one, in the form of m/n as the result of adding the unit fraction $1/n$ to itself m times.
2	C	Read and write fractions, including fractions greater than one, using standard form, numeral-word form and word form.
3	C	Represent and interpret unit fractions in the form $1/n$ as the quantity formed by one part when a whole is partitioned into n equal parts.
4	C	Represent and interpret unit fractions in the form $1/n$ as the quantity formed by one part when a whole is partitioned into n equal parts.
5	A	Represent and interpret unit fractions in the form $1/n$ as the quantity formed by one part when a whole is partitioned into n equal parts.
6	$1\frac{2}{3}$	Represent and interpret fractions, including fractions greater than one, in the form of m/n as the result of adding the unit fraction $1/n$ to itself m times.
7	3rd	Represent and interpret unit fractions in the form $1/n$ as the quantity formed by one part when a whole is partitioned into n equal parts.
8	4 parts shaded $\frac{4}{5}$	Represent and interpret fractions, including fractions greater than one, in the form of m/n as the result of adding the unit fraction $1/n$ to itself m times.
9	$\frac{5}{4}$, $1\frac{1}{4}$	Represent and interpret unit fractions in the form $1/n$ as the quantity formed by one part when a whole is partitioned into n equal parts.
10	7 parts shaded	Read and write fractions, including fractions greater than one, using standard form, numeral-word form and word form.

Understanding Fractions – Practice Set 5

Question	Answer	B.E.S.T Standard
1	D	Read and write fractions, including fractions greater than one, using standard form, numeral-word form and word form.
2	B	Represent and interpret fractions, including fractions greater than one, in the form of m/n as the result of adding the unit fraction $1/n$ to itself m times.
3	A	Represent and interpret unit fractions in the form $1/n$ as the quantity formed by one part when a whole is partitioned into n equal parts.
4	A	Read and write fractions, including fractions greater than one, using standard form, numeral-word form and word form.
5	B	Represent and interpret unit fractions in the form $1/n$ as the quantity formed by one part when a whole is partitioned into n equal parts.
6	$\frac{1}{3}$	Represent and interpret unit fractions in the form $1/n$ as the quantity formed by one part when a whole is partitioned into n equal parts.
7	2nd, 4th	Represent and interpret fractions, including fractions greater than one, in the form of m/n as the result of adding the unit fraction $1/n$ to itself m times.
8	point at $\frac{5}{6}$ $\frac{5}{6}$	Represent and interpret fractions, including fractions greater than one, in the form of m/n as the result of adding the unit fraction $1/n$ to itself m times.
9	$\frac{5}{3}, \frac{3}{4}, \frac{2}{10}, \frac{7}{5}$	Read and write fractions, including fractions greater than one, using standard form, numeral-word form and word form.
10	third square third rectangle	Represent and interpret unit fractions in the form $1/n$ as the quantity formed by one part when a whole is partitioned into n equal parts.

Fractions – Comparing and Ordering Fractions

Comparing and Ordering Fractions – Practice Set 1

Question	Answer	B.E.S.T Standard
1	$\frac{4}{6}$	Identify equivalent fractions and explain why they are equivalent.
2	C	Plot, order and compare fractional numbers with the same numerator or the same denominator.
3	A	Plot, order and compare fractional numbers with the same numerator or the same denominator.
4	$\frac{1}{2}, \frac{3}{6}$	Identify equivalent fractions and explain why they are equivalent.
5	point at $4\frac{3}{4}$	Plot, order and compare fractional numbers with the same numerator or the same denominator.
6	$2\frac{1}{2}$ or $2\frac{5}{10}$	Plot, order and compare fractional numbers with the same numerator or the same denominator.
7	middle two	Identify equivalent fractions and explain why they are equivalent.
8	$\frac{1}{3}$ and $\frac{2}{6}$ plotted $\frac{2}{6}$	Identify equivalent fractions and explain why they are equivalent.
9	3 parts, 7 parts $<$	Plot, order and compare fractional numbers with the same numerator or the same denominator.
10	2, 8	Identify equivalent fractions and explain why they are equivalent.

Comparing and Ordering Fractions – Practice Set 2

Question	Answer	B.E.S.T Standard
1	B	Plot, order and compare fractional numbers with the same numerator or the same denominator.
2	$\frac{1}{3}$	Identify equivalent fractions and explain why they are equivalent.
3	B	Plot, order and compare fractional numbers with the same numerator or the same denominator.
4	A	Identify equivalent fractions and explain why they are equivalent.
5	D	Plot, order and compare fractional numbers with the same numerator or the same denominator.
6	$\frac{1}{2}$	Plot, order and compare fractional numbers with the same numerator or the same denominator.
7	$\frac{2}{3}$ and $\frac{8}{12}$ plotted $\frac{8}{12}$	Identify equivalent fractions and explain why they are equivalent.
8	$\frac{2}{3} > \frac{1}{3}$	Plot, order and compare fractional numbers with the same numerator or the same denominator.
9	1 and 3 parts shaded	Identify equivalent fractions and explain why they are equivalent.
10	$\frac{2}{4}$ and $\frac{3}{6}$	Identify equivalent fractions and explain why they are equivalent.

Comparing and Ordering Fractions – Practice Set 3

Question	Answer	B.E.S.T Standard
1	A	Identify equivalent fractions and explain why they are equivalent.
2	A	Plot, order and compare fractional numbers with the same numerator or the same denominator.
3	D	Plot, order and compare fractional numbers with the same numerator or the same denominator.
4	$\frac{2}{3}$ and $\frac{4}{6}$	Identify equivalent fractions and explain why they are equivalent.
5	B	Plot, order and compare fractional numbers with the same numerator or the same denominator.
6	$2\frac{3}{4}$	Plot, order and compare fractional numbers with the same numerator or the same denominator.
7	$4\frac{3}{10}$ plotted	Plot, order and compare fractional numbers with the same numerator or the same denominator.
8	2 and 4 parts shaded	Identify equivalent fractions and explain why they are equivalent.
9	$\frac{3}{6} = \frac{2}{4}$	Identify equivalent fractions and explain why they are equivalent.
10	E	Identify equivalent fractions and explain why they are equivalent.

Comparing and Ordering Fractions – Practice Set 4

Question	Answer	B.E.S.T Standard
1	C	Identify equivalent fractions and explain why they are equivalent.
2	D	Identify equivalent fractions and explain why they are equivalent.
3	D	Plot, order and compare fractional numbers with the same numerator or the same denominator.
4	D	Identify equivalent fractions and explain why they are equivalent.
5	D	Plot, order and compare fractional numbers with the same numerator or the same denominator.
6	$1\frac{3}{4}$	Plot, order and compare fractional numbers with the same numerator or the same denominator.
7	1 and 2 parts shaded $>$	Plot, order and compare fractional numbers with the same numerator or the same denominator.
8	$\frac{1}{12}$	Plot, order and compare fractional numbers with the same numerator or the same denominator.
9	3 parts shaded $\frac{9}{12} = \frac{3}{4}$	Identify equivalent fractions and explain why they are equivalent.
10	$\frac{8}{10}$ plotted $\frac{8}{10}$	Identify equivalent fractions and explain why they are equivalent.

Comparing and Ordering Fractions – Practice Set 5

Question	Answer	B.E.S.T Standard
1	B	Plot, order and compare fractional numbers with the same numerator or the same denominator.
2	C	Identify equivalent fractions and explain why they are equivalent.
3	D	Plot, order and compare fractional numbers with the same numerator or the same denominator.
4	C	Identify equivalent fractions and explain why they are equivalent.
5	C	Plot, order and compare fractional numbers with the same numerator or the same denominator.
6	$2\frac{1}{4}$	Plot, order and compare fractional numbers with the same numerator or the same denominator.
7	8 parts shaded $\frac{4}{5} = \frac{8}{10}$	Identify equivalent fractions and explain why they are equivalent.
8	$\frac{7}{12}, \frac{1}{2},$ and $\frac{3}{4}$ plotted $\frac{3}{4}$	Plot, order and compare fractional numbers with the same numerator or the same denominator.
9	6, 8	Identify equivalent fractions and explain why they are equivalent.
10	$\frac{3}{4}$ and $\frac{6}{8}$ plotted $\frac{6}{8}$	Identify equivalent fractions and explain why they are equivalent.

Algebraic Reasoning – Multiplication and Division Problems

Multiplication and Division Problems – Practice Set 1

Question	Answer	B.E.S.T Standard
1	D	Solve one- and two-step real-world problems involving any of four operations with whole numbers.
2	C	Apply the distributive property to multiply a one-digit number and two-digit number. Apply properties of multiplication to find a product of one-digit whole numbers.
3	C	Apply the distributive property to multiply a one-digit number and two-digit number. Apply properties of multiplication to find a product of one-digit whole numbers.
4	25 × 5 5 × 25	Apply the distributive property to multiply a one-digit number and two-digit number. Apply properties of multiplication to find a product of one-digit whole numbers.
5	D	Solve one- and two-step real-world problems involving any of four operations with whole numbers.
6	$210	Solve one- and two-step real-world problems involving any of four operations with whole numbers.
7	1st, 4th	Apply the distributive property to multiply a one-digit number and two-digit number. Apply properties of multiplication to find a product of one-digit whole numbers.
8	1st – 3rd 2nd – 1st 3rd – 2nd	Apply the distributive property to multiply a one-digit number and two-digit number. Apply properties of multiplication to find a product of one-digit whole numbers.
9	$20, $52 $60, $156 $120, $312	Solve one- and two-step real-world problems involving any of four operations with whole numbers.
10	(4 × 55) + 30 $250	Solve one- and two-step real-world problems involving any of four operations with whole numbers.

Multiplication and Division Problems – Practice Set 2

Question	Answer	B.E.S.T Standard
1	D	Solve one- and two-step real-world problems involving any of four operations with whole numbers.
2	A	Apply the distributive property to multiply a one-digit number and two-digit number. Apply properties of multiplication to find a product of one-digit whole numbers.
3	C	Apply the distributive property to multiply a one-digit number and two-digit number. Apply properties of multiplication to find a product of one-digit whole numbers.
4	C	Solve one- and two-step real-world problems involving any of four operations with whole numbers.
5	32, 42, 30	Apply the distributive property to multiply a one-digit number and two-digit number. Apply properties of multiplication to find a product of one-digit whole numbers.
6	66	Solve one- and two-step real-world problems involving any of four operations with whole numbers.
7	$75, $107, $73	Solve one- and two-step real-world problems involving any of four operations with whole numbers.
8	(2 × 7) + (2 × 8) 14 + 16 30	Apply the distributive property to multiply a one-digit number and two-digit number. Apply properties of multiplication to find a product of one-digit whole numbers.
9	27 × 12 42 × 9 10 × 45 8 × 36	Apply the distributive property to multiply a one-digit number and two-digit number. Apply properties of multiplication to find a product of one-digit whole numbers.
10	(5 × 12) ÷ 3 20	Solve one- and two-step real-world problems involving any of four operations with whole numbers.

Multiplication and Division Problems – Practice Set 3

Question	Answer	B.E.S.T Standard
1	B	Apply the distributive property to multiply a one-digit number and two-digit number. Apply properties of multiplication to find a product of one-digit whole numbers.
2	B	Solve one- and two-step real-world problems involving any of four operations with whole numbers.
3	\$18	Solve one- and two-step real-world problems involving any of four operations with whole numbers.
4	B	Solve one- and two-step real-world problems involving any of four operations with whole numbers.
5	54, 8, 16	Apply the distributive property to multiply a one-digit number and two-digit number. Apply properties of multiplication to find a product of one-digit whole numbers.
6	48	Solve one- and two-step real-world problems involving any of four operations with whole numbers.
7	2nd, 5th	Apply the distributive property to multiply a one-digit number and two-digit number. Apply properties of multiplication to find a product of one-digit whole numbers.
8	18 × 3 3 × 18	Apply the distributive property to multiply a one-digit number and two-digit number. Apply properties of multiplication to find a product of one-digit whole numbers.
9	(5 × 4) + (5 × 9) 20 + 45 65	Apply the distributive property to multiply a one-digit number and two-digit number. Apply properties of multiplication to find a product of one-digit whole numbers.
10	(4 × 9) + (3 × 11) 36 + 33 69	Solve one- and two-step real-world problems involving any of four operations with whole numbers.

Multiplication and Division Problems – Practice Set 4

Question	Answer	B.E.S.T Standard
1	B	Apply the distributive property to multiply a one-digit number and two-digit number. Apply properties of multiplication to find a product of one-digit whole numbers.
2	C	Solve one- and two-step real-world problems involving any of four operations with whole numbers.
3	D	Solve one- and two-step real-world problems involving any of four operations with whole numbers.
4	49, 35, 32	Apply the distributive property to multiply a one-digit number and two-digit number. Apply properties of multiplication to find a product of one-digit whole numbers.
5	B	Solve one- and two-step real-world problems involving any of four operations with whole numbers.
6	6	Solve one- and two-step real-world problems involving any of four operations with whole numbers.
7	1st, 4th	Apply the distributive property to multiply a one-digit number and two-digit number. Apply properties of multiplication to find a product of one-digit whole numbers.
8	4 × 2 8 × 3 7 × 9	Apply the distributive property to multiply a one-digit number and two-digit number. Apply properties of multiplication to find a product of one-digit whole numbers.
9	(4 × 9) + (4 × 3) 36 + 12 48	Apply the distributive property to multiply a one-digit number and two-digit number. Apply properties of multiplication to find a product of one-digit whole numbers.
10	(12 × 12) – 105 144 – 105 \$39	Solve one- and two-step real-world problems involving any of four operations with whole numbers.

Multiplication and Division Problems – Practice Set 5

Question	Answer	B.E.S.T Standard
1	C	Solve one- and two-step real-world problems involving any of four operations with whole numbers.
2	B	Solve one- and two-step real-world problems involving any of four operations with whole numbers.
3	3, 6	Apply the distributive property to multiply a one-digit number and two-digit number. Apply properties of multiplication to find a product of one-digit whole numbers.
4	A	Apply the distributive property to multiply a one-digit number and two-digit number. Apply properties of multiplication to find a product of one-digit whole numbers.
5	D	Solve one- and two-step real-world problems involving any of four operations with whole numbers.
6	\$188	Solve one- and two-step real-world problems involving any of four operations with whole numbers.
7	1st, 4th	Apply the distributive property to multiply a one-digit number and two-digit number. Apply properties of multiplication to find a product of one-digit whole numbers.
8	1st – 3rd 2nd – 1st 3rd – 2nd	Apply the distributive property to multiply a one-digit number and two-digit number. Apply properties of multiplication to find a product of one-digit whole numbers.
9	6×17 5×53 11×87 22×64	Apply the distributive property to multiply a one-digit number and two-digit number. Apply properties of multiplication to find a product of one-digit whole numbers.
10	$(752 - 719) \times 2$ 33×2 \$66	Solve one- and two-step real-world problems involving any of four operations with whole numbers.

Algebraic Reasoning – Understanding and Using Equations

Understanding and Using Equations – Practice Set 1

Question	Answer	B.E.S.T Standard
1	B	Determine the unknown whole number in a multiplication or division equation, relating three whole numbers, with the unknown in any position.
2	C	Determine and explain whether an equation involving multiplication or division is true or false.
3	A	Determine the unknown whole number in a multiplication or division equation, relating three whole numbers, with the unknown in any position.
4	C	Restate a division problem as a missing factor problem using the relationship between multiplication and division.
5	C	Determine and explain whether an equation involving multiplication or division is true or false.
6	5	Restate a division problem as a missing factor problem using the relationship between multiplication and division.
7	1st, 5th	Determine and explain whether an equation involving multiplication or division is true or false.
8	20, 4, 7, 9	Determine the unknown whole number in a multiplication or division equation, relating three whole numbers, with the unknown in any position.
9	1st – 2nd 2nd – 3rd 3rd – 1st 4th – 4th	Determine the unknown whole number in a multiplication or division equation, relating three whole numbers, with the unknown in any position.
10	7×7	Restate a division problem as a missing factor problem using the relationship between multiplication and division.

Understanding and Using Equations – Practice Set 2

Question	Answer	B.E.S.T Standard
1	B	Restate a division problem as a missing factor problem using the relationship between multiplication and division.
2	A	Determine and explain whether an equation involving multiplication or division is true or false.
3	B	Determine the unknown whole number in a multiplication or division equation, relating three whole numbers, with the unknown in any position.
4	B	Determine the unknown whole number in a multiplication or division equation, relating three whole numbers, with the unknown in any position.
5	D	Determine and explain whether an equation involving multiplication or division is true or false.
6	12	Restate a division problem as a missing factor problem using the relationship between multiplication and division.
7	4th, 6th	Restate a division problem as a missing factor problem using the relationship between multiplication and division.
8	15, 28, 40, 27	Determine the unknown whole number in a multiplication or division equation, relating three whole numbers, with the unknown in any position.
9	9×2 6×3	Determine and explain whether an equation involving multiplication or division is true or false.
10	2, 35, 7, 30	Determine the unknown whole number in a multiplication or division equation, relating three whole numbers, with the unknown in any position.

Understanding and Using Equations – Practice Set 3

Question	Answer	B.E.S.T Standard
1	B	Determine and explain whether an equation involving multiplication or division is true or false.
2	B	Restate a division problem as a missing factor problem using the relationship between multiplication and division.
3	B	Determine and explain whether an equation involving multiplication or division is true or false.
4	B	Restate a division problem as a missing factor problem using the relationship between multiplication and division.
5	D	Determine the unknown whole number in a multiplication or division equation, relating three whole numbers, with the unknown in any position.
6	8	Determine the unknown whole number in a multiplication or division equation, relating three whole numbers, with the unknown in any position.
7	1st – 4th 2nd – 3rd 3rd – 1st 4th – 2nd	Determine the unknown whole number in a multiplication or division equation, relating three whole numbers, with the unknown in any position.
8	T, F, F, T	Determine and explain whether an equation involving multiplication or division is true or false.
9	8, 35, 9, 42	Determine the unknown whole number in a multiplication or division equation, relating three whole numbers, with the unknown in any position.
10	6 × 11	Restate a division problem as a missing factor problem using the relationship between multiplication and division.

Understanding and Using Equations – Practice Set 4

Question	Answer	B.E.S.T Standard
1	C	Determine the unknown whole number in a multiplication or division equation, relating three whole numbers, with the unknown in any position.
2	C	Restate a division problem as a missing factor problem using the relationship between multiplication and division.
3	C	Determine and explain whether an equation involving multiplication or division is true or false.
4	7	Restate a division problem as a missing factor problem using the relationship between multiplication and division.
5	C	Determine and explain whether an equation involving multiplication or division is true or false.
6	4	Determine the unknown whole number in a multiplication or division equation, relating three whole numbers, with the unknown in any position.
7	4th, 6th	Restate a division problem as a missing factor problem using the relationship between multiplication and division.
8	3, 40, 2, 48	Determine the unknown whole number in a multiplication or division equation, relating three whole numbers, with the unknown in any position.
9	2 × 10 4 × 5	Determine and explain whether an equation involving multiplication or division is true or false.
10	8, 4, 7, 6	Determine the unknown whole number in a multiplication or division equation, relating three whole numbers, with the unknown in any position.

Understanding and Using Equations – Practice Set 5

Question	Answer	B.E.S.T Standard
1	B	Restate a division problem as a missing factor problem using the relationship between multiplication and division.
2	B	Determine and explain whether an equation involving multiplication or division is true or false.
3	A	Determine the unknown whole number in a multiplication or division equation, relating three whole numbers, with the unknown in any position.
4	B	Restate a division problem as a missing factor problem using the relationship between multiplication and division.
5	A	Determine and explain whether an equation involving multiplication or division is true or false.
6	8	Determine and explain whether an equation involving multiplication or division is true or false.
7	12, 30, 14, 24	Determine the unknown whole number in a multiplication or division equation, relating three whole numbers, with the unknown in any position.
8	1st – 2nd 2nd – 1st 3rd – 3rd 4th – 4th	Determine the unknown whole number in a multiplication or division equation, relating three whole numbers, with the unknown in any position.
9	9 × 9	Restate a division problem as a missing factor problem using the relationship between multiplication and division.
10	6, 42, 5, 48	Determine the unknown whole number in a multiplication or division equation, relating three whole numbers, with the unknown in any position.

Algebraic Reasoning – Number Patterns

Number Patterns – Practice Set 1

Question	Answer	B.E.S.T Standard
1	D	Determine and explain whether a whole number from 1 to 1,000 is even or odd.
2	B	Determine whether a whole number from 1 to 144 is a multiple of a given one-digit number.
3	B	Determine and explain whether a whole number from 1 to 1,000 is even or odd.
4	24, 30	Determine whether a whole number from 1 to 144 is a multiple of a given one-digit number.
5	C	Identify, create and extend numerical patterns.
6	56	Determine whether a whole number from 1 to 144 is a multiple of a given one-digit number.
7	E, O, E, O, E, E	Determine and explain whether a whole number from 1 to 1,000 is even or odd.
8	\$21, \$27, \$33	Identify, create and extend numerical patterns.
9	22, 13, 14	Identify, create and extend numerical patterns.
10	10:05, 10:14, 10:23, 10:32 10:32 a.m.	Identify, create and extend numerical patterns.

Number Patterns – Practice Set 2

Question	Answer	B.E.S.T Standard
1	D	Determine and explain whether a whole number from 1 to 1,000 is even or odd.
2	B	Determine whether a whole number from 1 to 144 is a multiple of a given one-digit number.
3	C	Identify, create and extend numerical patterns.
4	C	Determine whether a whole number from 1 to 144 is a multiple of a given one-digit number.
5	C	Determine whether a whole number from 1 to 144 is a multiple of a given one-digit number.
6	35, 35	Identify, create and extend numerical patterns.
7	E, O, E, O, O, O	Determine and explain whether a whole number from 1 to 1,000 is even or odd.
8	10, 15, 25, 40	Identify, create and extend numerical patterns.
9	310, 312	Determine and explain whether a whole number from 1 to 1,000 is even or odd.
10	20, 24, 28, 32, 36, 40 40 pages	Identify, create and extend numerical patterns.

Number Patterns – Practice Set 3

Question	Answer	B.E.S.T Standard
1	B	Identify, create and extend numerical patterns.
2	C	Determine whether a whole number from 1 to 144 is a multiple of a given one-digit number.
3	B	Determine and explain whether a whole number from 1 to 1,000 is even or odd.
4	B	Determine whether a whole number from 1 to 144 is a multiple of a given one-digit number.
5	B	Identify, create and extend numerical patterns.
6	63	Determine whether a whole number from 1 to 144 is a multiple of a given one-digit number.
7	2nd, 4th	Determine and explain whether a whole number from 1 to 1,000 is even or odd.
8	1, 10, 24	Identify, create and extend numerical patterns.
9	69, 75, 67, 57	Determine and explain whether a whole number from 1 to 1,000 is even or odd.
10	3, 6, 9, 12, 15, 18, 21, 24, 27 27 novels	Identify, create and extend numerical patterns.

Number Patterns – Practice Set 4

Question	Answer	B.E.S.T Standard
1	B	Identify, create and extend numerical patterns.
2	D	Determine and explain whether a whole number from 1 to 1,000 is even or odd.
3	A	Determine whether a whole number from 1 to 144 is a multiple of a given one-digit number.
4	D	Determine and explain whether a whole number from 1 to 1,000 is even or odd.
5	90	Determine whether a whole number from 1 to 144 is a multiple of a given one-digit number.
6	12	Determine whether a whole number from 1 to 144 is a multiple of a given one-digit number.
7	O, E, E, E, O, O	Determine and explain whether a whole number from 1 to 1,000 is even or odd.
8	6, 9, 15, 24	Identify, create and extend numerical patterns.
9	41, 39 36, 41	Identify, create and extend numerical patterns.
10	Day 5 – 35 Day 6 – 30 Day 7 – 25 Day 8 – 20 20 treats	Identify, create and extend numerical patterns.

Number Patterns – Practice Set 5

Question	Answer	B.E.S.T Standard
1	D	Determine and explain whether a whole number from 1 to 1,000 is even or odd.
2	B	Determine whether a whole number from 1 to 144 is a multiple of a given one-digit number.
3	C	Identify, create and extend numerical patterns.
4	D	Determine whether a whole number from 1 to 144 is a multiple of a given one-digit number.
5	B	Determine whether a whole number from 1 to 144 is a multiple of a given one-digit number.
6	\$80, \$120, \$160	Identify, create and extend numerical patterns.
7	42, 29, 9	Identify, create and extend numerical patterns.
8	127, 121, 135	Determine and explain whether a whole number from 1 to 1,000 is even or odd.
9	E, O, E, O, E, O	Determine and explain whether a whole number from 1 to 1,000 is even or odd.
10	400, 200, 100, 50, 25 25 balloons	Identify, create and extend numerical patterns.

Measurement

Use Tools to Measure – Practice Set 1

Question	Answer	B.E.S.T Standard
1	C	Select and use appropriate tools to measure the length of an object, the volume of liquid within a beaker and temperature.
2	D	Select and use appropriate tools to measure the length of an object, the volume of liquid within a beaker and temperature.
3	A	Select and use appropriate tools to measure the length of an object, the volume of liquid within a beaker and temperature.
4	C	Select and use appropriate tools to measure the length of an object, the volume of liquid within a beaker and temperature.
5	15	Select and use appropriate tools to measure the length of an object, the volume of liquid within a beaker and temperature.
6	400	Select and use appropriate tools to measure the length of an object, the volume of liquid within a beaker and temperature.
7	30	Select and use appropriate tools to measure the length of an object, the volume of liquid within a beaker and temperature.
8	1st, 4th	Select and use appropriate tools to measure the length of an object, the volume of liquid within a beaker and temperature.
9	$2\frac{3}{4}$ shown $4\frac{1}{2}$ shown	Select and use appropriate tools to measure the length of an object, the volume of liquid within a beaker and temperature.
10	B	Select and use appropriate tools to measure the length of an object, the volume of liquid within a beaker and temperature.

Use Tools to Measure – Practice Set 2

Question	Answer	B.E.S.T Standard
1	B	Select and use appropriate tools to measure the length of an object, the volume of liquid within a beaker and temperature.
2	5	Select and use appropriate tools to measure the length of an object, the volume of liquid within a beaker and temperature.
3	12	Select and use appropriate tools to measure the length of an object, the volume of liquid within a beaker and temperature.
4	C	Select and use appropriate tools to measure the length of an object, the volume of liquid within a beaker and temperature.
5	C	Select and use appropriate tools to measure the length of an object, the volume of liquid within a beaker and temperature.
6	25	Select and use appropriate tools to measure the length of an object, the volume of liquid within a beaker and temperature.
7	200	Select and use appropriate tools to measure the length of an object, the volume of liquid within a beaker and temperature.
8	25, 45, 18 shown	Select and use appropriate tools to measure the length of an object, the volume of liquid within a beaker and temperature.
9	5	Select and use appropriate tools to measure the length of an object, the volume of liquid within a beaker and temperature.
10	3, 1, 2, 5, 4	Select and use appropriate tools to measure the length of an object, the volume of liquid within a beaker and temperature.

Use Tools to Measure – Practice Set 3

Question	Answer	B.E.S.T Standard
1	B	Select and use appropriate tools to measure the length of an object, the volume of liquid within a beaker and temperature.
2	C	Select and use appropriate tools to measure the length of an object, the volume of liquid within a beaker and temperature.
3	22	Select and use appropriate tools to measure the length of an object, the volume of liquid within a beaker and temperature.
4	B	Select and use appropriate tools to measure the length of an object, the volume of liquid within a beaker and temperature.
5	B	Select and use appropriate tools to measure the length of an object, the volume of liquid within a beaker and temperature.
6	$4\frac{1}{2}$	Select and use appropriate tools to measure the length of an object, the volume of liquid within a beaker and temperature.
7	B	Select and use appropriate tools to measure the length of an object, the volume of liquid within a beaker and temperature.
8	32	Select and use appropriate tools to measure the length of an object, the volume of liquid within a beaker and temperature.
9	700 shown 200 shown	Select and use appropriate tools to measure the length of an object, the volume of liquid within a beaker and temperature.
10	6, 8, 4	Select and use appropriate tools to measure the length of an object, the volume of liquid within a beaker and temperature.

Use Tools to Measure – Practice Set 4

Question	Answer	B.E.S.T Standard
1	D	Select and use appropriate tools to measure the length of an object, the volume of liquid within a beaker and temperature.
2	D	Select and use appropriate tools to measure the length of an object, the volume of liquid within a beaker and temperature.
3	C	Select and use appropriate tools to measure the length of an object, the volume of liquid within a beaker and temperature.
4	B	Select and use appropriate tools to measure the length of an object, the volume of liquid within a beaker and temperature.
5	B	Select and use appropriate tools to measure the length of an object, the volume of liquid within a beaker and temperature.
6	4	Select and use appropriate tools to measure the length of an object, the volume of liquid within a beaker and temperature.
7	70	Select and use appropriate tools to measure the length of an object, the volume of liquid within a beaker and temperature.
8	$3\frac{1}{2}$ shown $5\frac{1}{4}$ shown	Select and use appropriate tools to measure the length of an object, the volume of liquid within a beaker and temperature.
9	900	Select and use appropriate tools to measure the length of an object, the volume of liquid within a beaker and temperature.
10	4, 2, 6, 5, 1, 3	Select and use appropriate tools to measure the length of an object, the volume of liquid within a beaker and temperature.

Use Tools to Measure – Practice Set 5

Question	Answer	B.E.S.T Standard
1	C	Select and use appropriate tools to measure the length of an object, the volume of liquid within a beaker and temperature.
2	D	Select and use appropriate tools to measure the length of an object, the volume of liquid within a beaker and temperature.
3	13	Select and use appropriate tools to measure the length of an object, the volume of liquid within a beaker and temperature.
4	D	Select and use appropriate tools to measure the length of an object, the volume of liquid within a beaker and temperature.
5	A	Select and use appropriate tools to measure the length of an object, the volume of liquid within a beaker and temperature.
6	7	Select and use appropriate tools to measure the length of an object, the volume of liquid within a beaker and temperature.
7	100	Select and use appropriate tools to measure the length of an object, the volume of liquid within a beaker and temperature.
8	180	Select and use appropriate tools to measure the length of an object, the volume of liquid within a beaker and temperature.
9	550 shown 850 shown	Select and use appropriate tools to measure the length of an object, the volume of liquid within a beaker and temperature.
10	6, 4, 8	Select and use appropriate tools to measure the length of an object, the volume of liquid within a beaker and temperature.

Measurement

Solving Measurement Problems – Practice Set 1

Question	Answer	B.E.S.T Standard
1	C	Solve real-world problems involving any of the four operations with whole-number lengths, masses, weights, temperatures or liquid volumes.
2	C	Solve real-world problems involving any of the four operations with whole-number lengths, masses, weights, temperatures or liquid volumes.
3	B	Solve real-world problems involving any of the four operations with whole-number lengths, masses, weights, temperatures or liquid volumes.
4	B	Solve real-world problems involving any of the four operations with whole-number lengths, masses, weights, temperatures or liquid volumes.
5	80	Solve real-world problems involving any of the four operations with whole-number lengths, masses, weights, temperatures or liquid volumes.
6	1,500	Solve real-world problems involving any of the four operations with whole-number lengths, masses, weights, temperatures or liquid volumes.
7	Thursday	Solve real-world problems involving any of the four operations with whole-number lengths, masses, weights, temperatures or liquid volumes.
8	42	Solve real-world problems involving any of the four operations with whole-number lengths, masses, weights, temperatures or liquid volumes.
9	170	Solve real-world problems involving any of the four operations with whole-number lengths, masses, weights, temperatures or liquid volumes.
10	$(8 \times 6) + 2 + 2$ 52	Solve real-world problems involving any of the four operations with whole-number lengths, masses, weights, temperatures or liquid volumes.

Solving Measurement Problems – Practice Set 2

Question	Answer	B.E.S.T Standard
1	C	Solve real-world problems involving any of the four operations with whole-number lengths, masses, weights, temperatures or liquid volumes.
2	B	Solve real-world problems involving any of the four operations with whole-number lengths, masses, weights, temperatures or liquid volumes.
3	B	Solve real-world problems involving any of the four operations with whole-number lengths, masses, weights, temperatures or liquid volumes.
4	D	Solve real-world problems involving any of the four operations with whole-number lengths, masses, weights, temperatures or liquid volumes.
5	$24	Solve real-world problems involving any of the four operations with whole-number lengths, masses, weights, temperatures or liquid volumes.
6	3	Solve real-world problems involving any of the four operations with whole-number lengths, masses, weights, temperatures or liquid volumes.
7	C	Solve real-world problems involving any of the four operations with whole-number lengths, masses, weights, temperatures or liquid volumes.
8	2	Solve real-world problems involving any of the four operations with whole-number lengths, masses, weights, temperatures or liquid volumes.
9	20	Solve real-world problems involving any of the four operations with whole-number lengths, masses, weights, temperatures or liquid volumes.
10	$20 - (3 \times 4)$ 8	Solve real-world problems involving any of the four operations with whole-number lengths, masses, weights, temperatures or liquid volumes.

Solving Measurement Problems – Practice Set 3

Question	Answer	B.E.S.T Standard
1	C	Solve real-world problems involving any of the four operations with whole-number lengths, masses, weights, temperatures or liquid volumes.
2	B	Solve real-world problems involving any of the four operations with whole-number lengths, masses, weights, temperatures or liquid volumes.
3	105	Solve real-world problems involving any of the four operations with whole-number lengths, masses, weights, temperatures or liquid volumes.
4	B	Solve real-world problems involving any of the four operations with whole-number lengths, masses, weights, temperatures or liquid volumes.
5	A	Solve real-world problems involving any of the four operations with whole-number lengths, masses, weights, temperatures or liquid volumes.
6	$8	Solve real-world problems involving any of the four operations with whole-number lengths, masses, weights, temperatures or liquid volumes.
7	5	Solve real-world problems involving any of the four operations with whole-number lengths, masses, weights, temperatures or liquid volumes.
8	55, 70, 85	Solve real-world problems involving any of the four operations with whole-number lengths, masses, weights, temperatures or liquid volumes.
9	20	Solve real-world problems involving any of the four operations with whole-number lengths, masses, weights, temperatures or liquid volumes.
10	B	Solve real-world problems involving any of the four operations with whole-number lengths, masses, weights, temperatures or liquid volumes.

Solving Measurement Problems – Practice Set 4

Question	Answer	B.E.S.T Standard
1	B	Solve real-world problems involving any of the four operations with whole-number lengths, masses, weights, temperatures or liquid volumes.
2	A	Solve real-world problems involving any of the four operations with whole-number lengths, masses, weights, temperatures or liquid volumes.
3	C	Solve real-world problems involving any of the four operations with whole-number lengths, masses, weights, temperatures or liquid volumes.
4	B	Solve real-world problems involving any of the four operations with whole-number lengths, masses, weights, temperatures or liquid volumes.
5	B	Solve real-world problems involving any of the four operations with whole-number lengths, masses, weights, temperatures or liquid volumes.
6	45	Solve real-world problems involving any of the four operations with whole-number lengths, masses, weights, temperatures or liquid volumes.
7	Friday Thursday 8	Solve real-world problems involving any of the four operations with whole-number lengths, masses, weights, temperatures or liquid volumes.
8	9	Solve real-world problems involving any of the four operations with whole-number lengths, masses, weights, temperatures or liquid volumes.
9	3	Solve real-world problems involving any of the four operations with whole-number lengths, masses, weights, temperatures or liquid volumes.
10	$(200 \times 4) - 500$ 300	Solve real-world problems involving any of the four operations with whole-number lengths, masses, weights, temperatures or liquid volumes.

Solving Measurement Problems – Practice Set 5

Question	Answer	B.E.S.T Standard
1	C	Solve real-world problems involving any of the four operations with whole-number lengths, masses, weights, temperatures or liquid volumes.
2	A	Solve real-world problems involving any of the four operations with whole-number lengths, masses, weights, temperatures or liquid volumes.
3	5	Solve real-world problems involving any of the four operations with whole-number lengths, masses, weights, temperatures or liquid volumes.
4	B	Solve real-world problems involving any of the four operations with whole-number lengths, masses, weights, temperatures or liquid volumes.
5	A	Solve real-world problems involving any of the four operations with whole-number lengths, masses, weights, temperatures or liquid volumes.
6	12	Solve real-world problems involving any of the four operations with whole-number lengths, masses, weights, temperatures or liquid volumes.
7	1 kg, 2 kg, 16 kg	Solve real-world problems involving any of the four operations with whole-number lengths, masses, weights, temperatures or liquid volumes.
8	3	Solve real-world problems involving any of the four operations with whole-number lengths, masses, weights, temperatures or liquid volumes.
9	D	Solve real-world problems involving any of the four operations with whole-number lengths, masses, weights, temperatures or liquid volumes.
10	4 × 80 × \$3 \$960	Solve real-world problems involving any of the four operations with whole-number lengths, masses, weights, temperatures or liquid volumes.

Measurement

Telling Time and Solving Time Problems – Practice Set 1

Question	Answer	B.E.S.T Standard
1	B	Using analog and digital clocks tell and write time to the nearest minute using a.m. and p.m. appropriately.
2	B	Solve one- and two-step real-world problems involving elapsed time.
3	B	Using analog and digital clocks tell and write time to the nearest minute using a.m. and p.m. appropriately.
4	A	Solve one- and two-step real-world problems involving elapsed time.
5	C	Using analog and digital clocks tell and write time to the nearest minute using a.m. and p.m. appropriately.
6	3:45	Using analog and digital clocks tell and write time to the nearest minute using a.m. and p.m. appropriately.
7	5, 8, 11	Using analog and digital clocks tell and write time to the nearest minute using a.m. and p.m. appropriately.
8	10:55 4:30 12:10	Using analog and digital clocks tell and write time to the nearest minute using a.m. and p.m. appropriately.
9	8:30, 2:00 5, 30	Solve one- and two-step real-world problems involving elapsed time.
10	3 × \$6 \$18	Solve one- and two-step real-world problems involving elapsed time.

Telling Time and Solving Time Problems – Practice Set 2

Question	Answer	B.E.S.T Standard
1	B	Using analog and digital clocks tell and write time to the nearest minute using a.m. and p.m. appropriately.
2	C	Solve one- and two-step real-world problems involving elapsed time.
3	D	Using analog and digital clocks tell and write time to the nearest minute using a.m. and p.m. appropriately.
4	C	Solve one- and two-step real-world problems involving elapsed time.
5	2nd, 3rd, 5th	Solve one- and two-step real-world problems involving elapsed time.
6	1:50	Using analog and digital clocks tell and write time to the nearest minute using a.m. and p.m. appropriately.
7	11:20 6:00 2:40	Using analog and digital clocks tell and write time to the nearest minute using a.m. and p.m. appropriately.
8	3, 45	Solve one- and two-step real-world problems involving elapsed time.
9	10:30 and 2:00 shown	Using analog and digital clocks tell and write time to the nearest minute using a.m. and p.m. appropriately.
10	\$12 × 4 \$48	Solve one- and two-step real-world problems involving elapsed time.

Telling Time and Solving Time Problems – Practice Set 3

Question	Answer	B.E.S.T Standard
1	B	Solve one- and two-step real-world problems involving elapsed time.
2	B	Using analog and digital clocks tell and write time to the nearest minute using a.m. and p.m. appropriately.
3	C	Using analog and digital clocks tell and write time to the nearest minute using a.m. and p.m. appropriately.
4	A	Solve one- and two-step real-world problems involving elapsed time.
5	C	Using analog and digital clocks tell and write time to the nearest minute using a.m. and p.m. appropriately.
6	9	Solve one- and two-step real-world problems involving elapsed time.
7	3:00 9:00 6	Solve one- and two-step real-world problems involving elapsed time.
8	3:05 1:50 9:15	Using analog and digital clocks tell and write time to the nearest minute using a.m. and p.m. appropriately.
9	8:30 and 4:00 shown	Using analog and digital clocks tell and write time to the nearest minute using a.m. and p.m. appropriately.
10	45 × 4 = 180 180 min = 3 hrs 6:00 p.m.	Solve one- and two-step real-world problems involving elapsed time.

Telling Time and Solving Time Problems – Practice Set 4

Question	Answer	B.E.S.T Standard
1	B	Using analog and digital clocks tell and write time to the nearest minute using a.m. and p.m. appropriately.
2	C	Solve one- and two-step real-world problems involving elapsed time.
3	B	Using analog and digital clocks tell and write time to the nearest minute using a.m. and p.m. appropriately.
4	C	Solve one- and two-step real-world problems involving elapsed time.
5	4th	Solve one- and two-step real-world problems involving elapsed time.
6	8:25	Using analog and digital clocks tell and write time to the nearest minute using a.m. and p.m. appropriately.
7	8:35 5:25 7:45	Using analog and digital clocks tell and write time to the nearest minute using a.m. and p.m. appropriately.
8	1st – 5th 2nd – 3rd 3rd – 2nd 5th – 4th	Using analog and digital clocks tell and write time to the nearest minute using a.m. and p.m. appropriately.
9	1, 45	Solve one- and two-step real-world problems involving elapsed time.
10	51 min 51 – 45 = 6 6 minutes	Solve one- and two-step real-world problems involving elapsed time.

Telling Time and Solving Time Problems – Practice Set 5

Question	Answer	B.E.S.T Standard
1	A	Using analog and digital clocks tell and write time to the nearest minute using a.m. and p.m. appropriately.
2	D	Solve one- and two-step real-world problems involving elapsed time.
3	A	Using analog and digital clocks tell and write time to the nearest minute using a.m. and p.m. appropriately.
4	C	Solve one- and two-step real-world problems involving elapsed time.
5	B	Using analog and digital clocks tell and write time to the nearest minute using a.m. and p.m. appropriately.
6	4:15	Using analog and digital clocks tell and write time to the nearest minute using a.m. and p.m. appropriately.
7	6:00 shown 12:30 shown	Using analog and digital clocks tell and write time to the nearest minute using a.m. and p.m. appropriately.
8	3:00 6:00 3	Solve one- and two-step real-world problems involving elapsed time.
9	12:35 2:00 11:10	Using analog and digital clocks tell and write time to the nearest minute using a.m. and p.m. appropriately.
10	2:30 to 6:30 4 × \$8 = \$32 \$32	Solve one- and two-step real-world problems involving elapsed time.

Geometric Reasoning

Lines, Quadrilaterals, and Symmetry – Practice Set 1

Question	Answer	B.E.S.T Standard
1	B	Draw line(s) of symmetry in a two-dimensional figure and identify line-symmetric two-dimensional figures.
2	C	Describe and draw points, lines, line segments, rays, intersecting lines, perpendicular lines and parallel lines. Identify these in two-dimensional figures.
3	C	Draw line(s) of symmetry in a two-dimensional figure and identify line-symmetric two-dimensional figures.
4	B	Describe and draw points, lines, line segments, rays, intersecting lines, perpendicular lines and parallel lines. Identify these in two-dimensional figures.
5	A	Draw line(s) of symmetry in a two-dimensional figure and identify line-symmetric two-dimensional figures.
6	2	Identify and draw quadrilaterals based on their defining attributes. Quadrilaterals include parallelograms, rhombi, rectangles, squares and trapezoids.
7	1st, 3rd	Describe and draw points, lines, line segments, rays, intersecting lines, perpendicular lines and parallel lines. Identify these in two-dimensional figures.
8	line at center	Draw line(s) of symmetry in a two-dimensional figure and identify line-symmetric two-dimensional figures.
9	rhombus, square	Identify and draw quadrilaterals based on their defining attributes. Quadrilaterals include parallelograms, rhombi, rectangles, squares and trapezoids.
10	2 by 3 rectangle drawn	Identify and draw quadrilaterals based on their defining attributes. Quadrilaterals include parallelograms, rhombi, rectangles, squares and trapezoids.

Lines, Quadrilaterals, and Symmetry – Practice Set 2

Question	Answer	B.E.S.T Standard
1	parallel	Describe and draw points, lines, line segments, rays, intersecting lines, perpendicular lines and parallel lines. Identify these in two-dimensional figures.
2	B	Describe and draw points, lines, line segments, rays, intersecting lines, perpendicular lines and parallel lines. Identify these in two-dimensional figures.
3	B	Draw line(s) of symmetry in a two-dimensional figure and identify line-symmetric two-dimensional figures.
4	B	Identify and draw quadrilaterals based on their defining attributes. Quadrilaterals include parallelograms, rhombi, rectangles, squares and trapezoids.
5	C	Identify and draw quadrilaterals based on their defining attributes. Quadrilaterals include parallelograms, rhombi, rectangles, squares and trapezoids.
6	1st, 2nd, 4th	Draw line(s) of symmetry in a two-dimensional figure and identify line-symmetric two-dimensional figures.
7	2nd, 8th, 10th	Draw line(s) of symmetry in a two-dimensional figure and identify line-symmetric two-dimensional figures.
8	1st – 4th 2nd – 1st 3rd – 2nd 4th – 3rd	Identify and draw quadrilaterals based on their defining attributes. Quadrilaterals include parallelograms, rhombi, rectangles, squares and trapezoids.
9	second half shaded	Draw line(s) of symmetry in a two-dimensional figure and identify line-symmetric two-dimensional figures.
10	3 o'clock 9 o'clock	Describe and draw points, lines, line segments, rays, intersecting lines, perpendicular lines and parallel lines. Identify these in two-dimensional figures.

Lines, Quadrilaterals, and Symmetry – Practice Set 3

Question	Answer	B.E.S.T Standard
1	B	Draw line(s) of symmetry in a two-dimensional figure and identify line-symmetric two-dimensional figures.
2	B	Describe and draw points, lines, line segments, rays, intersecting lines, perpendicular lines and parallel lines. Identify these in two-dimensional figures.
3	D	Draw line(s) of symmetry in a two-dimensional figure and identify line-symmetric two-dimensional figures.
4	A	Identify and draw quadrilaterals based on their defining attributes. Quadrilaterals include parallelograms, rhombi, rectangles, squares and trapezoids.
5	A	Draw line(s) of symmetry in a two-dimensional figure and identify line-symmetric two-dimensional figures.
6	2nd, 4th, 5th	Describe and draw points, lines, line segments, rays, intersecting lines, perpendicular lines and parallel lines. Identify these in two-dimensional figures.
7	line at center	Draw line(s) of symmetry in a two-dimensional figure and identify line-symmetric two-dimensional figures.
8	1st – 1 2nd – 2 3rd – 0	Describe and draw points, lines, line segments, rays, intersecting lines, perpendicular lines and parallel lines. Identify these in two-dimensional figures.
9	trapezoids	Identify and draw quadrilaterals based on their defining attributes. Quadrilaterals include parallelograms, rhombi, rectangles, squares and trapezoids.
10	4 by 4 square drawn	Identify and draw quadrilaterals based on their defining attributes. Quadrilaterals include parallelograms, rhombi, rectangles, squares and trapezoids.

Lines, Quadrilaterals, and Symmetry – Practice Set 4

Question	Answer	B.E.S.T Standard
1	A	Describe and draw points, lines, line segments, rays, intersecting lines, perpendicular lines and parallel lines. Identify these in two-dimensional figures.
2	C	Identify and draw quadrilaterals based on their defining attributes. Quadrilaterals include parallelograms, rhombi, rectangles, squares and trapezoids.
3	C	Draw line(s) of symmetry in a two-dimensional figure and identify line-symmetric two-dimensional figures.
4	B	Identify and draw quadrilaterals based on their defining attributes. Quadrilaterals include parallelograms, rhombi, rectangles, squares and trapezoids.
5	B	Draw line(s) of symmetry in a two-dimensional figure and identify line-symmetric two-dimensional figures.
6	A, E	Draw line(s) of symmetry in a two-dimensional figure and identify line-symmetric two-dimensional figures.
7	2nd, 4th	Describe and draw points, lines, line segments, rays, intersecting lines, perpendicular lines and parallel lines. Identify these in two-dimensional figures.
8	bottom left	Describe and draw points, lines, line segments, rays, intersecting lines, perpendicular lines and parallel lines. Identify these in two-dimensional figures.
9	second half drawn	Draw line(s) of symmetry in a two-dimensional figure and identify line-symmetric two-dimensional figures.
10	square, rectangle	Identify and draw quadrilaterals based on their defining attributes. Quadrilaterals include parallelograms, rhombi, rectangles, squares and trapezoids.

Lines, Quadrilaterals, and Symmetry – Practice Set 5

Question	Answer	B.E.S.T Standard
1	C	Draw line(s) of symmetry in a two-dimensional figure and identify line-symmetric two-dimensional figures.
2	DE, BC	Describe and draw points, lines, line segments, rays, intersecting lines, perpendicular lines and parallel lines. Identify these in two-dimensional figures.
3	B	Draw line(s) of symmetry in a two-dimensional figure and identify line-symmetric two-dimensional figures.
4	D	Describe and draw points, lines, line segments, rays, intersecting lines, perpendicular lines and parallel lines. Identify these in two-dimensional figures.
5	B	Draw line(s) of symmetry in a two-dimensional figure and identify line-symmetric two-dimensional figures.
6	trapezoid	Identify and draw quadrilaterals based on their defining attributes. Quadrilaterals include parallelograms, rhombi, rectangles, squares and trapezoids.
7	3rd, 5th	Describe and draw points, lines, line segments, rays, intersecting lines, perpendicular lines and parallel lines. Identify these in two-dimensional figures.
8	parallelogram drawn	Identify and draw quadrilaterals based on their defining attributes. Quadrilaterals include parallelograms, rhombi, rectangles, squares and trapezoids.
9	line at center	Draw line(s) of symmetry in a two-dimensional figure and identify line-symmetric two-dimensional figures.
10	rhombus shaded, rectangle shaded	Identify and draw quadrilaterals based on their defining attributes. Quadrilaterals include parallelograms, rhombi, rectangles, squares and trapezoids.

Geometric Reasoning

Area and Perimeter – Practice Set 1

Question	Answer	B.E.S.T Standard
1	B	Find the area of a rectangle with whole-number side lengths using a visual model and a multiplication formula.
2	B	Solve mathematical and real-world problems involving the perimeter and area of rectangles with whole-number side lengths using a visual model and a formula.
3	A	Explore area as an attribute of a two-dimensional figure by covering the figure with unit squares without gaps or overlaps. Find areas of rectangles by counting unit squares.
4	D	Solve mathematical and real-world problems involving the perimeter and area of rectangles with whole-number side lengths using a visual model and a formula.
5	C	Find the area of a rectangle with whole-number side lengths using a visual model and a multiplication formula.
6	14	Explore area as an attribute of a two-dimensional figure by covering the figure with unit squares without gaps or overlaps. Find areas of rectangles by counting unit squares.
7	50 78	Solve mathematical and real-world problems involving the perimeter and area of composite figures composed of non-overlapping rectangles with whole-number side lengths.
8	24, 42, 36	Solve mathematical and real-world problems involving the perimeter and area of rectangles with whole-number side lengths using a visual model and a formula.
9	2 × (500 + 500) = 2000 2000 mm	Solve mathematical and real-world problems involving the perimeter and area of rectangles with whole-number side lengths using a visual model and a formula.
10	16 × 20 = 320 12 × 12 = 144 320 – 144 = 176 176 sq. in.	Solve mathematical and real-world problems involving the perimeter and area of rectangles with whole-number side lengths using a visual model and a formula.

Area and Perimeter – Practice Set 2

Question	Answer	B.E.S.T Standard
1	A	Solve mathematical and real-world problems involving the perimeter and area of rectangles with whole-number side lengths using a visual model and a formula.
2	2nd, 5th	Solve mathematical and real-world problems involving the perimeter and area of rectangles with whole-number side lengths using a visual model and a formula.
3	A	Explore area as an attribute of a two-dimensional figure by covering the figure with unit squares without gaps or overlaps. Find areas of rectangles by counting unit squares.
4	B	Solve mathematical and real-world problems involving the perimeter and area of rectangles with whole-number side lengths using a visual model and a formula.
5	B	Explore area as an attribute of a two-dimensional figure by covering the figure with unit squares without gaps or overlaps. Find areas of rectangles by counting unit squares.
6	60	Solve mathematical and real-world problems involving the perimeter and area of rectangles with whole-number side lengths using a visual model and a formula.
7	$(4 \times 2) + (6 \times 1)$ $8 + 6$ 14	Solve mathematical and real-world problems involving the perimeter and area of composite figures composed of non-overlapping rectangles with whole-number side lengths.
8	12, 35, 27	Find the area of a rectangle with whole-number side lengths using a visual model and a multiplication formula.
9	$9 \times 4 = 36$ 36	Find the area of a rectangle with whole-number side lengths using a visual model and a multiplication formula.
10	22	Solve mathematical and real-world problems involving the perimeter and area of composite figures composed of non-overlapping rectangles with whole-number side lengths.

Area and Perimeter – Practice Set 3

Question	Answer	B.E.S.T Standard
1	A	Solve mathematical and real-world problems involving the perimeter and area of rectangles with whole-number side lengths using a visual model and a formula.
2	D	Solve mathematical and real-world problems involving the perimeter and area of rectangles with whole-number side lengths using a visual model and a formula.
3	C	Solve mathematical and real-world problems involving the perimeter and area of rectangles with whole-number side lengths using a visual model and a formula.
4	B	Solve mathematical and real-world problems involving the perimeter and area of rectangles with whole-number side lengths using a visual model and a formula.
5	C	Explore area as an attribute of a two-dimensional figure by covering the figure with unit squares without gaps or overlaps. Find areas of rectangles by counting unit squares.
6	29	Explore area as an attribute of a two-dimensional figure by covering the figure with unit squares without gaps or overlaps. Find areas of rectangles by counting unit squares.
7	50 66	Solve mathematical and real-world problems involving the perimeter and area of composite figures composed of non-overlapping rectangles with whole-number side lengths.
8	72, 24, 35	Find the area of a rectangle with whole-number side lengths using a visual model and a multiplication formula.
9	$9 \times 4 = 36$ 36	Find the area of a rectangle with whole-number side lengths using a visual model and a multiplication formula.
10	$20 \times 9 = 180$ $4 \times 2 = 8$ $180 - 8 = 172$ 172 sq. ft	Solve mathematical and real-world problems involving the perimeter and area of rectangles with whole-number side lengths using a visual model and a formula.

Area and Perimeter – Practice Set 4

Question	Answer	B.E.S.T Standard
1	A	Find the area of a rectangle with whole-number side lengths using a visual model and a multiplication formula.
2	A	Solve mathematical and real-world problems involving the perimeter and area of rectangles with whole-number side lengths using a visual model and a formula.
3	B	Explore area as an attribute of a two-dimensional figure by covering the figure with unit squares without gaps or overlaps. Find areas of rectangles by counting unit squares.
4	B	Solve mathematical and real-world problems involving the perimeter and area of rectangles with whole-number side lengths using a visual model and a formula.
5	A	Explore area as an attribute of a two-dimensional figure by covering the figure with unit squares without gaps or overlaps. Find areas of rectangles by counting unit squares.
6	18	Find the area of a rectangle with whole-number side lengths using a visual model and a multiplication formula.
7	(2 × 2) + (3 × 3) 4 + 9 13	Solve mathematical and real-world problems involving the perimeter and area of composite figures composed of non-overlapping rectangles with whole-number side lengths.
8	34, 46, 20	Solve mathematical and real-world problems involving the perimeter and area of rectangles with whole-number side lengths using a visual model and a formula.
9	500 + 500 + 850 + 850 = 2700 2,700 mm	Solve mathematical and real-world problems involving the perimeter and area of rectangles with whole-number side lengths using a visual model and a formula.
10	28	Solve mathematical and real-world problems involving the perimeter and area of composite figures composed of non-overlapping rectangles with whole-number side lengths.

Area and Perimeter – Practice Set 5

Question	Answer	B.E.S.T Standard
1	A	Solve mathematical and real-world problems involving the perimeter and area of rectangles with whole-number side lengths using a visual model and a formula.
2	C	Solve mathematical and real-world problems involving the perimeter and area of rectangles with whole-number side lengths using a visual model and a formula.
3	120	Solve mathematical and real-world problems involving the perimeter and area of rectangles with whole-number side lengths using a visual model and a formula.
4	D	Solve mathematical and real-world problems involving the perimeter and area of rectangles with whole-number side lengths using a visual model and a formula.
5	A	Explore area as an attribute of a two-dimensional figure by covering the figure with unit squares without gaps or overlaps. Find areas of rectangles by counting unit squares.
6	18	Explore area as an attribute of a two-dimensional figure by covering the figure with unit squares without gaps or overlaps. Find areas of rectangles by counting unit squares.
7	$(3 \times 2) + (5 \times 2)$ $6 + 10$ 16	Solve mathematical and real-world problems involving the perimeter and area of composite figures composed of non-overlapping rectangles with whole-number side lengths.
8	18, 32, 90	Find the area of a rectangle with whole-number side lengths using a visual model and a multiplication formula.
9	$9 \times 7 = 63$ 63	Find the area of a rectangle with whole-number side lengths using a visual model and a multiplication formula.
10	24	Solve mathematical and real-world problems involving the perimeter and area of composite figures composed of non-overlapping rectangles with whole-number side lengths.

Data Analysis and Probability

Collect and Represent Data – Practice Set 1

Question	Answer	B.E.S.T Standard
1	B	Collect and represent numerical and categorical data with whole-number values using tables, scaled pictographs, scaled bar graphs or line plots. Use appropriate titles, labels and units.
2	B	Collect and represent numerical and categorical data with whole-number values using tables, scaled pictographs, scaled bar graphs or line plots. Use appropriate titles, labels and units.
3	B	Collect and represent numerical and categorical data with whole-number values using tables, scaled pictographs, scaled bar graphs or line plots. Use appropriate titles, labels and units.
4	C	Collect and represent numerical and categorical data with whole-number values using tables, scaled pictographs, scaled bar graphs or line plots. Use appropriate titles, labels and units.
5	B	Collect and represent numerical and categorical data with whole-number values using tables, scaled pictographs, scaled bar graphs or line plots. Use appropriate titles, labels and units.
6	2nd, 5th	Collect and represent numerical and categorical data with whole-number values using tables, scaled pictographs, scaled bar graphs or line plots. Use appropriate titles, labels and units.
7	5 – 2 points 6 – 2 points 7 – 3 points 8 – 3 points	Collect and represent numerical and categorical data with whole-number values using tables, scaled pictographs, scaled bar graphs or line plots. Use appropriate titles, labels and units.
8	B	Collect and represent numerical and categorical data with whole-number values using tables, scaled pictographs, scaled bar graphs or line plots. Use appropriate titles, labels and units.
9	symbols from top to bottom – 9, 6, 7, 7	Collect and represent numerical and categorical data with whole-number values using tables, scaled pictographs, scaled bar graphs or line plots. Use appropriate titles, labels and units.
10	60, 70, 110, 120 graphed	Collect and represent numerical and categorical data with whole-number values using tables, scaled pictographs, scaled bar graphs or line plots. Use appropriate titles, labels and units.

Collect and Represent Data – Practice Set 2

Question	Answer	B.E.S.T Standard
1	B	Collect and represent numerical and categorical data with whole-number values using tables, scaled pictographs, scaled bar graphs or line plots. Use appropriate titles, labels and units.
2	A	Collect and represent numerical and categorical data with whole-number values using tables, scaled pictographs, scaled bar graphs or line plots. Use appropriate titles, labels and units.
3	C	Collect and represent numerical and categorical data with whole-number values using tables, scaled pictographs, scaled bar graphs or line plots. Use appropriate titles, labels and units.
4	D	Collect and represent numerical and categorical data with whole-number values using tables, scaled pictographs, scaled bar graphs or line plots. Use appropriate titles, labels and units.
5	C	Collect and represent numerical and categorical data with whole-number values using tables, scaled pictographs, scaled bar graphs or line plots. Use appropriate titles, labels and units.
6	5	Collect and represent numerical and categorical data with whole-number values using tables, scaled pictographs, scaled bar graphs or line plots. Use appropriate titles, labels and units.
7	12 – 2 points 13 – 4 points 14 – 3 points 15 – 2 points	Collect and represent numerical and categorical data with whole-number values using tables, scaled pictographs, scaled bar graphs or line plots. Use appropriate titles, labels and units.
8	4, 8, 6, 2, 5	Collect and represent numerical and categorical data with whole-number values using tables, scaled pictographs, scaled bar graphs or line plots. Use appropriate titles, labels and units.
9	300, 500, 800, 1,100 graphed	Collect and represent numerical and categorical data with whole-number values using tables, scaled pictographs, scaled bar graphs or line plots. Use appropriate titles, labels and units.
10	symbols from top to bottom – 7, 6, 8	Collect and represent numerical and categorical data with whole-number values using tables, scaled pictographs, scaled bar graphs or line plots. Use appropriate titles, labels and units.

Collect and Represent Data – Practice Set 3

Question	Answer	B.E.S.T Standard
1	2nd, 5th	Collect and represent numerical and categorical data with whole-number values using tables, scaled pictographs, scaled bar graphs or line plots. Use appropriate titles, labels and units.
2	A	Collect and represent numerical and categorical data with whole-number values using tables, scaled pictographs, scaled bar graphs or line plots. Use appropriate titles, labels and units.
3	28	Collect and represent numerical and categorical data with whole-number values using tables, scaled pictographs, scaled bar graphs or line plots. Use appropriate titles, labels and units.
4	B	Collect and represent numerical and categorical data with whole-number values using tables, scaled pictographs, scaled bar graphs or line plots. Use appropriate titles, labels and units.
5	C	Collect and represent numerical and categorical data with whole-number values using tables, scaled pictographs, scaled bar graphs or line plots. Use appropriate titles, labels and units.
6	73 – 2 points 74 – 1 point 76 – 1 point 78 – 1 point 80 – 1 point	Collect and represent numerical and categorical data with whole-number values using tables, scaled pictographs, scaled bar graphs or line plots. Use appropriate titles, labels and units.
7	5, 4	Collect and represent numerical and categorical data with whole-number values using tables, scaled pictographs, scaled bar graphs or line plots. Use appropriate titles, labels and units.
8	7, 8, 4, 1 graphed	Collect and represent numerical and categorical data with whole-number values using tables, scaled pictographs, scaled bar graphs or line plots. Use appropriate titles, labels and units.
9	symbols from top to bottom – 6, 7, 8, 5	Collect and represent numerical and categorical data with whole-number values using tables, scaled pictographs, scaled bar graphs or line plots. Use appropriate titles, labels and units.
10	80, 100, 90, 60 graphed	Collect and represent numerical and categorical data with whole-number values using tables, scaled pictographs, scaled bar graphs or line plots. Use appropriate titles, labels and units.

Collect and Represent Data – Practice Set 4

Question	Answer	B.E.S.T Standard
1	C	Collect and represent numerical and categorical data with whole-number values using tables, scaled pictographs, scaled bar graphs or line plots. Use appropriate titles, labels and units.
2	C	Collect and represent numerical and categorical data with whole-number values using tables, scaled pictographs, scaled bar graphs or line plots. Use appropriate titles, labels and units.
3	A	Collect and represent numerical and categorical data with whole-number values using tables, scaled pictographs, scaled bar graphs or line plots. Use appropriate titles, labels and units.
4	D	Collect and represent numerical and categorical data with whole-number values using tables, scaled pictographs, scaled bar graphs or line plots. Use appropriate titles, labels and units.
5	C	Collect and represent numerical and categorical data with whole-number values using tables, scaled pictographs, scaled bar graphs or line plots. Use appropriate titles, labels and units.
6	6	Collect and represent numerical and categorical data with whole-number values using tables, scaled pictographs, scaled bar graphs or line plots. Use appropriate titles, labels and units.
7	12 – 4 points 13 – 2 points 14 – 1 point 15 – 2 points	Collect and represent numerical and categorical data with whole-number values using tables, scaled pictographs, scaled bar graphs or line plots. Use appropriate titles, labels and units.
8	7, 5, 3, 10, 9	Collect and represent numerical and categorical data with whole-number values using tables, scaled pictographs, scaled bar graphs or line plots. Use appropriate titles, labels and units.
9	symbols from top to bottom – 3, 4½, 3, 4	Collect and represent numerical and categorical data with whole-number values using tables, scaled pictographs, scaled bar graphs or line plots. Use appropriate titles, labels and units.
10	7, 9, 8, 5 graphed	Collect and represent numerical and categorical data with whole-number values using tables, scaled pictographs, scaled bar graphs or line plots. Use appropriate titles, labels and units.

Collect and Represent Data – Practice Set 5

Question	Answer	B.E.S.T Standard
1	C	Collect and represent numerical and categorical data with whole-number values using tables, scaled pictographs, scaled bar graphs or line plots. Use appropriate titles, labels and units.
2	B	Collect and represent numerical and categorical data with whole-number values using tables, scaled pictographs, scaled bar graphs or line plots. Use appropriate titles, labels and units.
3	24	Collect and represent numerical and categorical data with whole-number values using tables, scaled pictographs, scaled bar graphs or line plots. Use appropriate titles, labels and units.
4	8	Collect and represent numerical and categorical data with whole-number values using tables, scaled pictographs, scaled bar graphs or line plots. Use appropriate titles, labels and units.
5	C	Collect and represent numerical and categorical data with whole-number values using tables, scaled pictographs, scaled bar graphs or line plots. Use appropriate titles, labels and units.
6	3 – 3 points 5 – 1 point	Collect and represent numerical and categorical data with whole-number values using tables, scaled pictographs, scaled bar graphs or line plots. Use appropriate titles, labels and units.
7	15, 25, 40 graphed	Collect and represent numerical and categorical data with whole-number values using tables, scaled pictographs, scaled bar graphs or line plots. Use appropriate titles, labels and units.
8	2nd	Collect and represent numerical and categorical data with whole-number values using tables, scaled pictographs, scaled bar graphs or line plots. Use appropriate titles, labels and units.
9	symbols from left to right – 3, 4	Collect and represent numerical and categorical data with whole-number values using tables, scaled pictographs, scaled bar graphs or line plots. Use appropriate titles, labels and units.
10	7, 8, 5, 4 graphed	Collect and represent numerical and categorical data with whole-number values using tables, scaled pictographs, scaled bar graphs or line plots. Use appropriate titles, labels and units.

Data Analysis and Probability

Interpret Data – Practice Set 1

Question	Answer	B.E.S.T Standard
1	3	Interpret data with whole-number values represented with tables, scaled pictographs, circle graphs, scaled bar graphs or line plots by solving one- and two-step problems.
2	A	Interpret data with whole-number values represented with tables, scaled pictographs, circle graphs, scaled bar graphs or line plots by solving one- and two-step problems.
3	14	Interpret data with whole-number values represented with tables, scaled pictographs, circle graphs, scaled bar graphs or line plots by solving one- and two-step problems.
4	11	Interpret data with whole-number values represented with tables, scaled pictographs, circle graphs, scaled bar graphs or line plots by solving one- and two-step problems.
5	Leanne	Interpret data with whole-number values represented with tables, scaled pictographs, circle graphs, scaled bar graphs or line plots by solving one- and two-step problems.
6	6	Interpret data with whole-number values represented with tables, scaled pictographs, circle graphs, scaled bar graphs or line plots by solving one- and two-step problems.
7	D	Interpret data with whole-number values represented with tables, scaled pictographs, circle graphs, scaled bar graphs or line plots by solving one- and two-step problems.
8	90%	Interpret data with whole-number values represented with tables, scaled pictographs, circle graphs, scaled bar graphs or line plots by solving one- and two-step problems.
9	2	Interpret data with whole-number values represented with tables, scaled pictographs, circle graphs, scaled bar graphs or line plots by solving one- and two-step problems.
10	600	Interpret data with whole-number values represented with tables, scaled pictographs, circle graphs, scaled bar graphs or line plots by solving one- and two-step problems.

Interpret Data – Practice Set 2

Question	Answer	B.E.S.T Standard
1	C	Interpret data with whole-number values represented with tables, scaled pictographs, circle graphs, scaled bar graphs or line plots by solving one- and two-step problems.
2	10	Interpret data with whole-number values represented with tables, scaled pictographs, circle graphs, scaled bar graphs or line plots by solving one- and two-step problems.
3	C	Interpret data with whole-number values represented with tables, scaled pictographs, circle graphs, scaled bar graphs or line plots by solving one- and two-step problems.
4	$45	Interpret data with whole-number values represented with tables, scaled pictographs, circle graphs, scaled bar graphs or line plots by solving one- and two-step problems.
5	A	Interpret data with whole-number values represented with tables, scaled pictographs, circle graphs, scaled bar graphs or line plots by solving one- and two-step problems.
6	dog	Interpret data with whole-number values represented with tables, scaled pictographs, circle graphs, scaled bar graphs or line plots by solving one- and two-step problems.
7	130	Interpret data with whole-number values represented with tables, scaled pictographs, circle graphs, scaled bar graphs or line plots by solving one- and two-step problems.
8	9	Interpret data with whole-number values represented with tables, scaled pictographs, circle graphs, scaled bar graphs or line plots by solving one- and two-step problems.
9	650	Interpret data with whole-number values represented with tables, scaled pictographs, circle graphs, scaled bar graphs or line plots by solving one- and two-step problems.
10	60	Interpret data with whole-number values represented with tables, scaled pictographs, circle graphs, scaled bar graphs or line plots by solving one- and two-step problems.

Interpret Data – Practice Set 3

Question	Answer	B.E.S.T Standard
1	D	Interpret data with whole-number values represented with tables, scaled pictographs, circle graphs, scaled bar graphs or line plots by solving one- and two-step problems.
2	3	Interpret data with whole-number values represented with tables, scaled pictographs, circle graphs, scaled bar graphs or line plots by solving one- and two-step problems.
3	C	Interpret data with whole-number values represented with tables, scaled pictographs, circle graphs, scaled bar graphs or line plots by solving one- and two-step problems.
4	red, green	Interpret data with whole-number values represented with tables, scaled pictographs, circle graphs, scaled bar graphs or line plots by solving one- and two-step problems.
5	37	Interpret data with whole-number values represented with tables, scaled pictographs, circle graphs, scaled bar graphs or line plots by solving one- and two-step problems.
6	English	Interpret data with whole-number values represented with tables, scaled pictographs, circle graphs, scaled bar graphs or line plots by solving one- and two-step problems.
7	12	Interpret data with whole-number values represented with tables, scaled pictographs, circle graphs, scaled bar graphs or line plots by solving one- and two-step problems.
8	5	Interpret data with whole-number values represented with tables, scaled pictographs, circle graphs, scaled bar graphs or line plots by solving one- and two-step problems.
9	$18	Interpret data with whole-number values represented with tables, scaled pictographs, circle graphs, scaled bar graphs or line plots by solving one- and two-step problems.
10	Supreme	Interpret data with whole-number values represented with tables, scaled pictographs, circle graphs, scaled bar graphs or line plots by solving one- and two-step problems.

Interpret Data – Practice Set 4

Question	Answer	B.E.S.T Standard
1	D	Interpret data with whole-number values represented with tables, scaled pictographs, circle graphs, scaled bar graphs or line plots by solving one- and two-step problems.
2	105	Interpret data with whole-number values represented with tables, scaled pictographs, circle graphs, scaled bar graphs or line plots by solving one- and two-step problems.
3	B	Interpret data with whole-number values represented with tables, scaled pictographs, circle graphs, scaled bar graphs or line plots by solving one- and two-step problems.
4	A	Interpret data with whole-number values represented with tables, scaled pictographs, circle graphs, scaled bar graphs or line plots by solving one- and two-step problems.
5	C	Interpret data with whole-number values represented with tables, scaled pictographs, circle graphs, scaled bar graphs or line plots by solving one- and two-step problems.
6	brownies, pies	Interpret data with whole-number values represented with tables, scaled pictographs, circle graphs, scaled bar graphs or line plots by solving one- and two-step problems.
7	softball swimming, hockey	Interpret data with whole-number values represented with tables, scaled pictographs, circle graphs, scaled bar graphs or line plots by solving one- and two-step problems.
8	5	Interpret data with whole-number values represented with tables, scaled pictographs, circle graphs, scaled bar graphs or line plots by solving one- and two-step problems.
9	C	Interpret data with whole-number values represented with tables, scaled pictographs, circle graphs, scaled bar graphs or line plots by solving one- and two-step problems.
10	pepperoni	Interpret data with whole-number values represented with tables, scaled pictographs, circle graphs, scaled bar graphs or line plots by solving one- and two-step problems.

Interpret Data – Practice Set 5

Question	Answer	B.E.S.T Standard
1	D	Interpret data with whole-number values represented with tables, scaled pictographs, circle graphs, scaled bar graphs or line plots by solving one- and two-step problems.
2	C	Interpret data with whole-number values represented with tables, scaled pictographs, circle graphs, scaled bar graphs or line plots by solving one- and two-step problems.
3	A	Interpret data with whole-number values represented with tables, scaled pictographs, circle graphs, scaled bar graphs or line plots by solving one- and two-step problems.
4	7	Interpret data with whole-number values represented with tables, scaled pictographs, circle graphs, scaled bar graphs or line plots by solving one- and two-step problems.
5	pizza	Interpret data with whole-number values represented with tables, scaled pictographs, circle graphs, scaled bar graphs or line plots by solving one- and two-step problems.
6	$450	Interpret data with whole-number values represented with tables, scaled pictographs, circle graphs, scaled bar graphs or line plots by solving one- and two-step problems.
7	8	Interpret data with whole-number values represented with tables, scaled pictographs, circle graphs, scaled bar graphs or line plots by solving one- and two-step problems.
8	rabbit	Interpret data with whole-number values represented with tables, scaled pictographs, circle graphs, scaled bar graphs or line plots by solving one- and two-step problems.
9	$36	Interpret data with whole-number values represented with tables, scaled pictographs, circle graphs, scaled bar graphs or line plots by solving one- and two-step problems.
10	5	Interpret data with whole-number values represented with tables, scaled pictographs, circle graphs, scaled bar graphs or line plots by solving one- and two-step problems.

Made in United States
Orlando, FL
09 January 2025

57085993R00196